CARING
FOR THE
NURSING
HOME
PATIENT

Clinical and Managerial Challenges for Nurses

673790

Charlotte Eliopoulos

AN ASPEN PUBLICATION®
Aspen Publishers, Inc.

1989

Rockville, Maryland
Royal Tunbridge Wells

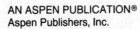

Library of Congress Cataloging-in-Publication Data

Eliopoulos, Charlotte.
Caring for the nursing home patient: clinical and managerial
challenges for nurses/Charlotte Eliopoulos.
p. cm.
"An Aspen publication."
Includes bibliographies and index.
ISBN: 0-8342-0047-3
1. Geriatric nursing. 2. Nursing home patients--Care. I. Title
[DNLM: 1. Geriatric Nursing. 2. Nursing Care--in old age.
3. Nursing Homes--United States. WY 152 E42c]
RC954.E43   1989   610.73'65--dc19
DNLM/DLC
for Library of Congress
88-38207
CIP

The authors have made every effort to ensure the accuracy of the information herein, particularly with regard to drug selection and dose. However, appropriate information sources should be consulted, especially for new or unfamiliar procedures. It is the responsibility of every practitioner to evaluate the appropriateness of a particular opinion in the context of actual clinical situations and with due consideration to new developments. Authors, editors, and the publisher cannot be held responsible for any typographical or other errors found in this book.

Editorial Services: Marsha Davies

Library of Congress Catalog Card Number: 88-38207
ISBN: 0-8342-0047-3

Printed in the United States of America

1 2 3 4 5

Dedicated to my brother,
Manuel Eliopoulos

Table of Contents

Preface

Currently, there are more than 25,000 nursing homes in the United States that serve more than 1.5 million people. This care setting, long stigmatized and misunderstood by the general public and professionals alike, is now becoming a major force in health care delivery. Growing numbers of persons are using nursing home services as more of the population survives to advanced age—a period in which the prevalence of serious chronic illness and disabilities peaks. Because of changes in the acute care reimbursement system hospitals are turning to nursing homes for their discharged patients in need of continuing care. Because of increased participation of women in the work force more families are seeking nursing home care as a necessary alternative to family care giving.

The reality is that nursing home care will grow in intensity and scope; consequently, more and better prepared nurses will be needed to meet the demands of this practice setting. Today's nursing home nurse typically received no formal classroom or field experience in long-term care to prepare for the clinical and managerial challenges that abound in the nursing home. The trial and error of on-the-job education is no longer sufficient to prepare nurses for nursing home nursing. Increased educational opportunities and resources must exist to increase nursing competencies in long-term care facilities.

The purpose of *Contemporary Nursing Home Nursing: Clinical and Managerial Challenges* is to serve as a resource for nurses as they prepare for and implement services in the nursing home setting. The book provides a basic understanding of the unique aspects of nursing home nursing. The clinical and managerial challenges faced by the nursing home nurse are reviewed in a practical manner

- To acquaint nurses with the unique practice of nursing within the nursing home setting

- To provide the knowledge and skills that will enhance the nurse's success in this setting, thereby reducing the risk of burnout and poor quality of care
- To increase the understanding of the complexities of nursing home nursing so that the status of the specialty will be enhanced
- To promote compliance with regulations and high standards of care within the nursing home

The book is divided into three parts. In Part I facts are separated from myths as the realities of the nursing home industry and consumers of this service are presented. The role of nurses in the development of nursing homes is discussed to give insight into the current problems and challenges that face nursing home nurses.

In Part II the unique features of applying the nursing process to an elderly nursing home population are reviewed. To aid this application, specific clinical problems are accompanied by care plans. Finally, the unique characteristics of the employee and patient population are considered in Part III, as topics such as legal risks, ethical dilemmas, performance appraisal, and public relations are discussed.

To the novice to nursing home nursing, this book will provide an understanding of the multifaceted responsibilities and complexities of nursing in this setting. To the experienced nursing home nurse, this book will strengthen the existing knowledge base and, it is hoped, give new perspectives to old problems.

Part I

Introduction to Nursing Home Nursing

Chapter 1

Nursing Home Nursing

Isn't it depressing to work with sick old people?
Wasn't a job available in a hospital?
Are you working in a nursing home because it's easier than hospital nursing?
Why ever would you want to work in an old-age home?

Many nursing home nurses have confronted these types of questions and found themselves in the position of justifying their decision to be employed in a long-term care facility. The same people questioning nurses' decision to work in the nursing home setting most likely would not ask psychiatric nurses if they selected their specialty to avoid physical work, nor suggest to shock trauma nurses that they must prefer machine management to human interaction. Somehow, though, they do not consider it equally offensive to imply that nursing home nurses are less competent, energetic, dynamic, or worthy than their colleagues in other settings. Is it any wonder that it is difficult to attract nurses to work in long-term care facilities?

The attitudes toward nursing home nurses may be related to society's attitude toward aging in general. Despite tremendous efforts to sensitize the public about the realities and virtues of the elderly, the United States remains a youth-oriented society. New, young, and change are the buzzwords. Perfectly functional clothing and furnishings are discarded and replaced by "new styles." Advertisers understand that a person with a beautiful, young body will do more to sell cars, sodas, and other products than will a factual presentation of the product's reliability, safety, and value. The millions of dollars spent on antiaging creams, face lifts, and hair transplants testify to the reluctance society has to growing old. In this climate elderly adults represent that which most of society seeks to avoid. And if healthy,

3

active elderly persons make our youth-oriented society uncomfortable, nursing home residents—who represent the extreme aged who are the most frail and dependent—must be an extremely difficult reality to accept.

As though the attitudes stemming from a youth-oriented society were not enough, they are compounded by attitudes toward nursing home care. Institutional care has always been viewed as the option of last resort. Most people believed that families who loved their elders would take care of them and certainly not "put them in a home." Even with the current realities of mobile nuclear families, more women employed outside the home, and greater numbers of persons surviving to old age, the aversion to institutional care continues. For many people, attitudes toward nursing homes have been molded by headlines and television exposés of the abuses perpetrated by a small minority of facilities.

The health care system also has contributed to the negative attitude about nursing homes. Interest, technology, and resources invested in saving lives have far exceeded the commitment to the quality of those lives that have been saved. Leaders in health care aggressively use the media to promote organ transplants and new technology that will benefit a small minority while ignoring the chronic underfunding and related problems faced by nursing homes. Few nursing and medical schools offer meaningful clinical experiences in nursing homes. Perhaps worst of all, health care professionals, whose opinions are valued by society, unfairly criticize, make generalizations, and perpetuate stereotypes of nursing homes.

Against this backdrop nursing home nurses must work. The low value society places on its elderly citizens transfers to the value placed on nurses who work with this population. Nursing home nurses carry the stigma of an industry whose history has been laced with scandals and abuses. The omission of meaningful education and clinical experiences in nursing home care reflects the perceived importance of this form of care to professional schools. These are tremendous obstacles for nursing home nurses to overcome; however, there is reason for optimism. Growing numbers of persons are using nursing home services and having their misconceptions dispelled. The media are paying more attention to positive aspects of nursing home life and increasing the public's awareness of the constraints within which nursing homes work. The legitimacy of gerontologic nursing as a specialty is increasing, and more and more nurses are realizing the challenges and satisfactions of working in nursing homes. Nursing home nurses are now at important crossroads and, like the butterfly emerging from a dark cocoon, are ready to spread their wings and fly.

SCOPE OF PRACTICE

Before becoming employed in the nursing home setting few nurses fully understand the roles and responsibilities they will assume. They soon learn the complexity and diversity of demands that await them. Few practice settings demand the wide range of clinical and managerial competencies of nurses that nursing homes do.

The special population being cared for in the nursing home is the first challenge. Although adults of any age can be institutionalized, most nursing home residents are elderly adults. This necessitates that nurses be knowledgeable of the normal aging process and the unique manifestations of illness in the aged. For instance, nurses must understand the action of medications in the aging body, how rest and sleep requirements differ for the aged, environmental modifications that should be made to compensate for sensory deficits, and methods for detecting complications in the absence of classic signs that middle-aged persons may display. This specialized knowledge in gerontology and geriatrics must be superimposed on general nursing knowledge for the management of health problems as nursing home nurses aid patients in managing a variety of medical and psychiatric illnesses. Thus nursing home nurses must be current in the care of patients with such disorders as congestive heart failure, parkinsonism, depression, cerebrovascular accident, dementia, diabetes mellitus, and hypertension, as well as a host of other disorders.

Regardless of the medical diagnosis, most of the care needs of nursing home patients are nursing in nature, that is, within the realm of nursing to assess, diagnose, and treat independently. Potential for injury, alterations in nutrition, alterations in bowel elimination, alterations in patterns of urinary elimination, self-care deficits, and disturbances in self-concept are among the major problems that absorb most care activities in the nursing home; interestingly, all are nursing diagnoses. Nursing home nurses must be competent and confident in their independent nursing practice.

Unlike the hospital setting, the nursing home becomes a residence for many of the patients. Thus a different set of concerns regarding the quality of life emerges. Nurses must aid patients in developing new roles and relationships in the nursing home setting, in establishing meaningful life styles, and in maintaining individuality and privacy. Attractiveness, safety, function, and comfort of the environment must be given priority.

Patients who reside in long-term care facilities are not immune to emergencies or crises in their health status, such as falls, delirium, myocardial infarctions, pulmonary emboli, suicidal attempts, cerebrovascular accidents, and insulin shock. In the nursing home, nurses do not have ready access to physicians, laboratories, radiology departments, and other resources; thus they must rely on their own assessment and decision-making skills. An error in judgment could lead to serious complications and even death for patients.

Nurses assume responsibility for coordinating the efforts of the health care team in the nursing home. As examples, changes in status and the need for alterations in drug therapy are communicated to the physician by nurses; the patient's need to a family problem with the social worker may be identified by nursing staff; a. irses may advise the priest of a patient's religious needs. Nurses ensure that all disciplines' pieces of care responsibility fit together into a sensible whole.

Another challenge to nursing home nurses is the responsibility to the families of residents. Families need assistance as they adjust to patients' admission and changing status. They need support as they work through their guilt, anger, depression, and other feelings associated with having a loved one in a nursing home. They need patience and understanding as they displace their feelings to staff. The nurse must consider the entire family unit as "the patient" in assessing, planning, giving, and evaluating care.

For the protection of their patients, the facility, and themselves, nursing home nurses must be cognizant of the legal and ethical aspects of their practice. Nurses may identify specific problems or be confronted by patients and families with questions related to competency, consent, appropriateness of life-sustaining measures, protection of assets, and abuse. Recognizing these problems and seeking assistance in their management are essential.

As though the wide range of clinical issues were not challenge enough to nursing home nursing practice, nurses also must exercise managerial skills. Nurses represent a minority of nursing staff in the nursing home and often must delegate to and supervise a large number of unlicensed personnel. Hiring such personnel, assuring their competencies, promoting their motivation, supervising their activities, evaluating their performance, and correcting their problems demand considerable management expertise.

Some of the potential responsibilities of nursing home nurses are listed in Exhibit 1-1. Not all nurses will be involved in all functions, and the lists are not inclusive. However, one fact is certain: nursing home nursing, if practiced competently and conscientiously, is a highly complex specialty requiring a wide range of knowledge and skills. As more nurses enter this practice setting and become aware of the realities of nursing home care, there will be a greater understanding that nursing's "cream of the crop" rather than its "rejects" are needed to work in long-term care facilities.

THE FUTURE

In recent years dramatic changes have occurred in the nursing home sector, and change can be expected to continue. Although the number of elderly in institutional settings is predicted to remain at approximately 5% of the elderly population, that percentage will represent larger numbers as the aging population becomes a greater proportion of society. Thus additional nursing home beds may be created and may be in new settings, such as acute hospitals and life care centers. The reduced lengths of hospital stays will cause hospitals to look to the nursing

Exhibit 1-1 Potential Responsibilities of Nursing Home Nurses

---

Clinical
Screen applicants for admission.
Perform comprehensive nursing assessment.
Identify nursing problems and diagnoses.
Differentiate normal from abnormal findings.
Develop plan of care.
Communicate plan of care to caregivers.
Delegate care responsibilities.
Supervise subordinates' care-giving activities.
Evaluate plan of care.
Monitor patients' status.
Identify and initiate care of emergency situations.
Promote and maintain safe, therapeutic environment.
Identify and make referrals for needs for other services.
Educate patients, caregivers, and families.
Communicate relevant patient information to physician.
Prepare and administer medications.
Recognize side effects, adverse reactions to therapy.
Support plan of care of other disciplines.
Counsel and support families and significant others.
Document nursing activities.
Comply with standards of professional practice.

Managerial
Recruit staff.
Interview applicants for employment.
Check references, current licensure.
Hire, discipline, evaluate, and fire nursing staff.
Orient new personnel.
Arrange for and provide in-service education.
Motivate and guide staff.
Develop and maintain nursing service standards, policies, procedures, and job descriptions.
Identify and recommend staffing needs.
Schedule nursing personnel according to staffing needs.
Monitor absenteeism and tardiness.
Identify and recommend budgetary needs for nursing services.
Promote and implement cost-containment practices.
Order supplies.
Evaluate and recommend new patient care products.
Develop and implement quality assurance program.
Assure and promote competency of subordinates.
Receive and investigate complaints.
Document and report incidents and accidents.
Serve as liaison between administration and caregivers.
Communicate, plan, and problem solve with other departments.
Serve on committees.
Represent facility at community functions.

Exhibit 1-1 continued

Assure compliance with regulations; correct deficiencies identified by surveyors.
Promote and practice good public relations.
Prevent, identify, and seek correction of legal risks.
Participate in facility's planning activities.
Identify need for new services, potential revenue-generating programs.
Keep current on legislation, regulations, and changes affecting practice.

home setting for continued care of their stable, but very ill, patients. The growing number of persons who age with psychiatric disorders or who survive to those advanced years in which the prevalence of mental impairments increases will influence the demand for increased psychiatric services in the nursing home. Nursing homes also will be looked to as a cost-effective site for caring for postoperative, ventilator-supported, and other special groups of patients. The complexity and diversity of care provided in this setting will definitely grow.

Many nursing homes will be expanding their services as well. Geriatric day care centers, home health care, assessment services, retirement housing, and primary care clinics may be some of the programs that will branch from the nursing home. With their experience and expertise in geriatric care, nursing home staff may provide consultation related to the care of the chronically ill aged to hospitals and home health agencies.

Increasing numbers of caregivers will be needed to work in nursing homes, and a greater proportion of them are going to be licensed nurses. Along with the higher quantity of nurses will be the need for those nurses to be of the highest quality. Nursing home nurses must prepare themselves for the wide range of clinical and managerial issues they will confront and ensure that the quality of nursing services delivered is a caliber of which the profession can be proud.

BIBLIOGRAPHY

Brock, A.M. 1988. The necessity of change. *J Gerontol Nurs* 14:7.

Carter, M.A. 1988. Professional nursing in the nursing home. *J Prof Nurs* 3:325, 376.

Chandler, J., J. Rachal, and R. Kazelskis. 1986. Attitudes of long term care nursing personnel toward the elderly. *Gerontologist* 26:551–55.

Fulmer, T.T. 1987. Lessons from a nursing home. *Am J Nurs* 87:332–33.

Kalisch, P.A., and B.J. Kalisch. 1987. *The changing image of the nurse*. Menlo Park, Calif.: Addison-Wesley Publishing Co.

Snape, J. 1986. Nurses' attitudes to the care of the elderly. *J Adv Nurs* 11:569–72.

Tinsdale, S. 1988. Harvest moon. Portrait of a nursing home. *Am J Nurs* 88:296–300.

Yager, D. 1988. Long term facilities feel the nursing shortage, too. *Am J Nurs* 88:450.

Chapter 2

Understanding the Nursing Home

Nursing homes are a significant part of the total health care system. Currently, the number of nursing homes, as well as the number of nursing home beds, exceeds those of hospitals (see Table 2-1). As inpatient hospital care is declining, the demand for long-term institutional care continues to grow. But, what are these institutions: rest homes? scaled-down hospitals? warehouses for the unwanted? Many myths emerge when nursing homes are discussed. Actually, long-term care facilities are unique care settings that are rapidly changing to meet the demands of an increasingly complex population. To understand fully what nursing homes are, it is useful to review how they developed into their existing form.

DEVELOPMENT OF NURSING HOMES

Although the number of people who reached advanced age in the past was few, various forms of long-term care have existed throughout history. It is believed that early Greek and Roman civilizations had special temples to provide such care. In 369 A.D. the Romans developed *gerocomeia*, a system of old age homes for the privileged class (George Washington University, 1969). The Renaissance brought a new interest in health care, including greater concern for the aged and poor. The English Poor Law of 1601 stimulated the development of almshouses for the needy or misfits of society; the poor aged without family resources resided in these almshouses with orphans, the insane, prostitutes, criminals, and persons with various handicaps.

The almshouse concept crossed the ocean with the pilgrims, and soon these institutions were established in the colonies. Charitable contributions and local governments provided the support for these facilities. Thus resources were slim,

9

Table 2-1 Comparison of Total Number of Nursing Homes and of Nursing Home Beds to Those of Hospitals

	No. of Institutions	No. of Beds (1,000)
Nursing homes	25,849	1,642
Hospitals	6,888	1,350

Source: *Statistical Abstracts of the United States*, 108th ed., No. 152, p. 97, U.S. Department of Commerce, Bureau of the Census, Washington, D.C., 1988.

and care was basic at best. Little progress in long-term care was made during the next two centuries. In the late 1800s there began to appear old age homes that had better living conditions and care services, but these were available only to the upper class of society.

In the early part of the twentieth century almshouses and mental hospitals were the major sources of long-term care for the poor aged. Elderly persons with resources lived in private homes for the aged. Because most old people were not eager to enter the less than desirable environments of mental hospitals and almshouses and few could afford private homes for the aged only a small percentage of this population resided in institutions. However, this situation changed dramatically with the advent of Social Security in 1935. With this new financial resource more elderly persons had the means to afford private institutional care and, in response, boarding homes, rest homes, and similar facilities emerged. During this period, the number of elderly persons was growing (see Table 2-2), leading to an increased demand for this form of care. Eager to stimulate growth of nursing homes, the federal government provided funds for

Table 2-2 Growth in Population Age 65 Years and Older

Year	No. of Persons Age 65 Years and Older (Millions)
1900	3.0
1910	3.9
1920	4.9
1930	6.6
1940	9.0
1950	12.2
1960	16.7
1970	20.1
1980	25.7
1983	27.4

Source: *Current Population Reports,* Series P-25, Nos. 519 and 949, U.S. Department of Commerce, Bureau of the Census, Washington, D.C., 1986.

their development through the Hill-Burton Act of 1946. (At this time, the first licensing of nursing homes began in an effort to correct the poor conditions that were surfacing in many of these facilities.) The growth in nursing homes during this period was significant: in 1940 there were 1,200 nursing homes with 25,000 beds; by 1960 there were 9,582 facilities with 390,000 beds.

The greatest influence on the growth of nursing home beds was the introduction of Medicare and Medicaid in 1965. At this time, the medical community wanted something to be done to alleviate the problem faced when patients who required long-term care had no place to be transferred and consequently had to remain in acute care hospital beds. Pressure was put on the federal government to stimulate long-term care by providing a means of reimbursement. Congress responded by enacting Medicare and Medicaid, and with a guaranteed form of reimbursement, entrepreneurs responded by expanding this industry. Between 1960 and 1970 the number of nursing homes more than doubled, and the number of beds in this sector tripled. As the number of persons served increased so did the costs associated with nursing home care: $500 million was spent in 1960, $4.7 billion in 1970.

Many persons who owned and operated nursing homes were caring and conscientious, but some were more concerned with bottom-line profits than with the means to achieve that end. During the 1960s and 1970s the problems of some nursing homes made the headlines, and exposés flourished. The public began to view long-term care institutions as inhumane warehouses for the aged and dreaded the thought of using this form of care for their own loved ones. Even health care professionals shunned nursing homes (which did nothing to help improve the quality and quantity of staff employed in long-term care facilities).

In response to public pressure federal and state governments placed tighter regulations on this sector and continue to closely supervise nursing home care. Fortunately, the conditions in many facilities, as well as the perceptions of the public and professionals, have improved. Growing numbers of persons view nursing homes as an important form of care. Because of increased emphasis on geriatric care and shrinking job opportunities in the hospital sector more health care workers appreciate the challenges of long-term institutional care. As nursing homes continue to evolve to meet the new demands of the population, the importance and complexity of this care setting will receive greater understanding.

WHAT ARE NURSING HOMES?

Nursing homes are unique facilities. They are not like hospitals, where people spend a short time for diagnosis and treatment of their health problems. Neither are they primarily residences where the aged obtain room and board. They are *care centers for the long-term treatment of stable patients who need assistance with activities of daily living (e.g., feeding, toileting, bathing, dressing, mobility) and it of health problems.* Although some patients reside in a long-term y only temporarily and then return to the community, many live the remainder of their lives in this setting. For these people the facility also serves as a home.

The reality of nursing homes being a care center and a residence confronts staff with special challenges. Staff members must not only provide expert services and comply with standards for health care institutions but also create a humane living environment. Staff members must adjust ideal practices to the unique preferences and needs of the residents of the facility. For example, it may be ideal to have all patients' room furnishings be identical, with washable surfaces and consistent with an overall decorating plan. However, to individualize the environment and enable the patient to have favorite and familiar items, the facility may allow patients to replace institutional furniture with their own pieces. Likewise, the nursing staff may schedule all baths during the day shift; however, flexibility must exist to honor the request of patients who prefer to bathe before bedtime. Sensitivity and flexibility can turn an impersonal, stiff institutional environment into a warm, comfortable home for patients.

Although nursing homes are health care centers, they are not equipped or staffed to manage acute care problems, as are hospitals. Patients who have unstable medical or psychiatric conditions, or who require emergency treatment, surgery, or other highly skilled care, are beyond the scope of nursing home treatment. In addition to not being licensed for acute care, nursing homes lack the resources to compete with hospital care (see Table 2-3). It is not unusual for nursing home patients to require transfer to a hospital when their conditions demand greater services than the nursing home can provide.

LEVELS OF CARE

In the total system of long-term care there are several different types of institutions. Facilities range from those providing services to persons with minimal care needs to those providing specialty hospital services. They include the following.

Table 2-3 Comparison of Resources of Nursing Homes and Hospitals

Resource	Nursing Homes	Hospitals
Staff per patient	0.57	3.6
Total expenditures (billions)	$38.1	$179.6

Source: Statistical Abstracts of the United States, 108th ed., No. 131, p. 88, U.S. Department of Commerce, Bureau of the Census, Washington, D.C., 1988.

- *Domiciliary Care Facility.* This type of facility provides roo
  basic supervision for persons who are able to care for themselves indepena-
  ently with minimal assistance.
- *Sheltered Housing.* In this type of facility the environment has been modified
  to accommodate the limitations of the frail or handicapped. Centralized
  services such as communal dining areas and emergency call systems are
  usually available, and assistive services may be brought to persons. Residents
  must be able to function without 24-hour care or supervision.
- *Intermediate Care Facility (ICF).* This type of facility is designed for persons
  who need care and services that exceed room and board (i.e., nursing home
  care), but do not require the intensity or professional level of service of a
  skilled nursing home or hospital. Unlike the preceding levels, intermediate
  care facilities must have health personnel present around the clock.
- *Skilled Nursing Facility (SNF).* Persons needing skilled care must be under
  the supervision of a physician and require the services of technical or
  professional personnel, such as a registered nurse, physical therapist, or
  speech pathologist. Twenty-four hour skilled nursing care must be needed.
- *Specialty Hospital.* Although less than 4% of the institutionalized population
  reside in specialty hospitals, this level of care is available in some states (e.g.,
  Maryland, Connecticut, and New Jersey). These facilities are called chronic
  disease or rehabilitation hospitals. Patients in a chronic disease hospital need
  an intensity of medical and nursing services that surpasses that provided in a
  skilled nursing home, such as ventilator support or hospice care. Persons in
  rehabilitation hospitals are usually there for a limited time; their function is
  improved so they can return to the community or to a nursing home.

Most nursing homes provide care for persons requiring intermediate or skilled
nursing care; however, institutions can provide combinations of any of the levels
of care described. In addition, increasing numbers of nursing homes are developing community-based or outreach services, such as adult day care, home health,
and geriatric assessment clinics.

WHAT MAKES THE NURSING HOME FUNCTION?

A wide range of talent is required for a nursing home to function. Each patient
has unique needs, necessitating that a variety of clinical services be provided to
meet all of the needs of this diverse population. Employees also have needs, for
fair labor practices and management of their work-related problems. Like any
housing structure, the physical plant has needs for maintenance and management.
Of course, agencies that regulate and pay for nursing home services also have their

set of demands that must be fulfilled. Departments supply the talent to meet this wide range of needs, and all are essential to the operation of the nursing home. They include the following.

- *Administration*. The administrator/chief executive officer/president, assistant administrators/vice-presidents, fiscal officer, accountants, and admission coordinators are among the personnel that may fall under the umbrella of administration. Administrative staff members plan, manage, monitor, and evaluate the overall activities of the facility. Some states have special licensing requirements for the administrator of a nursing home.
- *Dietary*. Because of the diversity of health problems of patients a variety of diets are needed. Meals must be planned to meet physicians' orders and be in accordance with the recommended daily allowances established by the Food and Nutrition Board of the National Research Council. Proper food storage, preparation, serving, and disposal is an important responsibility, particularly because problems in this area can be life threatening.
- *Housekeeping*. A safe, sanitary environment is crucial in a facility that has a sick, frail population. This department keeps patient rooms and other areas in the facility clean and in order.
- *Laundry*. Proper handling of linens is important in the prevention and control of infections. Laundry services may be provided as a department within the nursing home, as a component of the housekeeping department, or through contract with an outside agency.
- *Maintenance*. The physical plant and equipment are seldom given much thought, until they do not function. The maintenance department ensures the proper operation of plumbing, electrical, heating, and mechanical works, as well as facility compliance with the Life Safety Code of the National Fire Protection Association.
- *Medical Records*. Paper work is a necessary evil in any health care institution. Properly maintained patient records are valuable in communicating important information about patients that can promote safe, consistent, and individualized care. The quality of these records can influence reimbursement for care and, subsequently, the financial status of the facility. Also, in the event of litigation, the record serves as evidence of the events that transpired. In addition to organizing and storing patient records, the medical records department may collect statistics that can guide the facility in its planning.
- *Medicine*. All patients must have their own personal (attending) physician or a physician on the staff of the nursing home to provide their medical care. These physicians must examine patients when they are admitted, develop a plan of care (expressed as physicians' orders), visit patients as frequently as

required (at least every 60 days), and review patients' continued need for nursing home care on a regular basis. A nursing home must have a medical director who ensures that patients' medical needs are being met, acts as a liaison with all physicians serving patients, and ensures that staff are free from infection.

- *Nursing.* Nursing is the backbone of care in the long-term care facility. Twenty-four hour nursing services must be provided to ensure that patients are receiving basic personal care, medications, treatments, and other direct assistance. A licensed practical (vocational) nurse must be on duty every shift, and, in a skilled nursing facility, a registered nurse must be present at least during the day shift every day of the week. The director of nursing oversees all nursing services and assures the competency and sound practice of all nursing employees. Nursing staff develop patient care plans in collaboration with other disciplines and coordinate unit activities and needs with other departments.

- *Patient Activities.* In addition to the management of their health problems, patients require assistance in achieving meaningful emotional, social, spiritual, and intellectual stimulation as they reside in the facility. Music, art, dance, pet, and other therapies not only provide recreation but can be therapeutic to physical, mental, and social health. An activities coordinator assesses patients' needs and develops an activities program for the facility. If this person is not a qualified activities coordinator, he or she must receive regular consultation from a qualified person.

- *Personnel.* In addition to patient services, there are many needs that must be met pertaining to the employee population, such as hiring, firing, benefits, discipline, references, and employee record keeping. The facility must be in compliance with all labor laws and treat its employees fairly. These personnel functions may be part of the responsibilities of administration but are increasingly being assigned to a personnel expert under a separate department.

- *Pharmacy.* There are a considerable range and number of medications administered to nursing home patients. Pharmaceutical services ensure that drugs are properly ordered, stored, and administered. Although the nursing home is not required to have its own pharmacy on the premises, if it does not it must contract for pharmacy services and arrange for a pharmacist to review each patient's medication schedule at least monthly. Only the pharmacist can label and dispense medications; only physicians, licensed nurses, and certified medication aides can administer medications.

- *Purchasing.* A large volume of supplies are used for patient care, as well as for operating the facility. A purchasing agent or department may be assigned to coordinate supplies and equipment needs, match requests against budgeted

...op for the best buys, manage the review of new products, and monitor supply use.

- *Rehabilitation*. Patients may require physical, occupational, speech, or other therapy. If the facility does not have these rehabilitative specialists on staff, their services must be arranged when ordered by the physician.
- *Social Services*. Nursing home patients often have a variety of social and emotional needs as they adjust to their illnesses and institutionalization. Social service specialists are able to assess these needs, develop plans, and link patients and families with appropriate resources. If a social worker is not on staff, a person must be designated to provide social services, and this person must receive regular consultation from a qualified social worker.
- *Staff Development*. Every department has its unique educational needs that enable its staff members to stay current and competent. In addition, all employees must meet certain basic educational requirements, such as for fire

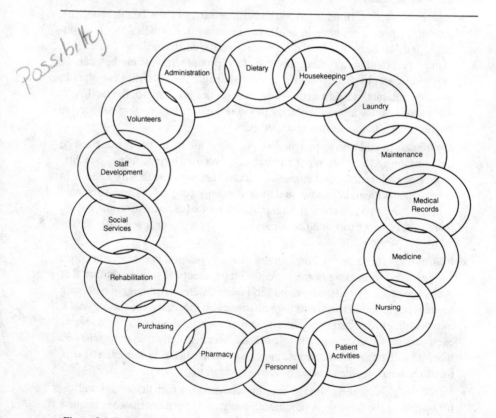

Figure 2-1 Departments Are Interrelated and Interdependent

and safety. Departments can provide in-service education individually or coordinate their efforts through a staff development or in-service educator. (Often this person is a member of the nursing department.) In addition to arranging for and providing in-service education, the person responsible for staff development must maintain records to reflect the content of educational programs and staff attendance.

- *Volunteers*. These unpaid resources are important members of the facility. They often "pick up the pieces," or perform tasks that might otherwise be left undone, and assist in improving the quality of patients' lives.

None of the departments can work in isolation. Each department's activities impact on the others' and are interrelated (Figure 2-1). Together they form a *team* that sets the level of quality within the nursing home. An understanding of the contributions of each department, as well as mutual respect, is essential to making this team work.

REFERENCE

George Washington University. 1969. *The evolution of long term care in the United States. A study of nursing homes and related facilities, monograph one*, 9-36. Washington, D.C.: George Washington University.

BIBLIOGRAPHY

Aiken, L. 1981. Nursing priorities for the 1980's: Hospitals or nursing homes. *Am J Nurs* 82:324–30.

Hogstel, M.O. 1983. *Management of personnel in long-term care*. Bowie, Md.: Robert J. Brady Co.

Johnson, C., and L. Grant. 1985. *The nursing home in American society*. Baltimore, Md.: Johns Hopkins University Press.

King, K., ed. 1985. *Long term care*. New York: Churchill-Livingstone.

LeSage, J. 1985. Teaching nursing homes. *Am J Nurs* 85:678–83.

Minkler, M. 1985. The nursing home; A neglected setting for health promotion. *Top Clin Nurs* 8:46–57.

Strahan, G. 1987. Nursing home characteristics. Preliminary data from the 1985 National Nursing Home Survey. *National Center for Health Statistics: Advance Data* 131:1–11.

Chapter 3

The Nursing Home Patient

Mr. Woods is an 82-year-old bilateral amputee who requires considerable assistance with his personal care and management of his medical problems. He has been a widower for 15 years and has been living with his daughter for the past 5 years because he is unable to care for himself. His daughter's family has enabled him to maintain his dignity and health status. The family is devoted to Mr. Woods, and he is grateful and proud to have the benefit of their love and support.

In the same neighborhood the estate of Miss Stevens is being sold. Miss Stevens, a single, 68-year-old retired secretary, has recently entered a nursing home because of her inability to care for herself independently after a small stroke.

Who becomes a nursing home resident? Victims of uncaring families? Minorities subjected to prejudicial treatment? Homeless people? A majority of the sick aged? The many myths that prevail regarding institutionalization do little to ease society's anxiety and negativism toward aging. By having a realistic understanding of the population they serve, nursing home nurses can clarify misconceptions that the public holds toward nursing home care.

PROFILE OF NURSING HOME PATIENTS

Persons of any age may require nursing home care; however, most nursing home residents are elderly—particularly the extremely aged. The risk of being institutionalized increases with each decade after age 65 years (Johnson and Grant,

1985); that is, 1.2% of 65- to 74-year-olds are institutionalized; 5.9% of 75- to 84-year-olds; and 23.7% of those older than age 85 years. From these figures it would seem that only a minority of elderly persons reside in nursing homes—less than 5%—at any given time. However, at least one in five aged who survive to the ''old-old'' years will spend some period in a nursing home.

Nursing home residents have a wide range of health problems (see Table 3-1), but for every person in a nursing home there are at least two persons equally sick and disabled that reside in the community. Therefore factors other than severity of illness and disability must influence institutionalization. Variables such as age, sex, marital status, and family support more frequently determine whether an ill person will be cared for in the nursing home or in a community setting.

The absence of a spouse is a significant factor influencing institutionalization. The Health Care Financing Administration (1981) discovered that widowed and single persons are the highest users of nursing homes; only 12% of the nursing home population is married. Because women enjoy a longer life expectancy than men (see Table 3-2), it is not surprising that they will have a greater likelihood of being widowed and, consequently, constitute a majority of nursing home patients.

Elderly blacks are known to have poorer health and greater functional disabilities than their white counterparts. Nevertheless, they have a significantly lower rate of institutionalization (see Table 3-3). This may be due in part to the fact that the lower life expectancy of the black population precludes blacks from obtaining the advanced years in which the risk of institutionalization significantly increases. Perhaps past prejudicial treatment and less financial resources play a

---

Table 3-1 Major Health Problems of Nursing Home Patients

Health Problem	Percentage of Patients with Disease
Arteriosclerosis	47.6
Heart trouble	34.5
Senility*	32.0
Chronic brain syndrome	24.9
Arthritis and rheumatism	24.6
Constipation	24.0
Hypertension	20.9
Edema	17.9
Stroke	16.4
Diabetes mellitus	14.5

*Terminology is that used in the survey.

Source: The National Nursing Home Survey 1977: Summary of the United States, National Center for Health Statistics, U.S. Department of Health and Human Services, Hyattsville, Md., 1979.

Table 3-2 Racial and Sexual Differences in Life Expectancy

Race	Life Expectancy (Yr.) Women	Men
Whites	78.5	71.1
Blacks	73.0	64.4

Source: *Vital Statistics of the United States,* National Center for Health Statistics.

Table 3-3 Institutionalization Differences between Blacks and Whites by Sex

Sex	Percentage of Persons Age 65 Years and Older in Nursing Homes Whites	Blacks
Women	5.1	2.9
Men	2.9	1.9

Source: *The Nursing Home in American Society* by C.L. Johnson and L.A. Grant, p. 40, Johns Hopkins University Press, © 1985.

part. Family commitment to elders also may be a significant factor. Blacks' utilization of nursing homes is expected to increase as financial gains are achieved and mobility of the young leaves a smaller pool of family support readily available. Other minority groups also are underrepresented in nursing homes, although this may change in the future.

REACTIONS TO INSTITUTIONALIZATION

There is little in life that prepares a person for entering an institutional setting. After a lifetime of making independent decisions, decorating an environment to satisfy personal style, practicing unique routines, and living with loved ones, patients enter the nursing home to find a severe cultural shock. The following description of a patient's admission highlights some of the adjustments faced.

Mrs. Evans is 79 years old and has been a widow for 1½ years. Her husband had been almost totally disabled from a dementia during his last 8 years of life, and Mrs. Evans provided direct care to him with only occasional assistance from her son and daughter-in-law. Mrs. Evans's own cardiac problems had been escalating during that time, and after several recent episodes of congestive heart failure she is now too frail to live alone. Her son and his wife have recently separated, and the uncertainty of his life prevents Mrs. Evans's son from taking her home. Several attempts to employ help in the home have proved unsuccessful, and it is now believed to be in Mrs. Evans's interest to enter a nursing home.

Mrs. Evans's son accompanied her to the nursing home. Although her steps are slow, Mrs. Evans has been ambulatory. Despite this, the admission clerk insists that Mrs. Evans be transferred to her room in a wheelchair. Mrs. Evans objects but eventually concedes.

As she travels to her room, Mrs. Evans gives smiles (unreturned) to staff who seem to be preoccupied with their own thoughts. A few of the patients offer blank looks, whereas others mumble incoherent messages to her. Her preadmission fantasies of having new friends with whom she could discuss books or play bridge quickly fade as she notes many patients pacing aimlessly and talking to unseen companions. She passes an opened door to spot a female patient sitting on a toilet in full view. Suddenly she is embarrassed for her son and on glancing at him notices tears streaming down his face. She grabs his hand to comfort him, but it only seems to cause him to become more upset.

Finally, she reaches her room. She had been prepared for the reality of having a roommate, but somehow did not envision her to be the unkempt person who welcomed her coldly with, "I see they didn't waste any time filling the bed with another one." After years of living with antiques, Mrs. Evans found the modern, built-in bedroom furniture stark and distasteful, not to mention that the room was smaller than anything in which she had ever lived.

Mrs. Evans was surprised by the number of staff who entered her room without asking permission or introducing themselves. One opened Mrs. Evans's closet and searched for something; another poked a head in and bellowed, "You'll let us know if you need go to the bathroom, won't you?" Someone else took her temperature and pulse while continuing a conversation with a co-worker on the buys she obtained at the local mall.

Mrs. Evans encouraged her son to leave and assured him that she would be just fine. After he left, her confidence dwindled as she began to wonder how she would manage living in such a strange new environment. She wondered if she should ask the staff members why they ignored a patient who had been screaming for help, make a special effort to introduce herself to staff and other patients, or explain her unique likes and dislikes. She feared her efforts would be resented, and, besides, she was not sure she had that kind of energy. She was not certain whether it was the fear of the unknown or the sadness and anger of spending her final days reduced to this form of living, but she felt a level of discontent never before experienced in her entire life.

Anger, fear, anxiety, depression, and regression often are manifested by patients entering a nursing home setting. This is understandable when some of the negative social and emotional consequences of institutionalization are considered.

- *Erosion of personal identity.* The status a person held in the community, the possessions and dress style that reflected his or her individuality, and the command over activities are lost when a person adapts to the "nursing home patient" role. Rather than the retired carpenter that the young, do-it-yourselfers sought for advice, the community activist who mobilized neighbors for good causes, or the avid collector of old quilts, the nursing home patient becomes one of many "diabetics," "total feeds," "tub baths," or "cancer patients."
- *Adoption of atypical behaviors.* Patients often discover that politely requesting a pain medication may not bring the rapid results of making a commotion at the nurses' station. Likewise, an otherwise gentle patient may resort to threatening mentally impaired patients to keep them from wandering into his or her room. Patients also learn that the assertiveness promoted in society at large is viewed as "noncompliance" in the nursing home.
- *Use of new survival skills.* Behaviors that may have been foreign to a person may be the same ones used to deal with the realities of nursing home life. For example, patients may resort to hoarding food in their clothing, to assure a snack when they are hungry; sharing their presents with staff to obtain favored treatment; or contriving ailments to get staff to pay more attention to them.
- *Disunity with society.* The institution serves not only as a physical barrier between patients and usual societal activities, but also as a psychologic one. It may be difficult for patients and their friends and families to find common current events or interests to share. Over time, visitors may decrease in their numbers or frequency of visits. Even with regular visitors, there can be isolation from the larger world.
- *Regression.* Physical, mental, and social competencies can be lost from lack of assistance or insufficient opportunity to use them. For instance, a patient without access to newspapers or stimulating conversation may lose track of current events; likewise, when a wheelchair is used to expedite mobility a patient's ambulation ability may decrease.

Entering a nursing home setting is known to produce a highly negative effect in some patients; that is, *relocation stress*. The trauma of entering a new environment can cause grief reactions and a heightening of health problems. Although it has been suggested that mortality rates after admission to a nursing home are high, results of most studies show no evidence of increased mortality related to relocation alone (Borup et al. 1983). Successful adjustment correlated with general health status, life satisfaction, and self-esteem (Doughtery et al. 1982). Like any profound stress, relocation can be an added stressor to others already present and have deleterious effects. This reinforces the necessity for nurses to assess comprehensively potential and newly admitted patients to identify stresses for which interventions must be planned.

HELPING PATIENTS ADJUST TO THE NURSING HOME

Preparing a person for the realities of nursing home life is one important measure to aid in reducing stress and facilitating adjustment. Sometimes this may not be possible because of the patient's status or the crisis nature of the admission. However, whenever possible, the element of surprise should be removed from the admission. This begins with being honest about the admission.

Patients should not be transferred to a nursing home without knowing their destination. Sometimes, in the belief that they are being kind or that the patient will not understand, or because of their own feelings about the placement, families will camouflage the admission by telling the patient, "The doctor's transferring you to a new hospital," "You're going to be transferred to a better place to live," or, worst of all, "You'll be going home tomorrow." Postponing the realization that a person is going to a nursing home only serves to escalate the stress associated with the admission and weaken the patient's credibility in persons he or she has trusted. Confronting the need for nursing home care is seldom easy, and nurses, social workers, and other professionals can serve as valuable resources in facilitating family discussions and clarifying misconceptions. The patient should have the maximum possible involvement in the selection of the facility and other decisions.

If possible, visiting the facility before admission can be beneficial for the patient. The patient can become familiar with the physical layout; meet some of the patients and staff; and learn about routines, activities, and other aspects of nursing home life. The nursing home will not be "just like home," and it would be dishonest to imply so. It is better to acknowledge that there are differences between a person's own home and a nursing home and that it normally takes time to adjust to the changes. Some of the positive aspects can be highlighted, such as activities, flexible visitation policies, and availability of medical and nursing care. The ability of patients to participate actively in decision making and in their care also should be emphasized.

Patients and families should be encouraged to bring small objects from home. Favorite knickknacks, quilts, wall hangings, pillows, and other items can make the patient's room more personal and familiar.

Ideally, patients should be paired with roommates with similar function and interests. It can be frustrating for an immobile patient who has high intellectual function to share a room with a severely demented patient. If similar roommates cannot be matched, a new patient should be paired with a "buddy" who resides elsewhere in the facility who can assist the patient in adjusting to nursing home life.

Particularly during the first few days after admission, staff should make an effort to check on the patient frequently and spend extra time with him or her. Questions from the patient should be encouraged; some patients may find a pen and paper left at the bedside a useful means of writing down questions and concerns as they emerge.

Entering a nursing home is one of the major and potentially traumatic adjustments persons may confront in their lives. At a time when they are experiencing multiple losses related to the aging process, the aged are particularly vulnerable to negative effects from admission to a nursing home. Special nursing assistance and support can minimize the risks associated with this process.

One thought bears remembering: The aged, although vulnerable to the negative effects of institutionalization, possess enormous coping strength. They have survived immigration to a new country, major wars, the Great Depression, and other hardships unknown to young adults today. This has left them with a strong foundation that can be built on to assist them in adapting to nursing home life. A satisfactory adjustment to the nursing home can facilitate sufficient improvement to enable some patients to return to the community, while providing a meaningful quality of life for those who will spend the remainder of their days in this setting.

REFERENCES

Borup, J., 1983. Relocation mortality research: Assessment, reply, and the need to refocus on the issues. *Gerontologist* 23:235–242.

Doughtery, L.M., I.K. Krauss, and K.M. Finello. 1982. Coping with anticipated relocation by the elderly. Paper presented at meeting, Gerontological Society of America, 21 November, Boston.

Health Care Financing Administration. 1981. *Long term care: Background and future directions.* HCFA Pub. No. 81-200047. Washington, D.C.: U.S. Department of Health and Human Services.

Johnson, C.L., and L.A. Grant. 1985. *The nursing home in American society*, 37–38. Baltimore, Md.: Johns Hopkins University Press.

BIBLIOGRAPHY

American Association of Retired Persons. 1988. *A profile of older Americans: 1988.* Washington, D.C.: American Association of Retired Persons.

Baurret, E. 1986. Improving patient care for the elderly through a geriatric consultation team. *Perspectives* 10:11–12.

Branch, L.G. 1984. Relative risk rates of nonmedical predictors of institutional care among elderly persons. *Compr Ther* 10:33–40.

Burnside, I. 1986. Some do not fly over the cuckoo's nest. *J Gerontol Nurs* 12:5.

Gallagher, L.P., and M.C. Kreidler. 1988. *Nursing and health: Maximizing human potential through the life cycle*. New York: John Wiley & Sons.

Howie, C. 1987. Helping the aged. *Nurs Times* 83:40–42.

Jones, D., and G. Van Amelsvoort Jones. 1986. Communication patterns between nursing home staff and the ethnic elderly in a long-term care facility. *J Adv Nurs* 11:265–72.

Phillips, L.R. 1987. Respect basic human rights. *J Gerontol Nurs* 13:36–39.

Chapter 4

Families as Partners in Care

Miss Billings is an 82-year-old spinster who lives alone in an apartment. Beginning her career as a teacher, she progressed to the position of assistant superintendent of the county school system. She has always been fiercely independent and is now frustrated by the frailty and dependency caused by her cardiac disease. She does not want to be a burden to her nieces and nephews by asking them to assist her; however, she has not had success in employing reliable and trustworthy help. After considering the options, Miss Billings decides to enter a local nursing home where her needs can be addressed and her decision-making control preserved.

Mr. and Mrs. Pall had enjoyed a fulfilling marriage of 40 years when Mrs. Pall was diagnosed as having Alzheimer's disease. The couple had never been apart, and Mr. Pall vowed to care for his wife at home. Keeping Mrs. Pall at home developed into a greater challenge than Mr. Pall ever anticipated. As Mrs. Pall's dementia progressed she wandered incessantly, often causing Mr. Pall to lose sleep in order to monitor her during the night. She resisted bathing and could not be trusted to stay alone. Mr. Pall found it difficult to obtain help and at one point, when he had to be hospitalized for 1 week, he needed to negotiate with five different caregivers to achieve 24-hour coverage. The physical and emotional stress of managing his wife's care was taking its toll, and Mr. Pall found that institutionalization of his wife would be necessary to meet her needs adequately and to maintain his own health.

Mrs. Dello agreed to take her mother, who had suffered a stroke, into the Dello household and assume care-giving responsibilities.

Mrs. Dello's two brothers agreed to assist financially but were unable to be involved in care-giving activities. Mrs. Dello had not anticipated the problems she faced when her mother joined the household: the formerly mild-mannered mother developed an irritable, demanding personality after her stroke and caused considerable friction in the household. Mr. Dello resented the time and energy his wife invested in her mother's care and finally gave an ultimatum that either his mother-in-law or he would have to leave. Mrs. Dello's brothers refused to accept their mother into their homes, claiming that their wives would not tolerate the arrangement. Hurt by her children's unwillingness to care for her, Mrs. Dello's mother agreed to nursing home placement, but told her children that she never wanted to see them again.

The roads to nursing home admission are varied and often rocky. Some patients make a conscious choice to enter a nursing home, whereas others have the decision made for them; some families exhaust multiple resources before using nursing home services, whereas others turn to nursing homes because of the lack of availability or knowledge of other options; and some patients and families recognize nursing home care as a constructive means to provide care beyond the capacity of the family, whereas others view it as a failure of the family to care for its own. Not surprisingly, families will have a wide range of feelings toward nursing home care.

An important point to remember is that nursing home placement is not the first choice of most families for the care of their ill relatives. It is usually after they have exhausted all other options that families turn to institutional care. As a result, families may become physically, emotionally, socially, and financially depleted by the time nursing home admission occurs.

REACTIONS TO ADMISSION

There are many factors that influence a family's reaction to the admission of a relative to a nursing home, such as the following.

- *Quality of relationship*. Family members who shared a close relationship and offered ongoing support and assistance to each other may feel that they are letting their loved ones down by having them cared for by strangers and feel frustrated, depressed, and angry. On the other hand, the fact that persons are related does not necessarily mean that they share a close relationship, or even like each other for that matter.

- *Care-giving experience*. Families who have attempted to care for ill relatives at home may be more receptive to nursing home care as they realize their limitations in meeting care-giving demands. At the other extreme, caregivers may view nursing home placement as an indication of their failure in fulfilling the care-giving role.

- *Resources available.* In a community where service options are limited, nursing home care may be accepted by families more readily than in communities where easily available home health, day care, or other services facilitate family care giving.
- *Experience with nursing homes.* Persons who have heard only negative reports of nursing home care may feel guilty that they are subjecting their relatives to a tragic ordeal. Persons who possess a realistic understanding of the nursing home environment may feel they are affording their loved one competent care.
- *Preparation for placement.* Families who have had the opportunity to discuss nursing home care, involve the relative in the decision, and select an appropriate facility for their needs may feel more comfortable with nursing home admission than families who had to make the decision in a crisis situation.
- *Promises.* Family members may have committed (to themselves or others) to never put their spouse or parent in a nursing home. Tremendous guilt and disappointment may arise when nursing home placement becomes a necessity.

Institutionalization can bring about changes in the roles and functions of the relative within the family system and result in a deep sense of loss. As with any significant loss, the family may grieve and manifest their grief through a variety of reactions.

Guilt is not an uncommon reaction to the institutionalization of a loved one. Family members may feel that if they had recognized the patient's problems earlier, been more involved with care, visited more frequently, or taken other actions, they may have avoided the consequence of institutionalization. Even if they have exhausted their physical, emotional, and economic resources in providing care, there may still be guilt at seeing the parent who sacrificed for them or the spouse with whom they shared decades of life now enter an impersonal environment to be cared for by strangers. This guilt can be compounded by the pleas, angry outbursts, tearful glances, and rejection from the patient. "What a shame you had to put her in a nursing home"; "Couldn't all of you children have found some way to keep your mother at home?"; "I could never do that to my parent"; and other comments from friends and neighbors further feed into guilt.

Anger, often displaced on staff, can be displayed by families. "Why do you have her sitting up so long?" "Can't you answer the call-light more quickly?" "You're getting paid to help patients, not sit at this desk!" Hostile outbursts, accusations, criticisms, and sarcasm are among the ways anger is vented. Family members may be angry that their loved one is ill, that no other care option is possible for them, that their lives are altered at having the responsibilities of a relative in a nursing home. They may be angry that the patient did not take better care of herself or himself, or that they are responsible for a relative with whom they never shared a close relationship. Although the family's anger is most commonly directed to staff, family members may display anger to other relatives or professionals for their actions in the situation.

The guilt, grief, frustration, and powerlessness families may feel can lead them to feelings of depression. Depression can affect their own physical and emotional health. They may lose their appetites; suffer from insomnia; and be disinterested in work, sex, or leisure activities. Some family members may cope with depression by withdrawing from the situation (e.g., not visiting for extended periods). Others try to overcompensate by visiting excessively or "overassisting" their loved one (i.e., doing tasks for the patient that the patient can do for herself or himself).

As families express reactions to the institutionalization of their loved ones, they need patience, support, and understanding. Staff must be sensitive to the fact that when they first encounter the family a distorted picture of the normal family may be presented. The stress associated with preparation for the admission and witnessing a loved one enter an institutional setting can cause some dysfunction of relatives. Family members may seem preoccupied, unable to answer basic questions, impatient with routine admission procedures, or demanding of staff. They may bicker among themselves or appear overwhelmed. With the many activities that must be performed to admit the patient to the facility it can be easy for the family to be overlooked and for their needs to be unmet.

CHALLENGES FOR THE FAMILY

One of the first challenges the family encounters is dealing with the patient's reaction to entering a nursing home. The patient may cry, sulk, withdraw, refuse to cooperate, beg to be taken home, or accuse relatives of being cold and uncaring. Such reactions are painful for relatives to witness and can be especially difficult if the patient displaces feelings on family members, as often happens. The feelings that family members are experiencing may limit their emotional reserves to accept the patient's reactions or offer support to the patient during this emotionally turbulent time.

Family members must be prepared for the guilt they may feel (or be made to feel) and learn ways to manage it. It can be helpful for staff to acknowledge the family's preadmission care-giving efforts and reinforce that the patient's care needs are of such a level to be met most appropriately in a health care facility. Stating to families that guilt is a common feeling that may reemerge periodically can be beneficial in helping families understand what they are experiencing.

Allowing families to ventilate their emotions or sitting in silence with them can provide support during times when guilt is exacerbated.

A new role—"visitor"—must be learned by family members when a loved one becomes a patient in a nursing home. Visitors are guests in the facility and must abide by definite rules of behavior. Rather than stopping on the way home from work to share a cup of coffee with mother or checking that a spouse's blanket has not slipped in the middle of the night, family members must adjust to seeing the patient during specified hours. There is no refrigerator from which family members can freely obtain a snack, nor a sofa on which they can comfortably lounge. A wife who wishes to cuddle in bed with her husband may be reluctant to do so in full view of others. The strange sights, sounds, and smells are constant reminders that the patient's new residence is hardly what home used to be. The best pie baker in town, skilled handyman, creative homemaker, and other roles that family members assumed in the household may be difficult or impossible to demonstrate to the patient in the nursing home environment. Very little prepares family members for the role of visitor.

Perhaps the greatest challenge for the family is to establish a meaningful role with the patient in which they can learn ways to enjoy this altered life style with the patient. Including families in facility activities and allowing them to participate in care-giving tasks (e.g., feeding, grooming, ambulating) can aid families in feeling that they are fulfilling a useful role during the visit. Families can be encouraged to keep the patient involved with family activities through discussion, photographs, and the patient's attendance at family events. Hobbies and games can provide enjoyable pastimes to make visitation meaningful. Of course, offering privacy and encouragement for family members to touch and demonstrate affection is important.

ASSISTING FAMILIES

Ideally, helping the family members adjust to nursing home care begins before their loved one enters the facility. The family should be guided in selecting a nursing home that most adequately meets their unique needs. Factors for the family to consider include proximity of the facility to family members; cost; level(s) of care provided; facility reputation; and cultural, religious, and ethnic similarity of residents to the patient. By contacting the institutional licensing division of the local health department families can obtain facts about how well the facility complies with standards. If possible, the family should select several facilities and visit each; factors that can be evaluated include the following.

- *Staffing*. How many licensed and unlicensed personnel are assigned to units? Are staff easily accessible to patients? Do staff communicate in a courteous, pleasant manner?

- *Physical plant.* Is the facility clean and odor free? Are there any safety hazards? Are rooms decorated to minimize an institutional look? Where is the dining room, activity area, and lobby in relation to patient rooms? Are there private bathrooms?
- *Patients.* Are patients clean and dressed in street clothes? How do patients spend their time? What are patients' impressions of the facility?
- *Meals.* Is food presented attractively? Do patients eat in their rooms or in a dining room? Can patients select their meals and make substitutions?
- *Administration.* Are the administrator and director of nursing located in an easily accessible area to patients and visitors? What is the mechanism for giving feedback to administration? Does administration have regular meetings with patients and families?

In most facilities visits are welcomed and questions are answered freely; families should be concerned when visits are discouraged or personnel are reluctant to answer questions.

Before admission, members of the facility should meet with and prepare the family and patient, reviewing issues such as billing procedures, visitation policies, and services provided and excluded. An average day for residents can be outlined, as can the realities of care. For instance, families can be informed that although general care will be provided (e.g., assistance with bathing, feeding, toileting) staff may not be able to spend the same amount of time with each resident as their family members did at home (e.g., escorting them for walks off the premises daily, giving backrubs every shift, setting their hair each night). This is not to imply that personalized attention to residents' needs is not promoted, but there are limitations to what the family can expect. The names of resource persons in the nursing, medical, social services, activities, dietary, and billing departments should be given to the family for future reference.

The orientation of the family should prepare them for the reaction they and the patient may experience. Telling family members that it is not unusual for the patient to cry, beg to be taken home, accuse the family of not caring, or demonstrate other negative feelings can help them understand that it is the situation, rather than them as individuals, to which the patient is reacting. The family also needs to know that during the first few months after the patient's admission, they may experience irritability, short attention spans, poor appetite, insomnia, crying episodes, nervousness, disinterest in activities, and doubts about the appropriateness of the decision. Knowing that these feelings usually subside as both patient and family adjust to placement can help put reactions into perspective.

Family orientation groups can be planned to offer information and support. Monthly sessions, led by a professional, can provide an opportunity for families to come together to develop relationships and understand their feelings. The following is a possible agenda.

Welcome and introduction of families.
Presentation of realities of nursing home life and of being a relative of a nursing home patient.

(10 minutes)

Sharing among families:
Families with relatives who have been institutionalized for a period explain what they and their relatives (patients) have experienced and share measures they have found helpful for adjustment.
Families of newly admitted patients express their concerns, ask questions.

(20 to 30 minutes)

Presentation and guided discussion of topic, such as managing guilt/ anger/depression, dealing with the reactions of other family members, realizing the importance of being selfish and meeting one's own needs, facing unresolved feelings toward the patient.

(30 minutes)

Facility news, open sharing.

(10 minutes)

These groups are useful for both families of new patients and families of patients who have resided in the facility for some time.

Linked to the family orientation and support groups can be a "buddy system" whereby new family members are matched to family members who have had a relative in the facility for an extended period. Ideally, the buddy system can begin before admission, with the more experienced family contacting the new family. Families may benefit more from learning about the personal experiences of their peers than from hearing the same information from a professional who has never been in a similar personal situation. Also, sometimes it is easier for families to ask questions of peers than to pose the same question to professionals. The buddy can meet the family on the day of admission and lend support during this difficult time. In addition to the support offered through a buddy system, families may develop friendships that can make visitation more meaningful and enjoyable.

Communication between staff and family members is crucial to efforts to assist the family. Family members have a lifetime of history about the patient and can be valuable resources to tap in assessing the patient and planning individualized care. Care plans and interventions should be explained to families so that the activities they see will be understood. Promptly informing families of changes in patients' status or unusual incidents can prevent unnecessary distress for the family and unnecessary problems for the facility.

CONCLUSION

Admission to a nursing home is a profound event for patients and their families. Regardless of how necessary this form of care is and how much the patient and family intellectually understand the necessity, nursing home care triggers a multitude of emotional responses. To protect families from the unhealthy effects that may result, stress interventions are necessary to provide information and support. The time and effort invested in assisting families can not only improve relationships between the facility and its consumers but, more importantly, enhance the quality of the relationship between the patient and family.

BIBLIOGRAPHY

Brody, E.M. 1985. Parent care as a normative stress. *Gerontologist* 25:19–29.

Brody, E.M., P.T. Johnsen, and M.C. Fulcomer. 1984. What should adult children do for elderly parents: Opinions and preferences of three generations of women. *J Gerontol* 39:736–46.

Brody, E.M., M.H. Kleban, P.T. Johnsen, C. Hoffman, and C.B. Schoonover. 1987. Work status and parent care: A comparison of four groups of women. *Gerontologist* 27:201–08.

Cantor, M.H. 1983. Strain among caregivers: A study of experience in the United States. *Gerontologist* 23:597–604.

Eliopoulos, C. 1989. Assessment of the family system. In *Health assessment of the older adult*, 2d ed., edited by C. Eliopoulos. Menlo Park, Calif.: Addison-Wesley Publishing Co.

Lipkin, L.V., and K.J. Faude. 1987. Dementia—Educating the caregiver. *J Gerontol Nurs* 13:23–27.

Rempusheski, V.F., and L.R. Phillips. 1988. Elders versus caregivers: Games they play. *Geriatr Nurs* 9:30–34.

Part II
Clinical Aspects

Chapter 5

Nursing Assessment

Assessment—the process of learning about the patient—has many important functions. By reviewing the unique physical, mental, and social aspects of the patient, nurses can plan care in an effective, individualized manner, thereby promoting a higher quality of care. A realistic determination of the appropriateness of the patient for the facility can be made. Resources can be used wisely in that services can be allocated for specific needs. Also, legal problems can be minimized through the early identification of risks and recognition of needs warranting intervention.

As many nurses know, data that other agencies share with the nursing home concerning the patient's status may bear little resemblance to the actual profile of the patient. Details such as the presence of a decubitus ulcer, a severe confusional state that requires constant monitoring, unstable vital signs, and incontinence may not be communicated to the nursing home. The unfortunate outcome of an incomplete data base can be refusal of admission by the nursing home once the patient is seen. If the nursing home does admit the patient, it may find itself saddled with more problems than bargained for. Ideally, the facility should have one of its nurses visit the patient before admission and assess the patient's status and appropriateness for the facility. If a preadmission visit is not possible, a nurse should call the patient's primary nurse or case manager and ask specific questions about the patient's status and level of function. The time invested in this preadmission evaluation can save considerable time, effort, and patient hardship in preventing inappropriate admissions.

PREPARING FOR ASSESSMENT

Although the data collected during the assessment may seem fairly basic and straightforward, there are many factors that can affect the quality of the informa-

37

tion obtained. Consideration of these factors in the preparation for the assessment can promote an effective experience.

Patients should be prepared for the assessment with a full explanation of what will occur, why data are being collected, and how much time will be required: "I will be spending the next hour asking you a lot of questions and examining you so that I can learn more about you and how the staff can best help you." This type of explanation can aid in alleviating anxieties; it also affords patients the opportunity to advise nurses of pain, fatigue, or other problems that could diminish participation in the assessment.

Casual conversation during the initial phase can help patients relax, as well as assist the nurse in identifying cognitive or language barriers that will interfere with data collection. Considering the variety of ethnic groups in some communities, lack of fluency in the English language is not unusual. Even when patients appear to be fluent in English, it is beneficial to ask if they are bilingual. Some persons resort to their primary (foreign) language when stressed or traumatized, and the interviewer should be prepared for this potential problem. Resources in the facility or the community can be located to assist with interpretation as needed.

Not only foreign languages but also medical jargon can create communication barriers. Some of the medical terminology that is now considered common may be unfamiliar to or misinterpreted by patients. For instance, a patient may not understand that hypertension refers to high blood pressure but instead think it has something to do with "being very tense"; a patient may answer positively to having a history of rheumatic fever because he or she believes this has something to do with his or her "rheumatism." Words like "void," "specimen," "diarrhea," and "sputum" may be unfamiliar to some patients. Likewise, patients may be unfamiliar with their formal medical diagnosis and omit contributing a history of the diagnosis as a result. Until the patient's level of understanding is ascertained it may be useful to couple the medical term with a lay term (e.g., diarrhea, watery stool; tuberculosis, consumption; diabetes, sugar; fainting, falling out).

The environment in which the assessment is conducted also impacts on the quality of the assessment. Older adults have a lower body temperature, which can cause them to feel cold in room temperatures that are comfortable for active, younger persons. Discomfort or preoccupation with a cold temperature can distract from the assessment. A room temperature of approximately 75°F should be maintained to promote comfort and relaxation. Lighting should be adjusted to prevent glare to which the aged are more sensitive. Many older persons suffer from hearing loss, and noisy environments can further limit hearing. Distractions should be controlled, even those to which staff have adapted, such as loud patients, paging systems, noisy equipment, ringing telephones, and heavy traffic flow. Also, not to be forgotten is the issue of privacy. Even if the patient in the next bed is too confused to understand or the staff member in the room will eventually have knowledge of what the patient is saying, the presence of those persons during the assessment can prohibit patients' open communication.

Families often can provide useful data about patients. It can be beneficial to arrange a meeting with family members so that they will have an opportunity to share their knowledge of the patient's norms, likes, and dislikes. This process also can provide an opportunity for families to have their questions answered and concerns addressed. From the start, families should know that they serve an important role in the patient's care process.

ASSESSMENT SKILLS

Nurses use a complex network of knowledge and skills during the assessment process. Often, these skills are so intrinsic to nursing practice that nurses give them little conscious thought. For instance, while passing a patient in the hall the nurse may note that his coloring is slightly altered, his breathing is shallow, and ambulation that did not bother him before now causes him to become short of breath; this may lead the nurse to evaluate vital signs and auscultate lung sounds. These seemingly basic actions required that the nurse know

- Normal anatomy and physiology
- Significance of alterations in coloring and chest expansion
- Physical examination skills of observation and auscultation
- Normal versus abnormal lung sounds

Nurses use a multitude of assessment skills during their routine daily activities.

Good interview skills are basic to the assessment. An interview is a structured verbal encounter for the purpose of exchanging information. Nurses may choose to follow the questions on a nursing history tool or ask questions in a less structured manner and document findings at a later time. Personal style and experience will influence the approach used.

Various styles of questions can be used during the interview, and some will be more effective than others in eliciting data. *Closed-ended questions* lend to concise responses and are useful when direct information, requiring no explanation, is desired:

What is your date of birth?
Do you ever have problems voiding?
When do you take this medication?
How many hours do you sleep?

Open-ended questions and comments demand more explanation:

You help yourself fall asleep by. . . ?
Will you describe your relationship with your wife?
Tell me more about your sleep problems.

Closed-ended questions allow a large volume of facts to be collected efficiently. Open-ended questions require more time for response, but are beneficial in that problems may surface that could otherwise go undetected and insight into patients' cognitive function may be gained. For example, a patient with a moderate degree of cognitive dysfunction may be able to respond satisfactorily to yes-and-no questions but, when asked to describe a problem, may reveal disjointed thinking:

Nurse: "Do you live alone?"
Patient: "No."
Nurse: "Do you live with family?"
Patient: "Yes."
Nurse: "Could you describe the family members with whom you live?"
Patient: "There is Bill, he is my father . . . I mean my . . . oh, what do you call it . . . my husband, I think . . . yes, he is my husband . . . and there are these other people . . . that man and woman. . . ."

This patient may have a cognitive impairment that prohibits her from remembering that she lives with her husband, son, and daughter-in-law. Stopping after the closed-ended question "Do you live with family?" may have prevented this dysfunction from surfacing at this time.

Physical examination of the patient is an important component of the nursing assessment. The primary purposes of the nursing assessment are to determine the patient's functional capacity, identify unique risks that require special attention, and recognize problems that may have been undetected during the medical examination. To assure accurate and comprehensive assessment of physical status the nurse must become competent in the skills of observation, percussion, palpation, and auscultation.

Observation is the conscious use of all senses to obtain information. This implies that observation encompasses more than inspecting or visualizing the patient's status. In addition to viewing the normalcy of structure, function, behavior, coloring, grooming, and hygienic practices, the nurse notes sounds, such as clicking dentures, cracking joints, gurgling intestines, and the tone and quality of speech. In addition, unusual odors are detected, such as breath that smells fruity (ketoacidosis), cloverlike (liver failure), or similar to urine (uremic acidosis); fecal or urine odors (poor hygiene or incontinence); and foul foot odors (infection or poor hygiene). Of course, the nurse's sense of touch will be used throughout the physical examination.

Percussion is the skill of tapping on body surfaces to assess the density, size, and location of underlying organs. Figure 5-1 demonstrates the correct method of percussion. The sounds detected through percussion are

Resonance: a clear, low-pitched, vibrant sound indicating an air-filled area (e.g., over the lungs and abdomen)
Dullness: a solid sound indicating little air in an area (e.g., over the heart and in lungs filled with fluid)
Flatness: an extremely dull sound indicating no air in an area (e.g., over a muscle)
Tympany: a clear, hollow, musical sound indicating air in the underlying tissue (e.g., over the bowel)
Hyperresonance: an abnormal, hollow, high-pitched sound indicating an over-inflated organ (e.g., with pneumothorax or emphysema)

Palpation is the touching and moving of body parts to determine their size, texture, and mobility. (See Figure 5-2.) Usually light palpation is followed by deeper palpation. Enlarged organs, masses, inflammation, pain, and other abnormalities can be detected through palpation.

Listening to internal body sounds with the aid of a stethoscope is referred to as *auscultation*. The diaphragm of the stethoscope is used to hear high-frequency sounds (e.g., respiratory and bowel sounds, blood pressure), and the bell portion is used to hear low-frequency sounds (e.g., murmurs).

THE ASSESSMENT: DIFFERENTIATING NORMAL FROM ABNORMAL

The purpose of the nursing assessment is not to diagnose medical problems, but to recognize deficits in the patient's functional capacity that necessitate nursing intervention. To identify deficits, nurses must be able to differentiate normal from abnormal findings as they use the basic skills of inspection, auscultation, palpation, and percussion to assess the patient. In the following sections normal and abnormal findings, as well as the skills required to assess each of the basic human needs, are reviewed.

Ventilation and Circulation

Assessment of the body's gaseous exchange begins during the initial observation of the patient. Coloring, breathing pattern, posture, and activity level can

If you are right handed, place the first joint of your left middle finger flat against the patient's body surface.

Flex the middle finger of your right hand and tap it against the left middle finger, withdrawing the right finger quickly. The movement should come from the wrist, not the finger.

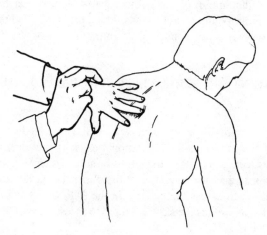

If left handed, reverse the function of each hand.

Figure 5-1 Procedure To Follow in Percussion. *Source:* Reprinted from *Nursing Administration of Long-Term Care* by C. Eliopoulos, p. 31, Aspen Publishers, Inc., © 1983.

For light palpation, indent the pads of your finger tips one-half inch into the body surface.

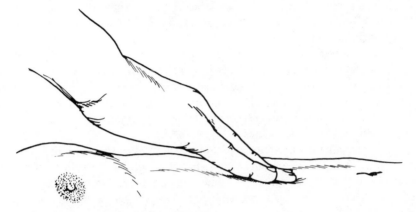

For deeper palpation, indent the pads of your finger tips more than one-half inch into the body surface. It may be useful to use the finger tips from your other hand to apply pressure to the palpating finger tips.

Figure 5-2 Positions of the Hand in Palpation. *Source*: Reprinted from *Handbook of Nursing Physical Assessment* by R. Kopf, p. 138, Aspen Publishers, Inc., © 1988.

indicate the status of cardiovascular and pulmonary systems. The patient should be asked about symptoms, such as chest or leg pain, shortness of breath, dyspnea, orthopnea, cough, hemoptysis, edema, dizziness and coldness, tingling, or numbness of extremities.

Inspect the coloring and vessels throughout the body. Check the quality of pulses in the extremities. Observe and palpate the carotid vessels. A weak carotid pulse can be associated with left ventricular failure, whereas a strong pulse can occur with anemia, fever, stress, aortic insufficiency, and complete heart block. Distention of the jugular veins should be noted and can indicate congestive heart failure or pericarditis.

Expose the trunk and inspect the anterior and posterior aspects of the chest. Spinal curvatures should be noted, particularly kyphosis, which can interfere with adequate respiration. An increased anteroposterior chest diameter, which gives the chest a barrel appearance, is indicative of chronic obstructive pulmonary disease (COPD). Watch the chest expand during respiration; note the rate, rhythm, depth, and length of respirations.

Begin palpating the posterior aspect of the chest by placing both hands on the area over the lower lobe of the lungs (thumbs alongside the spine and fingers fanned over the intercostal spaces) and gradually move toward the upper lobe region. Determine the depth and symmetry of respirations; note any massae and areas of sensitivity. A vibratory tremor (tactile fremitus) may be felt normally in the upper lobe region of the lungs; COPD and pneumothorax can cause these tremors to be diminished in the upper lobes, whereas pneumonia and massae can increase the vibrations felt in the lower lobes. (See Figure 5-3.)

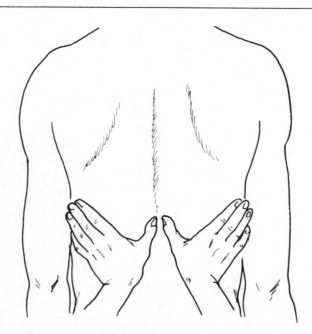

Figure 5-3 A Vibratory Tremor Can Be Felt Normally in the Upper Lobes of the Lungs. *Source:* Adapted from *Fundamentals of Nursing: Concepts and Procedures*, 3d ed., by B. Kozier and G.L. Erb, with permission of Addison-Wesley Publishing Company, © 1987.

Beginning at the upper lobe and moving downward, percuss the lungs. Alternate from one side to the other so that sounds can be compared. (See Figure 5-4.) Be sure to percuss over the intercostal spaces, rather than over the ribs. A clear, low-pitched sound (resonance) should be heard. A hollow, high-pitched sound (hyperresonance) occurs with emphysema and pneumothorax, whereas a solid sound (dullness) indicates filling of the air spaces, as may occur with a massa or pneumonia.

There are several types of normal breath sounds that can be auscultated:

Bronchial breath sounds: heard over the trachea; the inspiratory phase is shorter than the expiratory phase.
Vesicular breath sounds: heard over the entire lung field; the inspiratory phase is longer than the expiratory phase.
Bronchovesicular sounds: heard over the sternum and scapula; the inspiratory and expiratory phases are equal.

Crackling, rattling, or wheezing sounds are abnormal. When abnormal sounds are noted they should be described in terms of their characteristics and location. Some patients may always have some degree of abnormal breath sounds present;

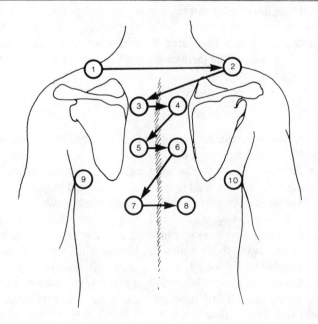

Figure 5-4 Alternate from One Side to the Other to Compare Percussion Sounds. *Source:* Reprinted from *Handbook of Nursing Physical Assessment* by R. Kopf, p. 92, Aspen Publishers, Inc., © 1988.

these sounds should be described thoroughly in the record so that other staff will understand this finding during their assessments and be able to identify changes from the patient's normal.

Examine the anterior aspect of the chest. Palpate the point of maximal impulse (PMI) in the apical or left ventricular area (at the fifth left intercostal space or slightly medial to the midclavicular line). COPD and kyphosis can displace the PMI downward; the PMI can be palpable at the anterior axillary line if there has been a considerable narrowing of chest size. Normally, the PMI should be 2 cm or less, and the sound should last for approximately 0.5 second.

Auscultate the heart for rate, rhythm, murmurs, and extra sounds. Although systolic murmurs are common in advanced age, diastolic murmurs signal cardiac disease and require further evaluation.

Obtain the blood pressure with the patient in three positions: lying, sitting, and standing. If a drop in blood pressure 20 mm Hg or greater is detected when the patient elevates from a supine position, orthostatic hypotension may be suspected. Repeated blood pressure values that exceed 140 mm Hg systolic and 90 mm Hg diastolic should be referred for evaluation.

Obtain the patient's resting heart rate, which can range from 60 to 100 beats per minute and does not normally change with age. Changes in the patient's usual resting heart rate should be reported to the physician. With age, there is a difference in the ability of the heart to recover from tachycardia, and it may take hours for heart rate to return to normal after experiencing an episode of tachycardia. If an elevated heart rate is discovered, the events of the preceding hours should be reviewed to determine if the tachycardia is a response to an earlier activity.

Nutrition

Although the facility's dietitian most likely will perform a comprehensive dietary assessment of the patient, it can be helpful to review the patient's dietary habits and preferences. The degree of independence in feeding should be determined, including the ability to hold utensils, cut meat, and grasp a cup.

Note clinical signs of malnutrition, such as muscle wasting, weight gain or loss, dull eyes, smooth tongue, ridged nails, rashes, and weakness. Values for hemoglobin, hematocrit, total iron-binding capacity, and transferrin saturation, as well as blood levels of vitamins and minerals, further aid in identifying malnutrition.

Ask about symptoms that could indicate gastrointestinal problems, such as difficulty swallowing, nausea, vomiting, regurgitation, indigestion, pain, flatus, diarrhea, and constipation. If such problems exist, explore how the patient usually manages them (e.g., uses antacid tablets for indigestion, ingests only liquids during episodes of regurgitation).

Observe the color, symmetry, and moisture of the lips. Blue lips can indicate anoxia or anemia, although dark-skinned persons can normally have a bluish hue to the lips. Because the oral cavity is a common site of cancers in the aged any sore or lesion on the lips warrants evaluation. Vitamin B complex deficiencies, or overclosure as a result of missing teeth or poorly fitting dentures, can cause a fissure at the corner of the mouth.

With the use of a gloved hand, examine the oral cavity. Any lesion or massa should be referred for evaluation. Note the condition of teeth and gums, and assess for bleeding and pain. The teeth may be discolored and appear longer than normal because of retracting of the gingival border. If dentures are present, evaluate the condition and fit.

Examine the tongue, which normally should be pink and well papillated. A smooth, red tongue can occur with a deficiency of iron, niacin, or vitamin B_{12}. White patches over the tongue may be associated with moniliasis; irregular, thick, white patches that have been present for at least several weeks could be a precancerous sign. Most carcinomas are apparent on the undersurface of the tongue. Also on the undersurface are varicosities; large varicosities can be due to cardiac or pulmonary disease.

Prepare the patient for examination of the abdomen by having him or her void; then expose the abdomen. Inspect the abdomen noting any discoloration, rash, asymmetry, bulges, dilated vessels, distention, or contractions. Silver or white striae (stretch marks) reflect old stretching (e.g., from pregnancies or weight changes). Recently acquired stretch marks tend to be pink or blue in color.

Auscultation of the abdomen should be performed before percussion and palpation to avoid stimulating bowel sounds. With the use of the diaphragm portion of the stethoscope, listen for normal peristaltic sounds, which are heard irregularly every 5 to 15 seconds. If no sounds are heard, listen for several minutes and then tap on the abdominal wall to stimulate intestinal motility. Bowel sounds can be absent with late bowel obstruction, peritonitis, electrolyte imbalances, and handling of the bowel during surgery. Early bowel obstruction, gastroenteritis, and diarrhea can increase bowel sounds.

Place the bell portion of the stethoscope over the major arteries (above the umbilicus) to auscultate vascular sounds. A heartbeat should be heard. A murmur could indicate an aneurysm and warrants prompt attention.

Percuss all quadrants of the abdomen (Figure 5-5). Normally, a drumlike sound (tympany) should be heard over air-filled spaces, and dullness should be heard over organs. Dullness over what should be an air-filled area could indicate the presence of abnormal solid material, such as a massa or ascites.

Palpate all quadrants of the abdomen, beginning with light touch and progressing to deep palpation. Pain, massae, rigidity, and enlarged organs are among the abnormalities that could be identified.

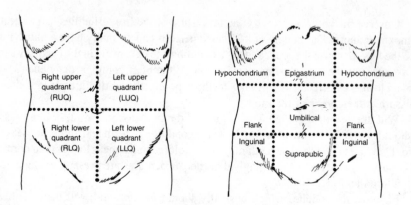

Figure 5-5 Percuss All Quadrants of the Abdomen. *Source:* Reprinted from *Handbook of Nursing Physical Assessment* by R. Kopf, p. 139, Aspen Publishers, Inc., © 1988.

Excretion

Bowel and bladder elimination can be affected by the ability of the patient to toilet himself or herself. Therefore assessment of excretion should include determining the degree of independence the patient has in recognizing the signal to eliminate, traveling to the bathroom or commode, transferring on and off the commode, and exercising good hygienic practices. For the patient who is unable to use bathroom facilities or a commode, the ability to reach for and use a urinal or bedpan independently should be assessed.

Review the patient's pattern of urinary elimination including frequency of voiding during the daytime and at night. Ask about the length of time between the patient's awareness of the need to void and the point at which bladder control can no longer be maintained. Explore problems in voiding, such as incontinence, hesitancy, retention, and burning. A urine specimen should be obtained. Urine testing for glucose can yield unreliable results in older adults; therefore blood samples are preferred for glucose screening. Note the characteristics of the urine specimen. (See Table 5-1).

Table 5-1 Abnormal Characteristics of Urine and Possible Causes

Urine Characteristics	Possible Cause
Dark, concentrated	Dehydration
Cloudy, odorous, alkaline	Urinary tract infection
Pink, red, dark-brown, black	Presence of blood
Cloudy	Infection; presence of prostatic fluid or sperm
Yellow-brown, green-brown	Jaundice; obstructive bile duct

The frequency of bowel elimination also should be reviewed. Ask the patient if laxatives, enemas, special foods, or other means have been used regularly to facilitate regular bowel elimination. Explore problems such as constipation, diarrhea, bloody or tarry stools, change in bowel habits, and pain or itching in the rectal area. A rectal examination may be done if it is consistent with facility policy. Obtain a stool specimen.

Activity

Assessment of the patient's level of activity begins from the moment the patient is first observed. Observe the patient's energy level, movements, gait, and ability to sit down and lift from a chair. Note deformities, weakness, and disuse of specific limbs. If a cane, walker, or wheelchair is used, determine when and how it was obtained and the appropriateness of use.

Inspect all joints. Bony nodules on the distal joints of the fingers (Heberden's nodes) are associated with osteoarthritis, the most common form of arthritis in late life. Red joints with subcutaneous nodules over bony prominences, atrophy of the surrounding muscle, and flexion contractures are associated with rheumatoid arthritis. Place all joints through a range of motion. (See Chapter 8.)

Review the patient's typical day to determine what the past activity level has been. Knowing whether the patient previously enjoyed gardening, reading, hiking, sewing, stamp collecting, swimming, or television viewing can be useful in planning activities to stimulate activity for the patient within the facility.

Continued observation of the patient can assist in assessing activity tolerance. Be aware of dramatic changes in pulse rate, rise in diastolic blood pressure (more than 15 mm Hg), shortness of breath, dyspnea, pallor, cyanosis, chest pain, dizziness, confusion, weakness, and excessive fatigue after activities.

Activity level can be affected by the patient's mental status. Some patients may be unmotivated to engage in activities because of depression; others may fear injuring themselves or demonstrating incompetence through activities. Altered cognition can impair a patient's ability to engage in activities. A thorough evaluation of mental status can give insight into activity status. (See Chapter 9.)

Rest and Sleep

Ask about the usual rest and sleep pattern, including frequency and length of naps, bedtime, amount of time to fall asleep after going to bed, interruptions to sleep, and awakening time. Several rest periods throughout the day may be necessary for older adults. Five to seven hours of night sleep are adequate for most elderly persons; longer periods of sleep can subject the patient to the hazardous effects of immobility. It is not uncommon for sleep to be interrupted by muscle cramps, nocturia, and environmental disturbances. Explore methods used by the patient to facilitate sleep, such as medications, baths, reading, and music.

As the patient adjusts to the institutional environment sleep problems and disorientation when awakening during the night may occur. Night lights and bedrails are among the measures that can prevent injury during this adjustment period. The night staff should observe the patient's sleep pattern and contribute their findings to the assessment.

Socialization and Solitude

Although institutionalization can dramatically affect the activities and roles that the patient will practice, learning about past patterns is useful in understanding behaviors and planning effective care. Ask the patient about typical social patterns: Did he or she belong to clubs, engage in regular activities with friends or family, attend meetings of any group, call or write any persons, or prefer staying at home alone? Obviously, it would be useful to plan opportunities for socialization for the patient in the nursing home that are most similar to those enjoyed in the community. Of course, it must be remembered that persons who did not enjoy group socialization throughout their lives may resist participation in group activities as nursing home patients.

Explore the patient's reactions to alterations in roles and activities. For instance, how is the patient coping with the separation from friends or the inability to spend weekends with grandchildren? Determine how the patient's current health status impacts on his or her ability to engage in usual roles and activities. For example: Does the patient have insufficient energy to stay awake during a 1-hour visit from family? Has hearing become so poor that engaging in normal conversation is too difficult? Has a disability caused the patient to be embarassed to meet new persons?

People need time alone, private time to reflect and relax. Explore the patient's individual pattern of solitude. Did he or she meet solitude needs by sitting on the patio with morning coffee and listening to the birds? by taking an extra-long bath? by walking through the woods? by listening to music after dinner? by meditating after meals? by lying across the bed in midafternoon? Plans should be developed to allow the patient to continue engaging in the same pattern of solitude, if possible.

Safety

Sensory function largely impacts on the ability of the patient to protect himself or herself from hazards. Determine the patient's visual capacity. Ideally, the results of ophthalmologic evaluation should be available in the patient's medical record. However, gross evaluation of the patient's vision can be done by having the patient look at a newspaper and, then, determining which lines of print he or she is able to see: smallest print? only bold, 1-inch headlines? If the patient is unable to see headline print, determine if he or she can see how many fingers you hold up, only shadows, or nothing at all. Explore how the patient manages visual deficits, such as with the use of reading glasses, magnifying lenses, large print books, or special lighting. Farsightedness; decreased peripheral vision; altered depth perception; poor night vision; slower accommodation; and poor discrimination of shades of green, blue, and violet are common in older adults. Review the patient's visual capacity at night; night shift staff can add to this assessment through direct observation. Ask about eye pain, restrictions in visual field, increased or absence of tearing, halos around lights, yellowing or blurring of vision, sudden appearance of flashes of light or spots, and recent changes in vision. Question the patient about eyeglasses, and review how old and effective the prescription is.

Throughout the interview an assessment of the patient's hearing can be made. Does the patient frequently ask for questions to be repeated? Are words misinterpreted? Is there a reliance on lip reading? Does the head cock to one side to enable the patient to hear better? Ask if the patient uses a hearing aid, and review how and when it was obtained and its effectiveness. Examine the ear with an otoscope, and look for a wax impaction. The harder consistency of the keratin in the cerumen can cause this to be a problem in the elderly.

Hearing and vision problems should be referred for further evaluation. In the interim these deficits should be communicated to staff to facilitate communication with the patient and reduce the risk of injury.

Other sensory deficits also can occur in older adults, such as decreased tactile sensation and reduced olfaction. Evaluate the patient's ability to differentiate hot from cold temperatures, sharp from dull objects, and coffee from a citrus scent. Determine if the patient, with eyes closed, can feel you gently touch different body parts (e.g., forehead, cheek, chin, extremities, finger tips).

The potential for skin breakdown also needs to be considered in assessing safety risks. The drier, more fragile skin of older persons can easily become irritated and torn. Inspect the skin throughout the body for moisture or dryness, integrity, and color. Note skin breaks, rashes, lesions, moles, discoloration, and other problems. Review the patient's usual skin care practices including frequency of bathing, and question about substances to which the skin is sensitive. Ask about cosmetic preferences so that the patient's usual practices can be maintained.

Do a careful review of medication practices. Ask the patient to describe all the prescription and over-the-counter drugs used. Determine if the patient has brought any medications into the facility. Keep in mind that some patients may not consider antacid tablets, analgesic ointments, cold capsules, and laxative suppositories as "medications"; therefore it may be necessary to be specific in the drug review.

Normalcy

Several important points must be considered when evaluating normalcy. First, what is normal for an older adult can be different from what is normal for a younger person. For example, normal findings in older persons that could be interpreted as abnormal in younger adults include

- Tachycardia for 1 hour after an activity
- Poor skin turgor
- Nocturia
- Decreased sensitivity to sweet and salty flavors
- Lower body temperature
- Poor short-term memory

Nursing staff must ensure that the patient's health status is evaluated against the norms for an older population.

Second, normal must be put in perspective of the patient's health status. The findings from the nursing assessment are significant in defining this perspective. Determine *the patient's* normal

- Breathing pattern
- Hygienic practices
- Appetite
- Food consumption
- Food preferences and intolerances
- Feeding ability
- Elimination pattern
- Toileting ability
- Energy level
- Mobility
- Sleep and rest requirements
- Vision and hearing capabilities
- Activity tolerance
- Sexual desires, practices, and needs

- Interests
- Mood
- Cognitive function

By understanding the patient's normal structure and function care can be planned effectively and changes in status identified more promptly.

PUTTING FINDINGS INTO PRACTICE

The many years of life and the multiple problems that patients possess when they enter a nursing home can yield extensive data for the nursing assessment. The value of these data is in their use as a guide to care activities. Therefore organization of findings is important. Data should be organized to follow a specific sequence, with like items (such as joint mobility restrictions or factors that cause shortness of breath) grouped together. Most likely there will be more problems discovered than time or ability to address them. Thus prioritization is essential.

The initial assessment gives insight into the patient's status at the time of admission. Often, the stresses associated with entering a nursing home and the effects of the illness and medications can cause the patient to interview poorly or demonstrate more disability than what usually exists. It can be advantageous to validate assessment findings after the patient has had a chance to adjust to the nursing home to assure accuracy.

In the next chapter how assessment findings are used in developing and implementing the care plan is discussed.

BIBLIOGRAPHY

Bower, F., and J. Patterson. 1986. A theory-based nursing assessment of the aged. *Top Clin Nurs* 8:22–32.

Burnside, I., ed. 1988. *Nursing and the aged. A self-care approach.* 3d ed. New York: McGraw-Hill Book Co.

Eliopoulos, C., ed. 1989. *Health assessment of the older adult.* 2d ed. Menlo Park, Calif.: Addison-Wesley Publishing Co.

Hallal, J. 1985. Nursing diagnosis: An essential step to quality care. *J Gerontol Nurs* 11:35–38.

Horgan, P.A. 1987. Health status perceptions affect health-related behaviors. *J Gerontol Nurs* 13:30–33.

Jessup, L. 1984. The health history. In *Handbook of gerontological nursing,* edited by B. Steffl. New York: Van Nostrand-Reinhold.

Jones, D. 1986. *Health assessment manual.* New York: McGraw-Hill Book Co.

Shepard, M., and J.R. Walsh. 1984. Clinical evaluation of the patient. In *Geriatric medicine.* vol. 2, 107–112, edited by C.K. Cassel and J.R. Walsh. New York: Springer-Verlag.

Chapter 6

Developing and Implementing Care Plans

Few words evoke the feelings of annoyance and dread in the practice setting as those of *care plan*. To some nurses, a care plan is a necessary evil, a form with numerous blanks to fill; to others, it is another piece of useless paper work that must be completed; and, to a few, it is the guessing game of selecting the best terminology to appease the surveyors' current preferences. It is unfortunate that problems and preoccupation with the structure of the care plan have shadowed the significance of this tool to the process of giving nursing services. Care plans can serve an important and useful function, and, because they are here to stay, it can be beneficial to learn to use them in an efficient and realistic manner.

WHY PREPARE A CARE PLAN?

A care plan is to nursing practice what a road map is to a cross-country trip. Care, like travel, can occur without planning, but imagine the added problems that could result from jumping into an automobile and beginning to drive without plans. Will there be enough money to cover expenses? Is the car in adequate condition to make the journey without breaking down? Will the most direct and comfortable driving route be selected? What landmarks can be used to determine if a person is moving toward his or her final destination? How would a person direct a friend, planning to begin the same trip a day later, to follow the path? A person need not have a vivid imagination to identify the potential headaches, added risks, and wasted time and resources that could arise from this unplanned venture.

Attempting to give care without a plan can lead to no fewer problems. Will all the supplies and assistance needed be available? Is there enough time to complete the tasks? Will care be given as efficiently and effectively as possible? What

55

indicators will aid in evaluating progress toward a goal? How will each person replicate activities when assigned to the same patient? A written plan for care is essential.

CHARACTERISTICS OF CARE PLANS

Care plans must be *individualized*. It is tempting to use a "model care plan," one that is well written and accepted by surveyors, for all patients. However, a model fails to capture the special aspects of caring for individual patients. A care plan is based on the unique capabilities, limitations, and diagnoses of the patient, as identified through the assessment process. Although similar nursing problems and diagnoses may exist among patients, goals and approaches must be tailored to the individual. For instance, two patients with Alzheimer's disease may have problems feeding themselves because they forget what to do with the food placed before them. The goal for both patients may be to maintain a good nutritional state by supervising their nutritional intake and reminding them to eat during mealtimes. However, the approach for one patient could be to have her sit next to more functional patients during mealtime so they can remind her to eat and she can imitate their behaviors, whereas the more effective approach for the other patient may be to have her eat in her room alone so there will be fewer distractions and she can focus solely on the food before her.

Care plans must be *realistic*. Patient goals "to return to the community" or "to improve function" sound admirable but may not be appropriate for all patients. Likewise, an approach to check on a patient every 15 minutes to control wandering may not be possible within the constraints of a busy workday. It is better to have a more basic, less impressive-looking care plan that is workable and attainable.

A reality-based care plan also is significant when the legal aspects of practice are considered. In the event of litigation, the care plan may be one of the documents used to judge the care given. For example, for the goal of maintaining the patient's weight between 125 and 130 pounds an approach may be listed to "check and record patient's intake and output of all food and fluids." If the patient suffers significant weight loss and there is no record or evaluation of intake and output evident, it could appear that the staff was negligent in following practices that they deemed essential to the patient's care.

"A plan of nursing care that includes goals derived from the nursing diagnosis is *developed in conjunction with the older adult or significant others*" (emphasis added) (American Nurses' Association, 1988). This important standard of practice makes good sense. Patients and their significant others have a right to know what goals of care are being sought and what approaches will be used; they also share a responsibility for being active participants and assisting in the plan of care.

Misunderstanding and noncompliance can be avoided by having the patient and significant others actively involved in the plan of care. For instance, a family member may object to the patient being ambulatory on days when the patient complains of arthritic pain if that relative is not aware of the importance of mobility to the goal of returning the patient to independent living. Instead of objecting to the ambulation, the family member may instead use the visiting time to encourage and assist the patient to walk down the hall.

Patients have a right to alter or object to the care plan. It is far more effective to have a compromised plan than an ideal one on paper that is resisted and rejected by the patient in reality.

Ideally, the care plan is *multidisciplinary*; that is, all disciplines contribute to the plan, and each discipline understands the goals and actions of all the others. For example, the social worker may plan to increase the patient's level of socialization by having the patient eat with other patients in the main dining room. Dietary and nursing staff need to be aware of this plan so they do not deliver the tray to the patient's room and allow the patient to eat there. Whenever possible, all disciplines should have actions that contribute to common goals. For instance, for the goal "patient will verbalize acceptance of the need for institutional care," various disciplines could use approaches that would facilitate this goal.

Discipline	*Approach*
Nursing	Allow maximum independence and decision making.
Social Services	Discuss realities and responsibilities of communal living.
Medicine	Control pain.
Psychiatry	Reduce depression.
Dietary	Provide ethnic foods to which patient is accustomed.

COMMUNICATING THE CARE PLAN

Of course, communication is the essence of the care plan. All members of the team need to be informed of goals and actions so that care of the patient can be individualized. Consistency of care also is gained through a well-communicated care plan; consistency can be significant to evaluating the effectiveness of the care plan. For example, the patient may have a sacral decubitus ulcer for which the goal is "to heal ulcer within 1 month." Without specific action guidelines to achieve this goal, a day shift nurse may keep the ulcer exposed to air and do nothing more; the evening shift nurse may apply wet-to-dry dressings; and the night nurse may use hydrogen peroxide irrigations and protective dressings. If, after 1 month, the decubitus ulcer is unimproved, it can be difficult to identify which specific technique was or was not effective and the exact change that could prove to be useful.

Documentation is basic to communicating the care plan to all members of the team. Frequently, facilities have their own standardized forms on which the care plan is written; the usual components are:

1. Brief profile:
   - Demographic data—name, date of birth, religion, contact person or next of kin
   - Capacity for activities of daily living—feeding, bathing, dressing, toileting, mobility
   - Mobility aids, assistive devices—use of canes, wheelchairs, walkers, eyeglasses, hearing aids, dentures
   - Diet
   - Sleep and rest patterns
   - Mental status, behavior, orientation
   - Allergies
2. Care plan guidelines:
   - Problems/needs
   - Goals—what is to be achieved in relation to problems
   - Date goal written
   - Target date—when goal is to be achieved
   - Approaches—actions/measures to achieve goal
   - Discipline—who is responsible for specific approaches
   - Evaluation/outcome—status of goal by target date

Although all caregivers should have access to and read the care plan, some will not. Others may read the plan but not fully understand the rationale or intent of the care. Therefore it is important to communicate and reinforce the plan verbally. This is achieved in a variety of ways.

- *On admission*. Discuss the plan of care with all caregivers. A multidisciplinary team meeting is an ideal forum for this.
- *Initial contact*. If possible, the charge or primary nurse who developed the care plan should work along with or guide staff during their first care-giving encounter with the patient.
- *During care*. Through informal discussions and spot checks the care plan can be reinforced and feedback on its appropriateness and effectiveness obtained.

- *After changes in status.* Team meetings and change of shift reports offer opportunities to inform staff of care plan alterations resulting from a change in the patient's status.

SURVEYORS' EXPECTATIONS

Because care plans reflect individual attention to care and guide daily activities surveyors view them as important documents. There are guidelines concerning nursing homes in the regulations that nursing homes must follow (summarized in Exhibit 6-1). Basically, surveyors will evaluate how well care plans meet the criteria described in the regulations, so there is really no mystery about their actions. Some of the factors they will examine include

- *Appropriateness.* Have needs identified during the assessment been addressed? Are goals and approaches current, realistic, and relevant? Have revisions to the care plan been made as the patient's status has changed?
- *Specificity of goals.* Global goals, such as "to improve function," "to maintain current status," and "to prevent problems," may be criticized as being too broad and difficult to evaluate. Measurable, specific goals are preferred, such as patient will "walk full length of hallway independently within 1 month," "continue to bathe and dress self with supervision," and "be free from skin breakdown."

Exhibit 6-1 Highlights of Regulatory Requirements for Care Plans

Every patient shall have a care plan developed on admission.

Nursing coordinates the development of the care plan with all other disciplines.

The care plan reflects the patient's needs, role of each discipline in meeting those needs, and approaches each discipline will use to accomplish goals of care.

The nursing component of the care plan is based on the nursing assessment or history.

The patient participates in the development and evaluation of the care plan to the fullest extent possible.

All caregivers should have access to the care plan.

Relevant information from the care plan is transferred to other agencies to whom the patient may be transferred or discharged.

The care plan is reviewed and revised as necessary.

Note: Individual state regulations may specify additional requirements regarding the care plan.

- *Evaluation of care plan.* Is the care plan truly a working tool, as evidenced by documented changes in the patient's condition or resolutions of problems? For instance, an approach of having the patient select favorite foods from the menu may be inappropriate if that patient now is strictly receiving nasogastric feedings.
- *Caregivers' knowledge of plan.* Recent changes in the survey process have brought surveyors to the bedside more, looking at the actual care being given. They may question nursing assistants on the approaches being used to meet a specific goal or explore if the nurse administering medications understands how a patient's psychotropic drug relates to the goals being sought.

Confidence in answering surveyors' questions and compliance with regulatory requirements are facilitated by the development of realistic care plans that are truly working tools.

IMPLEMENTING CARE

Care giving with chronically ill and aged patients presents a unique set of challenges. One of the first realities that must be faced is that more time is necessary to give care. Mealtime in the acute care hospital, for instance, may require staff to deliver and partially set up trays, as well as feed a few patients. In the nursing home, a majority of patients may need to be fed or coaxed to eat. Postural blood pressure changes, arthritic joints, unsteady gaits, slower responses, and sensory deficits extend the time for the activities of daily living to be completed. Because of mental and physical disabilities nursing home patients may require assistance with even the most minor tasks. Add to this the impact of pain, drug therapy, and the highly prevalent psychosocial problems of nursing home patients and it is not hard to understand why long-term care means care that takes a long time to give.

The changing status of patients can affect care giving. A patient who may be moderately independent in fulfilling activities of daily living may become highly dependent on days when pain, edema, shortness of breath, or other symptoms are present. Hypotension, hypoglycemia, hypoxia, and other problems that alter homeostasis can cause the patient to be too confused to participate in usual self-care activities. Motivation to engage in care can be reduced by depression over the lack of visitors or the loss of a loved one or valued object. There are a wide range of physical, mental, and social factors that can cause yesterday's care plan to be inappropriate today. With all the risks to which the nursing home patient is subject, frequent assessment of changes in status and revisions to the care plan are essential.

Most long-term care facilities depend on nonprofessional staff for direct care giving. Many are highly competent and skilled; however, they lack the professional preparation of the nurse. When care is delegated to nonprofessional staff their activities must be monitored closely to assure the care plan and proper procedures are followed. These caregivers also need opportunities to offer feedback about the appropriateness and effectiveness of the care plan. For example, the care plan may suggest that the patient be toileted every hour as part of a bladder training program, and a nursing assistant may follow this plan conscientiously. However, it may be discovered that the patient expends so much energy going to the bathroom and transferring to the toilet that she is too fatigued to engage in other activities of daily living. This frequency of activity also may be causing the nursing assistant to "shortchange" other patients' care because 15 minutes of every hour are invested in toileting this patient. By checking on delegated care the nurse could recognize the need to change the care plan.

PATIENT AND FAMILY INVOLVEMENT

Maximizing patient independence is inherent to nursing care in any setting; but for nursing home patients, who often are experiencing multiple losses and declines in health status, this becomes a crucial element. On busy days, when tasks to accomplish exceed available time, it can be quite tempting to dress a patient, rather than wait 15 minutes as she slowly puts on her clothing; to use a wheelchair to transport a patient to the dining room, rather than accompany him as he slowly shuffles down the hall; or to feed the patient rather than guide her in feeding herself. Staff must resist the temptation of "doing it faster themselves" and allow the patient to preserve independent function, regardless of how minor. Patients' efforts to remain independent should be recognized and rewarded.

In addition to having patients participate in their care, families also should be actively involved in care giving. This holds several benefits. The family members may better understand, support, and comply with the patient's plan of care if they are assisting with its implementation. Visitation can be a more fulfilling experience if the family can feel useful and integral to the patient's care, rather than sit passively. Also, the patient benefits by having the interest, contact, and perhaps extra attention from the family.

EVALUATING CARE

Ideally, all goals established for patients will be achieved using the recommended actions; unfortunately, that is hardly reality. Sometimes, unforeseen circumstances interfere with the care plan (e.g., the patient's medical condition worsens or the level of motivation plummets because of the death of a loved one). At times, care strategies that worked perfectly for one patient are unsuccessful with another (e.g., with Milk of Magnesia therapy for a decubitus ulcer). There also may be times when a care plan is ineffective because crucial data did not surface during the assessment process and later proved to be a block to planned efforts (e.g., hallucinations or restrictions because of pain that were noticed only after the patient had resided in the facility for several weeks). To be a working tool the care plan must be revised as necessary. Some of the points to consider in evaluating the care plan include

- *Effectiveness.* Did the care plan bring about the results desired? Were goals and approaches appropriate?
- *Efficiency.* Were results achieved with the least cost in terms of time, energy, and resources to patient and staff?
- *Impact.* What are the reactions of patient, family, and staff to the care?

Care planning is a cyclic process involving continuous reassessment, revision, implementation, and reevaluation. The documented care plan is a working tool that should be used by staff, not an academic paper neatly stored from the caregivers who need it. By gaining skill in the development of care plans the giving of a high standard of nursing care can be facilitated.

CARE PLAN GUIDES

There are no standardized goals and actions that will fit every patient with a similar problem or need. However, in the following pages a menu of goals and actions for 13 common geriatric nursing problems is offered as a guide for development of care plans. They can be used to stimulate ideas for the development of individualized care.

Problem: Risk of skin breakdown
Goal: Patient will maintain skin integrity.
Actions:
- Inspect skin surfaces every shift.
- Use nonirritating soaps for bathing.
- Apply skin moisturizers after baths.
- Keep skin clean and dry.
- Massage bony prominences every shift.
- Check for and correct wrinkles in bed linens, foreign objects in bed.

- Use alternating pressure mattress or water bed, if bedridden; pad bony prominences.
- Change position every 2 hours.
- Assure good protein, vitamin, and mineral intake.

Problem: Decubitus ulcer
Goals: Patient's ulcer will heal/decrease in size.
Patient will be free of secondary infection from ulcer.
Actions:

- Record stage/condition of ulcer every day.
- Follow prescribed protocol for specific stage of ulcer (e.g., protective dressing, chemical debridement).
- Follow actions listed under "Risk of skin breakdown."

Problem: Constipation
Goal: Patient will have bowel movements of normal consistency without straining every 3 days or more often.
Actions:

- Maintain record of bowel movements.
- Remind/assist with toileting at regular times.
- Increase fiber and bulk in diet.
- Increase fluid intake (unless contraindicated).
- Encourage/assist with increased activity.
- Educate about and discourage laxative use.

Problem: Self-care deficit (specify: eating, bathing, dressing, toileting, mobility)
Goals: Patient will perform self-care activities independently in _____ months.
Patient will perform self-care activities to maximum capacity and receive assistance to compensate for deficits.
Actions:

- Assess current self-care capacity and potential for increased self-care function.
- Assist as necessary:
  —Feed, set up tray.
  —Offer bedpan/urinal, assist to commode/toilet.
  —Provide bath basin, lift in/out of tub, bathe.
  —Lay out clothing, aid in clothing selection, dress.
  —Assist with ambulation, push in wheelchair.

- Obtain physical and occupational therapies evaluation.
- Provide and use assistive devices, mobility aids.

Problem: Immobility
Goals: Patient will increase level of mobility (specify; e.g., independently turn in bed, walk 20 feet with assistance within 1 month, learn to use wheelchair independently within 1 month).
Patient will be free of complications from immobility (e.g., contractures, decubiti, constipation, hypostatic pneumonia, depression).
Actions:

- Change position and have patient turn, cough, and deep breathe every 2 hours; maintain position chart.
- Maintain good body alignment.
- Perform/encourage range of motion exercises three times a day.
- Prevent dependent edema, obstructions to circulation.
- Check and massage bony prominences every 2 hours.
- Assure adequate intake of fluids, fiber.
- Monitor bowel movements, breath sounds, skin condition, joint mobility, intake, emotional state.

Problem: Impaired cognitive function
Goals: Cause of patient's cognitive dysfunction will be identified and corrected (to level possible).
Patient will be as oriented and functional as possible (specify).
Patient will be free from injury or complications resulting from inability to protect self from hazards.
Actions:

- Assess and record mental status every day.
- Refer for evaluation of causes of altered mental status.
- Support treatment plan to correct underlying cause (e.g., change medication, correct fluid and electrolyte imbalance, control pain).
- Orient to person, place, time; put calendar and clock in room.
- Adhere to routines, consistency of care.
- Minimize stimulation in environment (e.g., bright lights, noise, cold temperature).
- Protect from harming self and others.

- Provide safe area for walking/wandering.
- Safeguard environment (e.g., cover exposed outlets, remove solutions that could be accidentally ingested, secure screens on windows).
- Monitor intake and output, sleep and rest, activity.
- Reassure and explain realities of situation to family.
- Revise care plan as functional capacity changes.

Problem: Urinary incontinence
Goals: Patient will regain bladder control within _____ months.
            Patient will be dry and free of secondary problems (e.g., skin breakdown, falls, impaired social interactions).
Actions:

- Refer for evaluation for possible causes of incontinence.
- Monitor and record intake and output.
- Begin/adhere to bladder training program (if appropriate).
- Provide dignity and privacy in management of incontinent episodes.
- Toilet every 2 hours.
- Use adult diaper/brief (if appropriate); check diaper/brief every _____ hours.
- Assess skin condition every shift.
- Thoroughly cleanse urine from skin; keep skin dry.

Problem: Dehydration
Goal: Patient will have restored fluid and electrolyte balance within _____ days as indicated through absence of clinical signs of dehydration and blood chemistry studies within normal range.
Actions:

- Monitor and record intake, output, weight, mental status, and condition of skin and mucosa every day.
- Adhere to treatment plan to correct underlying cause (e.g., discontinue medication, control vomiting or diarrhea).
- Offer fluids; assure approximately 2,000 ml of fluid intake every day (unless contraindicated).
- Protect from secondary problems (e.g., skin breakdown, confusion).

Problem: Weight loss

Goals: Patient will gain _____ pounds per month until weight of _____ pounds is achieved.

Patient will maintain body weight between _____ and _____ pounds.

Patient will ingest _____ calories per day.

Patient's depression (or other potential cause of insufficient food intake) will be improved.

Actions:

- Evaluate and correct underlying cause of weight loss.
- Weigh weekly.
- Monitor and record daily caloric intake.
- Use measures to improve appetite (e.g., offer meals in main dining room, walk before meals, have family bring in favorite foods, offer mouth care before meals).
- Obtain nutritionist consult; follow recommendations.
- Provide foods of high nutritive value, rather than empty calories such as candy, cakes.
- Prevent and observe for secondary problems (e.g., skin breakdown, altered mental status, falls resulting from weakened state).

Problem: Obesity

Goals: Patient will lose _____ pounds per month until body weight of _____ pounds is achieved.

Patient will maintain body weight between _____ and _____ pounds.

Patient will verbalize principles of good nutrition.

Patient's anxiety (or other potential cause of excess nutritional intake) will be improved.

Actions:

- Identify and correct underlying cause for excess caloric intake (e.g., insufficient exercise, lack of knowledge of good eating habits, depression).
- Monitor and record weight weekly.
- Obtain nutritionist consult; follow recommendations.
- Educate about good nutritional practices.
- Help patient establish alternate ways of dealing with stress/anxiety/boredom/depression.
- Assure/assist with adequate exercise.
- Recognize and reinforce weight loss.

Problem: Anxiety
Goal: Patient will verbalize and demonstrate no discomfort or disruption in life from anxiety.
Actions:

- Identify and eliminate/control underlying cause (e.g., unfamiliarity with new surrounding, lack of knowledge of new diagnosis, symptoms of illness).
- Reduce environmental stimuli.
- Provide consistency in care.
- Explain/prepare for new activities, changes, procedures.
- Have contact with patient at least every 2 hours.
- Encourage/assist with use of relaxation techniques (e.g., deep breathing exercises, warm baths, backrubs).
- Refer for psychiatric consult.

Problem: Pain
Goals: Patient's source of pain will be eliminated.
Patient's pain will be sufficiently controlled to allow participation in activities of daily living.
Actions:

- Identify source of pain and correct (if possible).
- Administer analgesics as ordered.
- Assist patient in achieving comfortable position.
- Aid patient to develop pain control strategies (e.g., relaxation techniques, self-hypnosis).
- Provide massage and other comfort measures.

Problem: Risk of injury
Goal: Patient will be free from injury.
Actions:

- Obtain and assure proper use of assistive devices and mobility aids (e.g., eyeglasses, hearing aids, proper fitting cane).
- Supervise activities if patient lacks ability to detect dangers and protect self.
- Remove hazards from environment (e.g., faulty equipment, leaking pipe, cigarettes, chemicals).
- Check on patient's status every 2 hours.
- Place patient in room near nurses' station.

REFERENCE

American Nurses' Association. 1988. Standard III. In *Standards of gerontological nursing practice*, 6–7. Kansas City: American Nurses' Association.

BIBLIOGRAPHY

American Health Care Association. 1983. *Patient care management manual, long term care facility improvement program*. Chicago: American Health Care Association.

Caine, R.M., and P.M. Bufalino. 1987. *Nursing care planning guides for adults*. Baltimore, Md.: Williams & Wilkins.

Eliopoulos, C. 1984. A self-care model for gerontological nursing. *Geriatr Nurs* 5:366–69.

Eliopoulos, C. 1987. *A guide to the nursing of the aging*. Baltimore, Md.: Williams & Wilkins.

Petrucci, K.E., K.A. McCormick, and A.A.S. Scheve. 1987. Documenting patient care needs: Do nurses do it?'' *J Gerontol Nurs* 13:34–38.

Tucker, S.M., M.M. Canobbio, and E.V. Paquette. 1988. *Patient care standards: Nursing process, diagnosis, and outcome*. 4th ed. St. Louis: C.V. Mosby Co.

Ulrich, S.P., S.W. Canale, and S.A. Wendall. 1986. *Nursing care planning guides: A nursing diagnosis approach*. Philadelphia: W.B. Saunders Co.

Chapter 7

Safe Use of Medications

Growth in the scope and number of drugs over the last several decades has been remarkable. Nearly every ailment that humans can suffer has a medication that can either eliminate its cause or manage its symptoms. Thus it is not surprising that the aged, with the high rate of chronic illness they experience, would be major drug consumers.

In the nursing home setting each resident, on an average, receives six medications per day. Because this is an average, obviously, some patients receive far less, whereas others may receive 10, 15, or even more drugs daily. Although drugs can enable patients to live more comfortable, active, as well as longer, lives; they also can contribute new risks. The consumption of a large volume of drugs increases the likelihood of interactions that can have negative effects for the patient. (See Table 7-1.) Changes in the way in which body systems in the aged respond to drugs also can lead to problems. Add to this the large number of medications that a nurse typically administers during the drug pass and the limited time available to evaluate the patients' reactions to drugs and the risks are compounded further. Therefore nurses must be knowledgeable about special problems of drug use in the aged and take special steps to ensure safe drug use.

AGE-RELATED FACTORS

Changes that occur with the aging process affect drug administration, absorption, metabolism, detoxification, and elimination in a variety of ways. Difficulties can begin with the act of attempting to get the drug into the patient. Poor vision can prevent patients from seeing tablets or capsules that are placed into their hands for administration; reduced tactile sensation can cause them to be unable to feel the

69

Table 7-1 Potential Effects of Combining Medications

Effect	Examples
Synergistic—one drug potentiates another	Aspirin can increase the effects of oral anticoagulants, antidiabetic agents, and phenytoin. Alcohol can increase the effects of antianginals, anticoagulants, and sedatives.
Antagonistic—one drug reduces effects of another	Antacids can decrease effects of digoxin, iron preparations, penicillins, phenytoin, and tetracycline. Tricyclic antidepressants can decrease effects of antihypertensives.

drugs in their hands or know if they have successfully transferred all drugs from their hands to their mouths. The drier oral cavities of many elderly adults can cause swallowing of tablets and capsules to be problematic. As a result, drugs may adhere to the mucosa or dentures and dissolve in those sites or be expelled. If drugs do reach the stomach, the potential for altered absorption exists because of decreased gastric secretions and acidity.

Problems also are associated with other administration routes. Loss of muscle mass that occurs with age can reduce patients' ability to absorb the usual adult dose volume at a single site. Reduced tissue elasticity can decrease tissue sealing after the injection, causing a seepage of the medication from the injection site. Decreased cutaneous sensations can prevent elderly patients from detecting inflammation and other complications at the injection site.

Reduced circulation to the lower bowel and vagina slows the process of melting of suppositories in those sites. The therapeutic benefit of the suppository can be lost when it is expelled without dissolving.

A decrease in body fluids in advanced age can pose a problem when water-soluble substances such as vitamins B_1, B_2, B_6, and C are administered. Higher blood concentrations, even toxic levels, of these substances are achieved more easily. The increased proportion of fat tissue in the body lends to the accumulation of drugs that are fat soluble, such as barbiturates, diazepam, and lidocaine. The decreased concentration of albumin affects the distribution of protein-bound drugs (e.g., phenytoin, phenylbutazone, warfarin); that is, when administered concurrently, these drugs may compete for protein molecules. Also, with disease processes that decrease cardiac output, such as congestive heart failure, the volume of distribution of a drug is reduced, causing a higher concentration of the drug in the blood. Digoxin, furosemide, and lidocaine are among the drugs affected by this process.

A reduction in liver size and metabolism slows the metabolism of drugs and causes them to remain in the bloodstream for a longer period of time than would occur with a younger adult.

Metabolism and elimination of drugs are further influenced by age-related renal changes. There is a reduction in the number of nephrons, renal blood flow, and glomerular filtration rate. These changes slow the filtration of drugs from the bloodstream, which is particularly problematic with drugs eliminated in an unchanged form (e.g., digitalis and penicillin). The biologic half-life (i.e., the amount of time it takes for one half of the drug dose to be eliminated from the bloodstream) is longer, consequently; and a toxic level, causing an overdosing effect, can result.

Of course, disease states that impact on cardiovascular, respiratory, digestive, renal, hepatic, and endocrine functions can alter the normal course of drugs in the body.

Because of the overall changes to the body the aged have a decreased ability to manage negative outcomes from drug therapy. Adverse reactions that may cause only mild discomfort in young patients can cause major dysfunction and be life threatening to the aged. Drug therapy must be approached conservatively, starting therapy with the lowest dosage possible and monitoring responses closely.

STAFFING REALITIES

Most nursing home nurses would admit there are more responsibilities to fulfill than time to complete them. It would be wonderful if nurses had nothing more to do than focus on medications; however, administering and evaluating response to medications is just one of many responsibilities.

Staffing-related problems affecting drug use in the nursing home begin when the drug is first ordered. Often, it is nursing that determines if the drug will be ordered in the first place. For instance, a nursing assistant may complain to the nurse that a patient's behavior is worsening and difficult to control. In reality, the approach used by the nursing assistant may be triggering the problem, but detecting this may require direct observation by the nurse. Without adequate time available, the nurse may rely on the judgment of the nursing assistant and suggest to the physician that the patient be prescribed something to control the behavior. Likewise, nonpharmacologic approaches to manage problems, such as backrubs and relaxation exercises, may be overlooked or not attempted because they require more time than administering a medication. Although staffing and time limitations can be real obstacles to using alternate approaches, nurses should do whatever is realistically possible to avoid using medications when a nonchemical nursing approach can manage the problem. This is an important part of patient advocacy.

Staffing limitations also can interfere with adequate evaluation of patients' responses to medications. Therapeutic and adverse reactions to drugs can appear more subtly and slowly in elderly adults than in young persons. It can take longer to achieve therapeutic blood levels for a drug. Because of slowed metabolism and excretion the effects of a drug can continue for days after it has been discontinued. Adverse reactions can appear differently (e.g., altered mental status may be the first indication of a drug reaction). As normal aging and disease processes cause organ function to decline, dose levels that were once appropriate may need to be lowered. Only through astute nursing assessment can these factors be noted.

If nurses are unable to spend much time in direct care activities, they must ensure that they maximize every nurse-patient contact that they do have. For instance, when passing a medication, observing the patient in an activity, or talking with the patient in the hallway the nurse can note the patient's coloring, breathing pattern, mobility, mental status, and presence of new problems. Familiarity with the patient's medication orders can assist the nurse in evaluating if the intended effect of the drug is being achieved, such as the improvement of mobility in a patient who has been prescribed an analgesic for joint pain.

The necessity of delegating a considerable amount of direct care responsibilities to nonprofessional staff demands that nurses educate their subordinates about their patients' medications. Caregivers should be aware of

- Types of medications the patient is taking
- Desired effects of the medications
- Expected side effects and ways to assist the patient should they occur
- Potential adverse reactions that should be reported promptly

By educating and utilizing other caregivers to recognize the effects of medications nurses can extend their assessment "tentacles" and perhaps know the effects of drug therapy in a more timely manner.

REGULATORY REQUIREMENTS

In 1986, when the federal government revised the long-term care survey process, a giant step was taken to improve the practices pertaining to medication administration in the nursing home setting. Regulators were not only interested in checking that medications were signed off appropriately, but also that the storage, monitoring, passing, and understanding of drugs were consistent with safe, high-quality practices. This has caused anxiety for some nurses as surveyors have begun asking specific questions and accompanying nurses on the drug pass. (See Chapter 14 for a discussion of the survey process.) However, there is nothing to fear about the medication component of the survey process if a nurse is familiar with the regulations pertaining to this area of care. Some of the major aspects that nurses should know include the following.

- *Contract with pharmacist.* The nursing home must have an arrangement with a licensed pharmacist to provide pharmacy services. The pharmacist is responsible for preparing, dispensing, and maintaining records of patients' drugs. Nurses cannot pour drugs from a main supply in the pharmacy, label them, and dispense them; to do so is practicing pharmacy without a license. If obtaining drugs in a timely manner is a problem, the pharmacist may be able to prepare an emergency drug kit or interim box of commonly used drugs in unit dose form. The pharmacist also is responsible for ensuring that a formulary system exists in the facility and that patients' drugs and pharmacy practices are reviewed regularly.

- *Ordering of medications.* All medications administered to patients must be prescribed by a physician. Orders to administer medications p.r.n. (as needed) should specify the specific circumstances in which the drug should be administered, such as "for severe back pain" or "for temperature above 100°F."

- *Administration of drugs by approved personnel.* Only licensed nursing staff may administer medications. In states where specially trained and certified medication aides have been approved, these persons also may administer certain medications. (Check your specific state regulations concerning this.)

- *Storage of drugs.* All medications, including those stored in refrigerators, must be kept under lock and key. There are special requirements for the storage and management of narcotics and other controlled substances, including, usually, that they are to be double locked, counted, and each dose accounted for.

- *Drug review.* A pharmacist or registered nurse must regularly review the appropriateness of prescriptions, patients' reactions to drugs, drug monitoring practices, and other factors related to drug therapy. A record of these reviews, including recommendations made, should be maintained.

THE DRUG PASS

During an inspection, surveyors will pay particular attention to the drug pass procedure. In addition to compliance with regulations, the nurse will be observed for adherence to general principles of safe medication administration. The nurse will be required to know the regulations, policies, and procedures related to drug therapy, as well as to have a sound working knowledge of drugs and their effects.

Ensuring drug pass success begins with careful checking of the medication administration record. It can be very tempting, particularly on a busy day, for the nurse to pour the same set of drugs that he or she poured every previous day or automatically administer all unit dose drugs contained in the designated drawer for the given time without checking the record. However, a drug could have been discontinued or added, or its dosage could have been changed. Serious problems could result from not detecting these changes on the record. Some nurses find it helpful to mark off the drugs on the record as they check them, but signing off the drug at this time is inappropriate. One useful approach is to place a small dot in the designated box after the drug has been checked and initial or sign only after the drug has actually been administered.

The nurse should be familiar with all medications that he or she is administering. It is difficult to assess the patient's need for the drug, evaluate the appropriateness of the dose, or identify the expected and adverse effects without this knowledge. When in doubt, check your facility's drug formulary, the *Physicians' Desk Reference*, or other drug references. The pharmacist can also be a resource.

Even the simple act of pouring medications requires that certain principles be followed. Each drug must be identifiable until the time of administration. Thus, transferring a patient's drugs from their original containers and placing them all in one medicine cup, identified only by that patient's name and room number, is a poor practice because individual drugs can no longer be properly identified. This can be particularly dangerous when several patients' drugs are administered in this fashion. Most facilities safeguard against this problem by either using a unit dose medication system or drug carts that can be pushed to the patient's room for drug pouring before each patient's drug administration.

Swallowing large capsules and tablets can be problematic for some patients. In some cases it is acceptable to crush tablets and/or mix them with applesauce or other food. Care must be taken not to crush enteric-coated tablets or those marked "SR" (for sustained release) and to check that the medication will not interact with the food in which it is being mixed. Likewise, some capsules may be opened and their contents mixed with food, whereas others definitely should not be administered in this manner. Check the label, and consult the pharmacist before crushing tablets or opening capsules. Of course, when a medication is mixed in food or fluid, the total amount must be consumed to ensure that the patient has received the entire dose of the drug.

Liquid medications must be poured with care. Check the label to determine if the drug should be shaken before pouring, and follow the instructions as indicated. The cup in which the medication is to be poured should be placed on a flat surface at eye level to obtain an accurate reading of the calibrations on the cup. For small volumes (less than 10 ml) that may be difficult to determine accurately, a syringe can be used for measurement of the desired amount.

After the drugs are poured and before proceeding to the patient's bedside, the nurse should ensure that the drug cart is locked and no drugs are accessible. Even if the nurse will be in a patient's room only for a minute, this is enough time for another patient to accidentally take drugs on the cart and ingest them. (This is a particular risk in facilities that have confused patients.)

Throughout this process care must be taken so the patient's medications do not come in direct contact with the nurse's hands. To administer the medications, hand the patient the cup or pour the medications directly into the patient's hands for the patient to place in his or her mouth, unless the patient's status prevents this. To compensate for dry oral mucosa and facilitate swallowing of drugs, fluids may be offered before the drug is given. This also ensures a good fluid intake with the drug. If there is any doubt whether or not the patient has swallowed the drugs, inspect the oral cavity.

The nurse should wash his or her hands if any direct contact has occurred with a patient before proceeding to the next patient.

Document on the record that the medication was given as soon after administration as possible. Waiting to sign the medication administration record until all patients' drugs have been administered increases the risk of documentation errors and, possibly, may result in duplication of administration. For instance, if the nurse is called away in an emergency before documentation is completed, other staff, without proof that the specific drug has been given, could duplicate the administration. The full signature and title of the nurse should appear on every record that the nurse initials. Documentation also should reflect any drugs that were omitted or expelled by the patient.

Exhibit 7-1 provides a list of pitfalls that the nurse may want to guard against in the control and administration of drugs in the nursing home.

Exhibit 7-1 Pitfalls To Protect Against in Drug Control and Administration

Excessive dose (Age-related declines in organ function often require that lower dose levels be prescribed for the aged than those prescribed for the general adult population.)
Using a medication when a nonpharmacologic approach can alleviate or control the problem
Combining medications that have synergistic or antagonistic effects when those effects are undesired
Having nursing staff compound, prepare, dispense, or label drugs
Allowing unlicensed/uncertified persons to administer medications
Not checking the medication against the medication administration record each time administered
Administering a drug without knowledge of the drug's actions, interactions, and side effects
Carrying drugs in an unidentified form from the medication room to the bedside
Crushing tablets and opening capsules that should be swallowed whole
Leaving the medication cart unlocked when unattended
Not identifying the patient before administering medication
Forgetting to wash hands between patients when there has been direct contact
Forgetting to assess patient response to medications
Postponing documentation of medication administration to a later time, rather than immediately after the drug is administered
Administering the drug more than 1 hour before or 1 hour after the ordered time
Not having specific guidelines for the use of p.r.n. (as needed) medications
Storing medications in unlocked areas

Table 7-2 Interactions and Special Considerations for Major Drugs Used in Nursing Homes

Drug Group	Generic Name	Effects from Other Drugs	Effects on Other Drugs	Comments
Analgesic	acetaminophen	Phenobarbital decreases effects.	Increases effects of oral anticoagulants. (This is usually not a contraindication; acetaminophen is frequently given with anticoagulants.)	Extended use can lead to abnormal hemoglobin levels and anemia; periodic blood evaluation is advisable.
	codeine	Effects increased by aspirin, phenothiazines, and tricyclic antidepressants.	Increases effects of analgesics, antidepressants, narcotics, sedatives, and tranquilizers.	Drowsiness, lightheadedness, and constipation can occur. Alcohol use should be avoided.
	propoxyphene	Effects increased by acetaminophen and alcohol and aspirin.	Increases effects of alcohol, narcotics, sedatives, and tranquilizers.	Physical and psychologic dependency can occur if taken for extended time. Heavy cigarette smoking can reduce effects.
	salicylates	Effects increased by large doses of vitamin C. Effects decreased by antacids, phenobarbital, propranolol, and reserpine.	Increases effects of cortisone–like drugs, insulin, methotrexate, oral anticoagulants, oral hypoglycemics, penicillin, phenytoin, and sulfanomides. Decreases effects of probenecid, spironolactone, and sulfinpyrazone.	Extended use can cause erosion of stomach lining and chronic blood loss, manifested by anemia. Periodic evaluations of complete blood cell count (CBC) and liver function are advisable. Aspirin toxicity can result if taken with furosemide

Antacid	aluminum hydroxide	Increases effects of meperidine and pseudoephedrine.	and paraaminosalicylate (PAS). Risk of stomach ulceration is increased if taken with cortisone–like drugs, indomethacin, and phenylbutazone. Can decrease blood phosphates and promote osteomalacia.
	calcium carbonate		Can increase calcium level in blood, causing alkalosis.
	magnesium hydroxide	Increases effects of dicumarol.	Extended use can cause nervous system disorders.
	sodium bicarbonate	Increases effects of quinidine.	Extended use can cause recurrent urinary tract infections, sodium retention, edema, and hypertension.
		All antacids may decrease the effects of anticoagulants, chlorpromazine, digitalis, iron, isoniazid, penicillins, phenylbutazone, sulfonamides, tetracyclines, and vitamins A and C.	

Table 7-2 continued

Drug Group	Generic Name	Effects from Other Drugs	Effects on Other Drugs	Comments
Antianginal	nitroglycerin	Effects increased by propranolol.	Increases effects of atropine–like drugs and tricyclic antidepressants. Decreases effects of choline–like drugs.	Flushing of face, throbbing in head, tachycardia, and orthostatic hypotension can occur. Periodic evaluations of eyes, red blood cell count, and hemoglobin level are advisable. Severe drop in blood pressure (BP) can occur when taken with antihypertensives. Cigarette smoking can reduce effectiveness. Alcohol use should be avoided.
Antiasthmatic	theophylline		Increases effects of other antiasthmatic drugs. Decreases effects of allopurinol, lithium, and probenecid.	Nervousness and insomnia may occur, compounded by large intake of caffeine. More effective on empty stomach, although measures may be necessary to reduce potential gastric irritation. Should not be administered to persons with a peptic ulcer.

Anticoagulant			
warfarin	Effects can be increased or decreased by antihistamines, benzodiazepines, chloral hydrate, cortisone, phenylbutazone, and reserpine. Effects increased by acetaminophen, androgen, Antabuse, antibiotics, ethacrynic acid, glucagon, guanethidine, hydroxyzine, indomethacin, isoniazid (INH), methyldopa, methylphenidate, PAS, probenecid, salicylates, sulfonamides, sulfonylureas, thyroid preparations, and tricyclic antidepressants. Effects decreased by antacids, barbiturates, chlorpromazine, digitalis, estrogens, ethchlorvynol, furosemide, haloperidol, meprobamate, phenytoin, and vitamin C	Increases effects of insulin, phenytoin, and sulfonylureas.	Several weeks of trial and observation may be required to determine appropriate dose. Large intake of foods high in vitamin K can reduce effectiveness. Elevated body temperature and fluid loss can alter response.

Table 7-2 continued

Drug Group	Generic Name	Effects from Other Drugs	Effects on Other Drugs	Comments
Anticonvulsant	phenytoin	Effects increased by Antabuse, anticoagulants, aspirin, estrogens, Gantrisin, isoniazid, methylphenidate, PAS, phenothiazines, phenylbutazone, and tranquilizers. Effects decreased by alcohol, antihistamines, and glutethimide.	Increases effects of anticoagulants, antihypertensives, methotrexate, propranolol, and sedatives. Decreases effects of cortisone.	Sluggishness, drowsiness, anemia, photosensitivity, and discoloration of urine may occur. Periodic evaluation of CBC, lymph node, and liver function is advisable.
Antidepressant	amitriptyline	Thiazide diuretics increase effects.	Increases effects of anticoagulants, antihistamines, levodopa, narcotics, sedatives, and tranquilizers. Decreases effects of clonidine, guanethidine, and other antihypertensives, as well as phenytoin.	Four to six weeks of therapy are usually required for adequate response. Should not be used concurrently with monoamine oxidase (MAO) inhibitors or for persons with glaucoma. Periodic evaluations of CBC, electrocardiogram (ECG), BP, and liver function are advisable. Serious side effects can result when taken in

			combination with ethchlorvynol, MAO inhibitors, quinidine, or thyroid preparations.
Antidiabetic	chlorpropamide	Effects increased by oral anticoagulants, as well as chloramphenicol, MAO inhibitors, phenylbutazone, probenecid, propranolol, salicylates, and sulfisoxazole. Effects decreased by clorpromazine, cortisone, estrogens, isoniazid, thiazide diuretics, and thyroid preparations.	Increases effects of sedatives.	The aged are more likely to experience episodes of prolonged hypoglycemia when taking this drug. There may be a marked intolerance to alcohol. Dosage may need to be adjusted during periods of acute infection, trauma, or fluid loss.
	insulin	Effects increased by INH, MAO inhibitors, oral anticoagulants, oxyphenbutazone, salicylates (in large amounts), and sulfa drugs. Effects decreased by chlorthalidone, cortisone-like drugs, furosemide, phenytoin, thiazide diuretics, and thyroid preparations.		Propranolol can mask symptoms of hypoglycemia. Close monitoring of elderly diabetics is essential; they can be hyperglycemic without being glycosuric. Hypoglycemia is a greater threat to the aged than hyperglycemia.

Table 7-2 continued

Drug Group	Generic Name	Effects from Other Drugs	Effects on Other Drugs	Comments
	tolbutamide	Effects increased by oral anticoagulants, chloramphenicol, guanethidine, MAO inhibitors, phenylbutazone, probenecid, propranolol, salicylates, and sulfisoxazole. Effects decreased by chlorpromazine, cortisone, estrogens, ethacrynic acid, furosemide, isoniazid, thiazide diuretics, and thyroid preparations.	Increases effects of sedatives.	The aged are more likely to experience episodes of prolonged hypoglycemia when taking this drug. There may be a marked intolerance to alcohol. Dosage may need to be adjusted during periods of acute infection, trauma, or fluid loss. Extended use can reduce thyroid gland function. Photosensitivity may occur.
Antihypertensive	methyldopa	Effects increased by thiazide diuretics. Effects decreased by amphetamines.	Increases effects of oral anticoagulants and other antihypertensives. Decreases effects of levodopa.	Several weeks of therapy are required for response to be noted. Alcohol use should be avoided. Drowsiness, weakness, orthostatic hypotension, dry mouth, and nasal stuffiness can occur. Extended use can cause hemolytic anemia and

		sodium and fluid retention.
		Periodic evaluation of CBC and liver function is advisable.
		Severe hypertension can result when combined with tricyclic antidepressants.
reserpine	Increases effects of analgesics, antihistamines, narcotics, sedatives, and tranquilizers. Decreases effects of aspirin and levodopa.	Drowsiness, lethargy, reddening of eyes, dryness of mouth, nasal stuffiness, increased hunger contractions, indigestion, diarrhea, and fluid retention can occur.
	Effects increased by phenothiazines and propranolol.	Regular monitoring of BP and periodic evaluation of CBC and eye advisable.
		Prothrombin time can be altered when taken with anticoagulants.
		Seizure pattern can change when taken with anticonvulsants.
		Dysrhythmias can develop when combined with digitalis.

Table 7-2 continued

Drug Group	Generic Name	Effects from Other Drugs	Effects on Other Drugs	Comments
Antiinflammatory	phenylbutazone	Effects decreased by aspirin, barbiturates, and tricyclic antidepressants.	Increases effects of insulin, oral anticoagulants, oral hypoglycemics, penicillin, and sulfonamides. Decreases effects of antihistamines, barbiturates, and digitalis.	Gastrointestinal disturbances, photosensitivity, and diarrhea can occur.
Anti-Parkinson	levodopa	Effects increased by other anti-Parkinson drugs. Effects decreased by haloperidol, methyldopa, papaverine, phenothiazines, pyridoxine, and reserpine.	Increases effects of antihypertensives.	Several weeks of therapy are required for response to be noted. Lethargy, fatigue, discoloration of urine, and orthostatic hypotension can occur. Periodic evaluations of internal eye pressure, CBC, liver and kidney function, and regular monitoring of BP are advisable.
	trihexyphenidyl	Effects increased by antihistamines, meperidine, methylphenidate, and tricyclic antidepressants.	Increases effects of levodopa and tranquilizers.	Several weeks of trial and observation may be necessary to achieve appropriate dose. Nervousness, blurred vision, reduced

			perspiration, dryness of mouth, and constipation can occur. Extended use can cause glaucoma; regular eye examinations are recommended. Behavioral disturbances can occur if combined with phenothiazines.
Antitubercular	isoniazid	Increases effects of Antabuse, antihypertensives, atropine—like drugs, narcotics, oral hypoglycemics, phenytoin, sedatives, and stimulants.	Several months of therapy are necessary for full benefit. Can cause vitamin B_6 deficiency leading to peripheral nerve damage. Periodic CBC, liver function, and vision evaluations are advisable.
Cardiac glycoside	digoxin	Effects increased by guanethidine, phenytoin, propranolol, and quinidine. Effects decreased by antacids, laxatives, phenobarbital, and phenylbutazone.	Regular monitoring of pulse, ECG, intake and output, and blood potassium or digoxin levels is advisable. Dysrhythmias can result when combined with epinephrine and ephedrine.

Table 7-2 continued

Drug Group	Generic Name	Effects from Other Drugs	Effects on Other Drugs	Comments
				Digoxin toxicity is of high risk when combined with cortisone, diuretics, reserpine, and thyroid preparations; dehydration can also promote digoxin toxicity. Signs of digoxin overdose include anorexia, excessive salivation, diarrhea, nausea, vomiting, dysrhythmias, gastrointestinal bleeding, drowsiness, headache, delirium, and confusion. Persons with colostomies may have absorption problems.
Diuretic	hydrochlorothiazide	Effects decreased by cholestyramine. Effects increased by alcohol, analgesics, barbiturates, and MAO inhibitors.	Increases effects of antihypertensives and phenothiazides.	A 2- to 3-week period may be required for effects to be noted. Orthostatic hypotension, photosensitivity, increased blood glucose and blood uric acid levels, and decreased

Electrolyte replacement	potassium chloride	Effects decreased by thiazide diuretics.	blood potassium levels may occur. Periodic evaluation of liver function, CBC, and electrolytes is recommended. Can cause excessive drop in BP when taken with tricyclic antidepressants; can cause dysrhythmias when combined with digitalis. Can cause diarrhea if taken on an empty stomach; can have laxative effect on some persons. May decrease absorption of vitamin B_{12} leading to anemia. Periodic evaluation of hemoglobin level, blood potassium level, RBC, and ECG is advisable.
Sedative	chloral hydrate	Effects increased by analgesics, antihistamines, sedatives, and tranquilizers. Decreases effects of cortisone. Increases effects of oral anticoagulants.	Can cause gastric irritation. Physical and psychologic dependency can result from long-term therapy.

Table 7-2 continued

Drug Group	Generic Name	Effects from Other Drugs	Effects on Other Drugs	Comments
	phenobarbital	Effects increased by antihistamines, isoniazid, MAO inhibitors, oral hypoglycemics, and tranquilizers.	Increases effects of analgesics, antihistamines, narcotics, sedatives, and tranquilizers. Decreases effects of aspirin, cortisone, griseofulvin, oral anticoagulants, and phenylbutazone.	Extended use can cause anemia, photosensitivity and psychologic and physical dependency. Periodic CBC and liver function tests are advisable. Seizure activity can increase when taken with anticonvulsants. Alcohol use should be avoided.
Tranquilizer	chlordiazepoxide	Effects increased by tricyclic antidepressants.	Increases effects of anticoagulants, antihypertensives, narcotics, sedatives, and tranquilizers.	Several days of therapy required before full effects are noted. Photosensitivity, impaired bladder control, constipation, and confusion can occur. Physical and psychologic dependency can result from long-term therapy. Can increase seizure activity when combined with anticonvulsants.
	chlorpromazine		Increases effects of antidepressants, antihistamines, atropine,	Several weeks of therapy may be necessary for effects to be noted.

	methyldopa, narcotics, pargyline, phenytoin, reserpine, sedatives, and tranquilizers. Decreases effects of chlorphentermine, guanethidine, insulin, levodopa, oral anticoagulants, oral hypoglycemics, and phenmetrazine.	Can cause photosensitivity, impairment in temperature-regulating mechanisms, tardive dyskinesia, cataracts, and pigmentation of the skin and retina. Periodic eye exams, ECG, CBC, and liver function evaluations are advisable.
diazepam	Effects increased by tricyclic antidepressants. Increases effects of antidepressants, narcotics, oral anticoagulants, sedatives, and tranquilizers.	Can cause confusion, impaired bladder control, and constipation. Physical and psychologic dependency can result from long-term therapy. Periodic CBC and liver function evaluations are advisable. Seizure activity can increase when taken with anticonvulsants. Extreme sedation and convulsions can occur when taken with a MAO inhibitor. Extended use can produce impaired liver function, reductions in white blood cells, and

Table 7-2 continued

Drug Group	Generic Name	Effects from Other Drugs	Effects on Other Drugs	Comments
				physical and psychologic dependency. Periodic CBC and liver function tests are advisable.
				Several weeks of therapy may be required for results to be noted.
	fluphenazine	Effects increased by tricyclic antidepressants.	Increases effects of antidepressants, antihistamines, atropine, narcotics, sedatives, and tranquilizers. Decreases effects of appetite suppressants and levodopa.	Drowsiness, blurred vision, nasal stuffiness, dryness of the mouth, constipation, and impaired voiding are not unusual. Extended use can cause tardive dyskinesia, deposits in cornea and lens, impaired liver function, photosensitivity, and impairment of the temperature-regulating mechanism. Periodic chest film, ECG, CBC, liver, kidney, and vision evaluations are recommended.

haloperidol	Effects increased by alcohol, barbiturates, tranquilizers, and tricyclic antidepressants.	Increases effects of antihistamines, antihypertensives, narcotics, sedatives, and tranquilizers. Decreases the effects of guanethidine, levodopa, and oral anticoagulants.	Seizure activity can increase when taken with anticonvulsants. Several weeks of therapy may be required for result to be noted. Photosensitivity, impaired voiding, constipation, and a fall in BP may occur. Extended use can cause tardive dyskinesia. Periodic evaluation of CBC and liver function is advisable.
perphenazine	Effects increased by sedatives, tranquilizers, and tricyclic antidepressants.	Decreases effects of appetite suppressants and levodopa. Increases effects of antidepressants, antihistamines, atropine, MAO inhibitors, reserpine, sedatives, and tranquilizers.	Seizure activity can increase when combined with anticonvulsants. Several weeks of therapy are required for maximum benefit. Blurred vision, nasal congestion, dryness of the mouth, constipation, and impaired voiding can occur. Extended use can cause tardive dyskinesia, impairment of temperature-regulating mechanism, and photosensitivity.

Table 7-2 continued

Drug Group	Generic Name	Effects from Other Drugs	Effects on Other Drugs	Comments
				Periodic evaluations of CBC, ECG, and liver function are advisable. Seizure activity can increase when combined with anticonvulsants. When combined with antihypertensives, an excessive fall in BP can occur.
	thioridazine	Effects increased by tricyclic antidepressants.	Increases effects of antidepressants, antihistamines, atropine, narcotics, sedatives, and tranquilizers.	Blurred vision, dryness of the mouth, nasal congestion, constipation, impaired voiding, and photosensitivity may occur.
			Decreases effects of appetite suppressants and levodopa.	Extended use can cause pigmentation of retina, tardive dyskinesia, and impairment of temperature-regulating mechanism. Periodic evaluation of eyes, CBC, and ECG is advisable.

Source: Adapted from *Nursing Administration of Long-Term Care* by C. Eliopoulos, pp. 77–91, Aspen Publishers, Inc., © 1983.

DRUG REVIEW

With the thousands of drugs on the market today it would be impossible for any nurse to memorize every action, side effect, adverse response, and interaction of all medications. Instead, nurses should have a good working knowledge of drugs commonly administered and have current pharmacology resource books readily available. In Table 7-2 some of the interactions and special considerations for some of the major drug groups used in the nursing home setting are highlighted.

BIBLIOGRAPHY

Fruncillo, R.J. 1987. Drug therapy in the elderly. *Am Fam Physician* 35:225–28.

Goldberg, P.B., and J. Roberts, eds. 1983. *CRC handbook on pharmacology of aging*. Boca Raton, Fla.: CRC Press.

Lamy, P.P. 1986a. Drug interactions and the elderly. *J Gerontol Nurs* 12:36–37.

Lamy, P.P. 1986b. Geriatric drug therapy. *Am Fam Physician* 34:118–26.

Pagliaro, L.A., and A.M. Pagliaro, eds. 1983. *Pharmacologic aspects of aging*. St. Louis: C.V. Mosby Co.

Roberts, J. 1988. Pharmacodynamic basis for altered drug action in the elderly. *Clin Geriatr Med* 4:127–49.

Roberts, P.A. 1988. Extent of medication use in U.S. long term care facilities. *Am J Hosp Pharm* 45:93–100.

Simonson, W. 1984. *Medications and the elderly*. Rockville, Md.: Aspen Publishers.

Thomas, M. 1988. Directors of nursing speak out on LTC patients' drug therapy. *Contemp Longterm Care* 11:83–84,89.

Vestal, R.E., ed. 1984. *Drug treatment in the elderly*. Sydney, Australia: ADIS Health Science.

Chapter 8

Rehabilitative Nursing Care

With rare exception, nursing home residents are affected by chronic illnesses. By their nature, chronic diseases cannot be cured; instead, they must be managed to minimize their negative effects. Persons in whom chronic diseases have developed must learn and be assisted with special techniques to prevent unnecessary disability and dependency and to promote maximum independent function. Rehabilitative nursing care, therefore, becomes the foundation on which care of the nursing home resident is built.

Technically, *rehabilitation* is the return of persons to their maximum level of function. For some, this means their preinjury or preillness status will be regained, as with persons who will return to their jobs and independent living in the community after a period of convalescence. However, the unfortunate reality for a majority of nursing home patients is that full function will not be regained and regression of functional ability may be likely, as with victims of Alzheimer's disease. For these persons, the essence of rehabilitation is maintaining maximum independence and preventing or delaying declines in functional ability.

PRINCIPLES GUIDING REHABILITATIVE NURSING

Most of the general principles of rehabilitation are the same for nursing home patients as for patients in other care settings. However, some of the characteristics of older, chronically ill persons add more facets to care. The principles listed below can aid nursing home nurses in their rehabilitative efforts.

- *Functional capacity is highly individualized.* There is much diversity in functional capacity and limitations among patients. Regardless of their similarity, no two patients will demonstrate similar function. Age, diagnosis,

95

general physical and mental status, motivation, and family support are among the variables affecting a person's current and potential level of function; and they are important to assess in order to understand the unique needs and problems that will impact on rehabilitation efforts.

- *"Highest level of function" is relative.* The maximum independent function realistically achievable by patients must be put in perspective of their physical and mental status. Maximum independence is not measured by the ability of the patient to eat, dress, bathe, toilet, and ambulate without impairment or need for assistance. Instead, maximum independence implies the patient is participating in activities of daily living with as much independence as possible, which could mean grooming himself or herself using assistive devices, ambulating with a wheelchair, or holding a piece of bread while being fed.

- *Advanced age imposes some degree of functional limitations.* The slowing down of responses, decreased muscle strength, poorer vision, and other age-related changes affect the ability of patients to participate in activities of daily living. Of course, illness imposes another layer of limitations that further threatens independent function.

- *Capacities and limitations are in a changing state.* There is nothing stagnant about the functional capacity of the aged. Various physical, emotional, and social factors can influence a change in a patient's ability and willingness to function independently. This reinforces the importance of regular reassessment.

- *The aged require more time for rehabilitative activities.* The combination of age-related changes and illness-imposed limitations slows the patient's ability to engage in and achieve results from rehabilitative activities. Nurses need to allocate more time for assisting patients with rehabilitative activities and expect longer periods for outcomes to be achieved.

- *The aged experience a high risk of complications from the lack of rehabilitation efforts.* Disability, deformity, and dependency occur more quickly in the aged than in the young. To compensate for the high risk of complications, active attention must be paid to maintaining skin integrity, joint mobility, mental stimulation, and general functional ability.

- *Expectations of staff influence rehabilitation efforts.* Staff who feel it is quicker and easier to do for patients, rather than assist patients in doing for themselves, convey to patients an acceptance and preference for dependency, whereas staff who give time and support to allow patients to be as independent as possible can encourage higher levels of function in patients. It is important for patients to know that their caregivers hold hope for patients' independence and respect for whatever fragments of independent function exist.

ASSESSING REHABILITATION NEEDS

As discussed earlier, the functional capacity of each patient will differ, thus it is important to assess carefully the rehabilitation needs of each patient. A comprehensive assessment of physical and mental status (see Chapter 5) is essential to understanding the full capacities and limitations of each patient. From that information, the patient's degree of independence in engaging in activities of daily living can be evaluated. Specific areas to assess are described in Exhibit 8-1.

Exhibit 8-1 Assessment of Activities of Daily Living for the Nursing Home Patient

Bathing
Differentiation of hot and cold water temperatures
Transfer in/out of tub
Manipulation of washcloth and towel
Range of motion to reach all body parts
Cognitive ability to know how to bathe self

Dressing
Cognitive ability to select proper attire
Range of motion and coordination to place clothes on body, shoes on feet
Manipulation of buttons, ties, snaps, zippers

Feeding
Manipulation of utensils
Grasp of cups, glasses, finger foods
Chewing and swallowing ability
Cognitive ability to know what to do with food

Toileting
Recognition of signal to eliminate
Transfer on/off commode
Manipulation of urinal and/or bedpan
Range of motion to cleanse self
Cognitive ability to know steps of toileting

Continence
Sensation of need to eliminate
Motor and neurologic ability to control urination and defecation
Cognitive ability to recognize signal to eliminate and know how to act accordingly

Transfer/Mobility
Ability to roll, lift, sit, stand, walk, raise from bed or chair
Balance
Physical and cognitive ability to use mobility aid

Another important aspect to assess is the patient's attitude toward rehabilitation. Some patients enter the nursing home setting highly motivated to regain function, so they will not be dependent on others or, perhaps, so they eventually can be discharged from the facility. These patients will readily accept rehabilitation challenges and work hard toward rehabilitation goals. Other patients may believe they should be "taken care of," or that they should succumb to their disabilities. These patients may be reluctant to invest in efforts to improve their self-care capacity. Also, there are patients who use disability as a tool to manipulate others and find more advantages in being dependent than in increasing their functional ability. Reviewing how patients managed illness or disability in the past and asking what they expect during their nursing home stay can aid in gaining insight into patients' levels of motivation to engage in rehabilitative activities. Misconceptions also may surface, such as the beliefs that lost function cannot be regained and old people cannot learn new ways to function.

Relatives and other significant persons can influence patients' rehabilitative efforts. Nurses may want to determine if family members are suggesting that the patient do as little for himself or herself as possible because "that is what staff are being paid for," or encouraging the patient to be as independent as possible. Likewise, it can be useful to note if relatives accept the patient's excuses for not attempting to be independent or if they coax the patient to achieve higher levels of function. Family members' understanding of patients' conditions should be evaluated, and education and counseling should be provided as necessary. It is highly beneficial for families to be knowledgeable participants in the development of the care plan and involved actively in the patient's rehabilitation activities.

RECOGNIZING AND REINFORCING EFFORTS

Maintaining and improving function require a strong commitment from patients. Activities to promote functional independence can be difficult, uncomfortable, time consuming, and monotonous. A long time may pass before results are noted. In some circumstances, rehabilitative efforts may not increase function, but prevent regression; thus progress in the sense of "moving ahead" is not evident. New health problems or the worsening of existing ones can create new obstacles to overcome and interfere with rehabilitation activities. Psychosocial factors, such as a patient's learning that his or her home in the community has been sold or that a family member is moving and will be unable to visit daily, also can take the rehabilitation plan off course.

Nurses must acknowledge the efforts of patients to remain independent and improve function. Seemingly minor actions of a patient, such as calling for assistance to be toileted, combing hair, and propelling oneself in a wheelchair to an activity, should be praised. Patients with conditions that prohibit improvement may need to be reminded of how their rehabilitative efforts have prevented them from losing function or developing complications. Nurses should offer encouragement, optimism, and hope as patients engage in rehabilitation activities.

SPECIAL CARE PROBLEMS

Many of the most prevalent problems of nursing home patients are those that can severely jeopardize independent function. Nurses must plan interventions to prevent these problems, whenever possible, and effectively manage them once they occur. A discussion of some of these problems follows, accompanied by goals and actions that can aid in care planning. (See also Chapter 6 for guides to care plans for common geriatric nursing problems.)

Incontinence

Although incontinence is not a normal consequence of growing old, it is a problem that increases progressively with advanced age (Table 8-1). Because it often contributes to persons' becoming institutionalized and will affect nearly half of all nursing home residents, it is a nursing care problem that nursing home nurses frequently confront. A realistic understanding of the various causes and management approaches for incontinence is essential to effective care of patients with this problem.

What Is Incontinence?

Incontinence is an inappropriate or involuntary loss of urine and is usually quite evident through wet clothing and linens or urine puddles on the floor. However, some patients may attempt to hide the problem and it may only be through observations, such as the patient's reluctance to drink fluids, excessive toileting, or urine odor, that incontinence can be identified.

Table 8-1 Increasing Incidence of Incontinence with Age

Age Group (Yr.)	No. of Incontinent Persons (per 1,000)
45–64	7.5
65–74	17.3
75+	46.7

Source: Americans Needing Help To Function at Home by B. Feller, Vol. 92, pp. 1–12, National Center for Health Statistics, U.S. Department of Health and Human Services, Hyattsville, Md., September 14, 1983.

There are various types of incontinence, as outlined in Table 8-2. A comprehensive diagnostic evaluation is important to identify the specific type of incontinence so that a realistic nursing care plan can be developed. Diagnostic measures include urinalysis; evaluations of neurologic and mental status; and analysis of serum concentrations of glucose, as well as calcium and other electrolytes. A variety of urodynamic studies also may be done, such as:

- *Cystometry:* to test motor and sensory function of the bladder
- *Uroflometry:* to measure bladder pressures during filling and emptying of the bladder
- *Bonney's test:* to determine if a full bladder can contain urine under the stress of coughing or laughing

Secondary Problems

Incontinence opens the door to a new set of risks for the affected person, including the following.

- *Skin breakdown.* Moisture makes the skin more susceptible to breakdown; the irritation from urine further compounds this problem. Once a decubitus ulcer develops, incontinence can facilitate infection and slow the healing process.

Table 8-2 Types of Incontinence

Type	Characteristics	Causes
Stress	Urine is released when pressure from laughing, coughing, or sneezing occurs, because of ineffective closure of the urethra.	Weak supporting pelvic muscles secondary to pregnancy, obesity
Urgency	Sudden elimination of urine because of spasms or irritation of bladder wall	Urinary tract infection, prostatic hypertrophy, pelvic or bladder tumor, diverticulitis
Overflow	Excessive urine accumulation in bladder because of lack of bladder contraction or failure of periurethral muscles to relax during bladder contraction	Bladder neck obstructions, drugs
Neurogenic	Inability to sense need to void or control urine flow	Cerebral cortex lesions, multiple sclerosis, Parkinson's disease
Functional	Inability to interpret signal to void or reach toilet in time	Dementia, toileting dependency, sedation, inaccessible bathroom

- *Falls.* When urine puddles create a slippery floor surface, falls are a potential outcome. (It could be useful to review incident/accident reports involving falls to determine if the presence of urine on the floor was a contributing factor.) Studies have shown that 3% of all falls result in serious injury and 30% of nursing home patients who sustained a hip fracture died within 5 months of their injury; thus the seriousness of falls cannot be over-emphasized (Myers et al. 1987).
- *Dehydration.* Some patients erroneously believe that reducing fluid intake will decrease their incontinence and they become dehydrated as a result.
- *Social isolation.* Patients who are incontinent may be embarrassed to engage in social activities or travel from their rooms because of the threat of having an "accident." Likewise, other persons may be reluctant to socialize with the incontinent person.
- *Altered self-concept.* Lacking control of bladder function, wearing diapers, or "wetting" oneself are not considered normal adult behaviors. Incontinent persons may begin to believe they are regressing and not perceive themselves as normal. Feelings of being offensive, an embarrassment, or a burden may result.

Consequences such as these reinforce the importance of controlling or managing incontinence in a manner that minimizes risks and promotes a high quality of life.

Nursing Considerations

   Goal: Patient will have cause of incontinence identified.
   Actions:
- Review history for onset, ask about new factors (e.g., medications, weight gain, relocation, altered mental status).
- Refer patient for physical examination.

   Goal: Patient will regain bladder control.
   Actions:
- Obtain comprehensive physical and mental evaluations to determine if bladder control is realistic.
- Maintain record of time and amount of voiding and related factors (e.g., after meals, during ambulation).
- Identify patient's voiding pattern.
- Schedule toileting according to individual voiding pattern.
- Assure toilet facilities are readily available.

Goal: Patient will maintain skin integrity.
Actions:
- Inspect skin daily.
- Assure urine and feces are thoroughly cleansed from the skin after incontinent incidents.
- Change soiled clothing and linens promptly.

Goal: Patient will be free from injury.
Actions:
- Keep bathroom and path to bathroom well lighted and free of obstacles.
- Keep call light readily accessible, answer requests for assistance promptly.
- Use incontinence briefs that are effective in containing urine to avoid leaks to the floor.
- Clean urine spills from floors and furniture immediately.

Goal: Patient will have positive self-concept.
Actions:
- Do not discuss patient's incontinence in presence of other patients or visitors.
- Assist patient in using effective incontinence brief.
- Support patient's bladder training program.
- Control urine odors (e.g., change soiled clothing, assist with perineal cleansing).
- Encourage patient to engage in social activities.

Immobility

Many of the health problems that affect nursing home residents threaten their ability to be physically active. Weakness, structural deformities, shortness of breath, pain, missing limbs, paralysis, alterations in mental status, and imposed bed rest can significantly limit normal movement and exercise of the body. Impaired physical mobility is a risk for persons of any age (Exhibit 8-2), but it is particularly threatening to the aged because of the following factors.

- *More fragile skin.* Narrowing of the space between the dermis and the epidermis and decreased circulation cause the skin to break down more easily.

Exhibit 8-2 Effects of Immobility

Orthostatic hypotension
Hypostatic pneumonia
Decubitus ulcers
Thrombus formation
Anorexia
Constipation
Urinary stasis and infection
Loss of bone calcium and strength
Muscle atrophy
Contracture
Poor motivation
Depression

- *Decreased respiratory activity.* Weaker diaphragm and thoracic muscles, combined with reduced elasticity of the lungs, limit the lungs' ability to remove secretions effectively. Thus risk of infection is increased.
- *Less cardiac efficiency.* Because of increased rigidity of heart valves and muscle, reduced cardiac output, and less efficient oxygen utilization the heart is less able to respond to any additional burdens.
- *Increased peripheral vessel resistance.* Decreased elasticity and the presence of deposits on the walls of peripheral vessels can impair venous return and facilitate thrombus formation.
- *Loss of muscle mass.* Loss of muscle tissue and strength can decrease movement and cause muscles to fatigue, strain, and stiffen more easily.
- *Deterioration of cartilage surface of joints and slower bone production.* Stiff, painful joints are not uncommon in old age, and symptoms can worsen from inactivity. Lack of activity can increase the brittleness of bones.
- *Weaker intestinal musculature.* Slower peristalsis causes bowel elimination to be a problem; inactivity further decreases peristalsis.
- *Weaker bladder muscles.* Incomplete emptying of the bladder during voiding may result in some degree of urinary retention and lead to infection.

Age-related changes in themselves reduce bodily function and require that special attention be paid to activity. When illness imposes further restrictions on activity it is crucial that actions be implemented to prevent further restrictions to function, independence, and comfort.

Nursing Considerations

Goal: Patient will exercise all joints to maximum capacity.

Actions:

- Assess every joint for degree of passive and active movement.
- Perform range of motion exercises (Figure 8-1) at least three times each day.
- Encourage patient to participate in activities that promote exercise (e.g., dancing, walking).

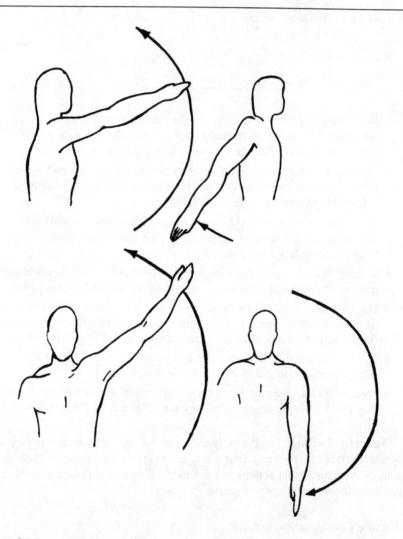

Figure 8-1 Range of Motion Exercises

Figure 8-1 continued

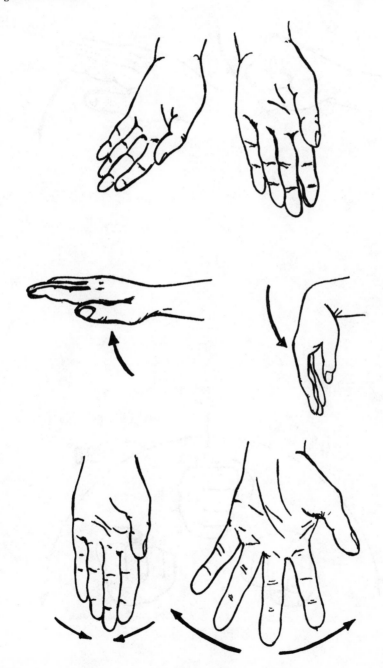

Figure 8-1 continued

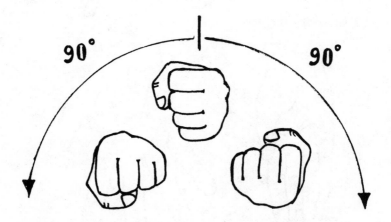

Figure 8-1 continued

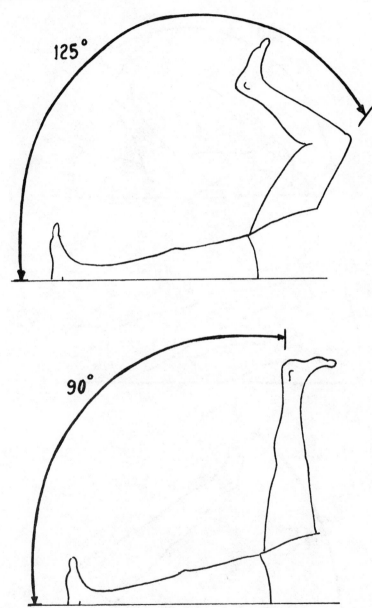

Figure 8-1 continued

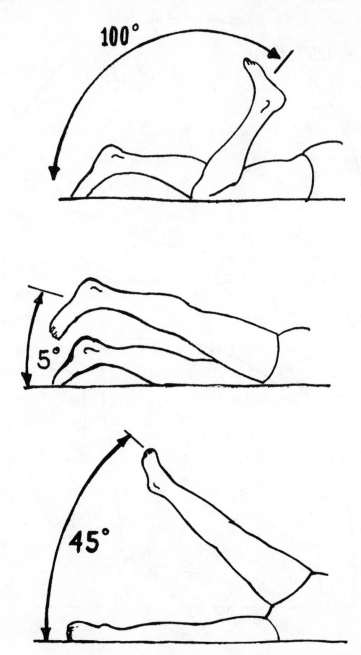

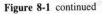

Figure 8-1 continued

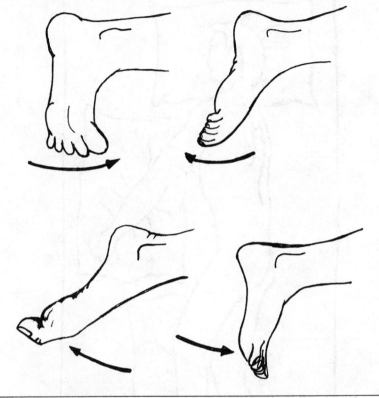

Goal: Patient will be free of complications from immobility.

Actions:

- Position body in good alignment (Figure 8-2).
- Ensure patient changes position and deep breathes at least every 2 hours.
- Assess daily for signs and symptoms of complications from immobility (e.g., skin status, joint mobility, bowel elimination, appetite, characteristics of urine, respiratory function).
- Protect and massage bony prominences; use air mattresses, sheepskin, heel protectors as needed.
- Assist patient in performing isometric exercises.
- Encourage good fluid and fiber intake.
- Adhere to regular toileting schedule.

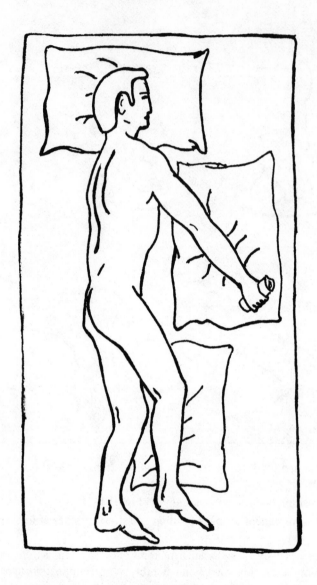

Figure 8-2 Proper Positioning

Figure 8-2 continued

Figure 8-2 continued

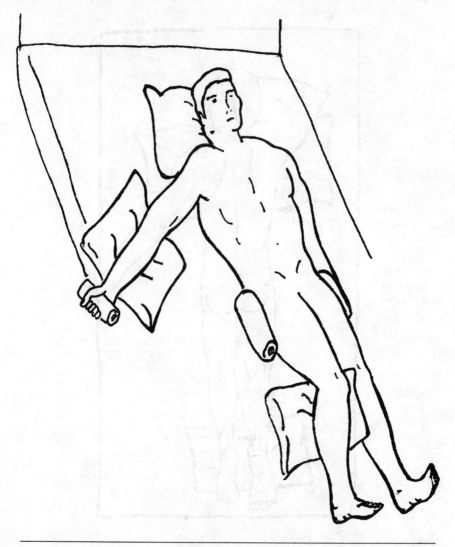

Goal: Patient will increase mobility.
Actions:

- Strengthen patient's capacity to tolerate activities (e.g., by ensuring good nutrition, adequate rest, pain control)
- Control obstacles to mobility (e.g., cluttered room; lack of, or inappropriate, mobility aid; poor fitting shoes or clothing).

- Refer to and follow recommendations of physical therapy.
- Obtain and use mobility aids (Figure 8-3).
- Reinforce and praise efforts that maintain and increase mobility.
- Instruct family members in techniques to assist patient with mobility.

Sensory Alterations

The sensory functions of vision, hearing, smell, taste, and touch aid in the interaction of persons with their environment. The senses allow for communication, protection, learning, enjoyment, stimulation, and a host of other activities.

A major problem for the older nursing home patient is an age-related decrease in the function of sensory organs. Farsightedness, opacity and yellowing of the lens, decreased peripheral vision, and other changes to the eye make visual interpretation of the environment more difficult. High frequency hearing loss distorts the perception of certain sounds. The loss of taste buds alters the perception of flavors. Reduced olfactory ability causes scents to be missed, whereas less acute tactile sensations reduce pleasures and warnings received through receptors in the skin.

Age-related sensory perception problems are compounded by illness and disease processes. For instance, glaucoma can blur vision and cause halos to be seen

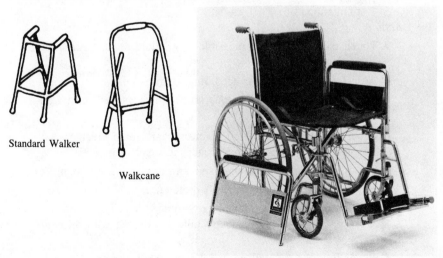

Standard Walker

Walkcane

Wheelchair with Detachable Arms

Figure 8-3 Mobility Aids

around lights; a cerebrovascular accident can dull or obliterate the sensations in a limb; and tumors or infections within the ear canal can block the transmission of sound. Adverse reactions to medications also can alter sensory function by dulling sensations, distorting vision, and damaging hearing.

Situations within the nursing home environment may further jeopardize good sensory perception and stimulation. Fluorescent lighting can create glare, which can make the eyes uncomfortable and give the perception of holes or spots on surfaces; shadows cast by lights can appear as strange items or people lurking. Extraneous noise can be annoying and prevent normal speech from being heard. Intercoms and paging systems can give the impression that invisible beings are speaking. Dietary restrictions can lead to bland meals, limited in textures and flavors. Often, the only olfactory stimulation results from the unpleasant odors of excrements. Few opportunities may exist to touch or be touched outside the realm of baths and treatments. Drab colors, formica table tops, vinyl-covered chairs, standardized furnishings, and the absence of decorations, pets, and live plants— which are characteristic of many institutional settings—do little to provide sensory pleasure. Recognizing that sensory deprivation can easily occur in institutional settings, nursing home nurses should incorporate mechanisms into care activities that stimulate the senses of patients.

Nursing Considerations

> *Goal:* Patient will have opportunities throughout the day for sensory
> stimulation.
> *Actions:*
> - Touch patient whenever possible (e.g., hold hand, hug, stroke cheek, pat back).
> - Adjust window coverings according to time of day.
> - Place fresh flowers, plants, aquariums, birdcages, pets in environment.
> - Decorate and periodically redecorate patient's room with the use of personal photographs and possessions as much as possible.
> - Use different color theme or designs for each resident's room.
> - Play music according to patient's preferences.
> - Incorporate different textures in environment (e.g., textured wall coverings, knitted lap blankets, pillows covered with different types of fabrics).
> - Flavor foods (e.g., with artificial sweeteners, lemon juice, cinnamon).
> - Provide clocks and calendars in environment.

- Bring sensory stimulation activities to the bedside of bedridden patients (e.g., fresh flowers; small stuffed items of different shapes, colors, and textures; caged birds; taped music).

Goal: Patient will have sensory deficits compensated.
Actions:

- Obtain and use corrective lenses, hearing aids.
- Provide adequate lighting.
- Eliminate extraneous noise from patient's environment.
- Approach patient from front, face when speaking.
- Obtain and use assistive devices (Figure 8-4).

Plate Guard

Suction Holder

Figure 8-4 Assistive Devices

Figure 8-4 continued

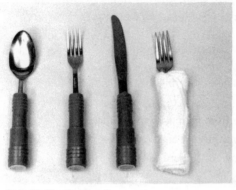

Built-Up-Handle Utensils

Long-Handled Utensils

Swivel Spoon

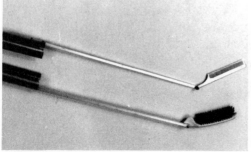

Universal Cuff

Long-Handled Comb and Brush

- Examine patient's body regularly for signs of pressure, irritation, injury.
- Provide consistency in location of items.
- Clarify sensory misperceptions.

Goal: Patient will not experience injury as a result of sensory deficits.
Actions:

- Ensure patient uses eyeglasses, hearing aids.
- Keep bathroom, hallways, stairways well lighted.
- Have call lights easily accessible in bedrooms and bathrooms.
- Ensure hot water temperature is controlled, color code faucets.
- Remove hazardous substances from environment.
- Do not use, or allow patient to use, extension cords, unapproved electrical appliances.
- Encourage patient to use handrails, bedrails.
- Clean up spills immediately.
- Examine patient's body regularly for signs of pressure, irritation, injury, infection.
- Reinforce and ensure patient understands directions.
- Check on patient frequently.
- Attempt to have patient share a room with someone who does not have similar sensory deficits.

Pressure Sores

Age-related changes to the skin, combined with the poor health state and reduced mobility commonly found in nursing home patients, lead to an increased risk of skin breakdown in this group. Pressure sores have a significant impact on patients and their providers. The patient's comfort, quality of life, and general health status can be significantly threatened from a decubitus ulcer. Care activities designed to heal the ulcer and prevent complications absorb considerable nursing time. The limited budget of the facility can be burdened as the cost of treating a decubitus ulcer is estimated to be as high as $40,000. Prevention of skin breakdown and effective management of decubiti once they do occur benefit all parties involved.

What Causes Pressure Ulcers?

Good circulation to the skin keeps it healthy and intact. When pressure is applied to the skin vascular insufficiency results, and the cells lack their necessary nourishment and die. (This can be demonstrated by tightly clenching a clear glass; the portion of the hand in contact with the glass will blanch as the pressure to the fingers inhibits circulation.) The bony prominences are common sites of skin breakdown because of the pressure that is exerted both from the external source and from the underlying bone. Mechanical destruction of the tissue also can result from a shearing force that occurs when two layers of skin move in opposite directions, as when a patient sitting upright gradually slides down. Pulling a patient across the surface of a bed or chair is an example of how friction can lead to decubiti by mechanically injuring the protective tissue surface. Moisture is yet another contributing factor to decubiti formation in that continuous wetness of the skin softens connective tissue and irritates and erodes the epidermis.

Stages of Decubitus Ulcers

In the example given earlier, in which blanching to the fingers occurred from clenching fingers around a glass, tissue color of the fingers returned to normal after the pressure was relieved. Likewise, any site of pressure, if relieved in a timely manner, will have circulation to the tissue restored. However, unrelieved pressure causes ischemia that destroys the skin. This skin destruction progresses through various stages (Exhibit 8-3).

Redness is an early indicator of pressure that is impeding adequate circulation to the tissues. Regular inspection of the patient's skin can aid in detecting redness early and relieving pressure so that circulation can be restored. If left uncorrected, pressure will cause the area to become edematous and blistering or erosion of the epidermis can result; once pressure is relieved it may require several days for erythema to disappear. If pressure to the site is sustained, ulceration will result, exposing subcutaneous tissue and requiring several weeks to heal. Severe problems result when deep ulceration is present and necrosis extends to the fascia and even the bone. In the latter stage, eschar is often present, and secondary complications such as osteomyelitis can develop.

Exhibit 8-3 Stages of Pressure Sores

> *Stage 1* Reactive hyperemia
> Redness, no induration
> *Stage 2* Nonblanching erythema
> Redness, edema, induration
> *Stage 3* Open lesion
> Subcutaneous tissue exposed
> *Stage 4* Open lesion
> Necrosis

Nursing Considerations

Goal: Patient will maintain skin integrity.
Actions:

- Assess patient's risk for skin breakdown at time of admission and on a regular basis thereafter (Exhibit 8-4).
- Change patient's position often; turn bedridden patients at least once every 2 hours; have patient in wheelchair shift weight, or lift the patient at least every 2 hours to relieve pressure from buttocks; use chart to document position change.
- Ensure good fluid intake and consumption of proteins and vitamins.
- Keep skin dry.
- Examine daily skin of patients at high risk.
- Avoid shearing force (e.g., do not pull patient across surface, limit time spent in Fowler's or high-Fowler's position).
- Use alternating pressure or eggcrate mattress for high-risk patients.
- Keep linens and clothing beneath the patient smooth.
- Do not use inflatable (doughnut) rings.
- Massage bony prominences (if reddened, massage around rather than on reddened area).
- Use heel and elbow protectors, sheepskin.

Goal: Patient will have existing decubiti heal.
Actions:

- Record daily location, size, and stage of decubiti.

Exhibit 8-4 Risk Factors for Skin Breakdown

Immobility
Incontinence
Excessive perspiration
Edema
Emaciation
Vitamin C deficiency
Hypoproteinemia
Anemia
Obesity
Paralysis

Exhibit 8-5 Sample Treatment Measures for Pressure Sores

Pressure relief:	Alternating pressure mattress, eggcrate, sheepskin, heel protectors, Clinetron beds
Protective dressing:	Op-site, Duoderm, Vigilon, Reston or adhesive foam with plastic covering
Debridement:	Wet-to-dry dressings, Elase, Travase, Santyl, surgery
Circulation and granulation stimulation:	Ultrasound, oxygen, insulin, Maalox, sugar, Gelfoam

- Follow actions to maintain skin integrity. (See goal to maintain skin integrity, described earlier.)
- Follow prescribed treatment plan (Exhibit 8-5).
- Do not break blisters.
- Keep ulcer moist to facilitate healing (Drying the ulcer and promoting the formation of a scab interfere with epithelial migration.); sterile dressing may aid in maintaining moist wound.
- Use absorbent dressing for draining ulcers.
- Consult physician regarding chemical or surgical debridement if eschar is present.
- Prevent and recognize secondary complications; monitor vital signs, mental status, white blood cell count.

REFERENCE

Myers, A.H., S.P. Baker, E.G. Robinson, H. Abbey, E. Timms, and S. Levenson. 1987. Injurious falls among institutionalized elderly. Findings of the Johns Hopkins Falls Study, Baltimore, Md.

BIBLIOGRAPHY

Neuberger, J. 1986. New for old . . . better design of clothing and furniture for elderly patients. *Nurs Times* 82:8-14.

Orr, A.L. 1987. The elderly visually impaired patient: What every health care provider should know. *Caring* 6:55–58.

Penn, N.D. 1988. Toilet aids. *Br Med J* 296:918–19.

Williams, T.F., ed. 1984. *Rehabilitation in the aging.* New York: Raven Press.

Wong, R.A. 1988. Geriatrics emphasis in physical therapy. A historical survey. *Phys Ther* 68:360–63.

Chapter 9

Mental Health Problems

Since the 1970s a dramatic increase in the number of nursing home patients with a diagnosis of mental illness has occurred. Some of this has been due to more people achieving advanced age when the risk of certain mental health problems rises. Medications and other improvements in treatment measures have enabled more mentally ill persons to survive to old age. Also, the policy of deinstitutionalization has shifted the care of the chronically mentally ill from mental hospitals to nursing homes and community agencies. It is currently estimated that as many as 80% of all nursing home patients have some form of cognitive dysfunction (Burnside, 1988).

The growing number of patients with mental illness has created some problems for nursing homes. The physical layout of most nursing homes is not conducive for close observation of depressed persons or protection of persons with dementia. Staffing levels that may be adequate to provide physical care are less than adequate to address the continuous, complex needs of mentally impaired patients. Reimbursement to achieve improved staffing has been sorely lacking. Regulatory bodies historically have not considered standards for mental health services in nursing homes to guide staff. Professional support has been minimal, partially because of the myth that a loss of mental function is normal in old age and therefore does not warrant psychiatric intervention, and partially because the nursing home has not been an environment in which psychiatrists and other mental health professionals have shown an interest to practice. Nursing homes are now faced with the challenge of developing resources and expertise to provide expert services to patients with psychiatric problems.

MENTAL STATUS ASSESSMENT

At the time the patient is admitted and on a regular basis thereafter, an assessment of his or her mental status is done. The assessment is beneficial both to identify problems that may require further evaluation and interventions and to provide insight into patients' capacities and limitations. The basic components of a mental status evaluation are described in Table 9-1.

There are a variety of tools that have been developed for mental status assessment, and many can be adopted or modified for use by a facility. Whatever tool or approach is used, the important factor is to use it consistently. For example, for Nurse A to judge Mr. J to be oriented because he engaged in a reasonably coherent conversation and then the next week for Nurse B to label Mr. J disoriented because he was unable to answer questions on the assessment tool pertaining to time and place does not provide comparable data. Knowing how Mr. J answered

---

Table 9-1 Components of a Mental Status Evaluation

Component	Methods for Assessment
General appearance and behavior	Observe appropriateness of dress, grooming, level of consciousness, body language.
Mood	Note general affect, tone of voice, fluctuations in mood.
History	Ask about hospitalizations or treatments for emotional problems, "bad nerves," "nervous breakdown."
Symptoms	Ask about delusions, hallucinations, suspiciousness, anxiety, depression, obsessions, compulsions, phobias; explore sleep disturbances, appetite or weight changes, constipation, nervousness, palpitations, hyperventilation.
Cognitive function: retention and recall	Ask patient to remember three unrelated words (e.g., pen, car, bird); immediately ask the patient to repeat the words; ask for recall again at 5- and 15-minute intervals.
Orientation	Ask questions pertaining to person (e.g., Who is the president? Who am I?), place (e.g., What city are we in? What is this building that we are in?), and time (What day is this? What is the season?).
Judgment	Present a situation and ask what the patient's actions would be (e.g., What would you do if you noticed the trash can in this room was on fire?).
Three-stage command	Ask the patient to perform three simple functions (e.g., "Pick up that piece of paper, fold it in half, and put it in that box.").
Calculation	Ask the patient to count backward from 100 by 5s or 7s
Language	Point to several objects and ask the patient to name them; ask the patient to repeat a sentence or phrase; write a simple instruction on a piece of paper and ask the patient to read and follow it; write a sentence and ask the patient to copy it. (Put findings in perspective of educational level.).

the same orientation-related questions on different occasions provides more relevant data to use in determining changes in mental function. Staff should be instructed in how to conduct a mental status examination and comply with a consistent method.

Although evaluation of mental status provides valuable data pertaining to patients' functional abilities, nurses must realize that it indicates patients' function at the time the evaluation was done, which may or may not reflect patients' general status. For example, a newly admitted patient may be so overwhelmed by the unfamiliar institutional environment that he does not concentrate on the interview and scores badly on his mental status evaluation. Likewise, a patient with dementia may vary in mental function throughout the day because of fluctuations in cerebral circulation, level of blood glucose, or effects of medications. Findings must be put in perspective of the total circumstance.

Findings of altered mental function demand further evaluation; essential is a thorough physical examination, including electrocardiogram and laboratory studies of blood and urine. Many alterations in mental status are outgrowths of physical problems, thus identification of potentially treatable causes is important.

The impact of medications on mental function should be assessed regularly. As shown in Exhibit 9-1, drugs can cause mood and cognition to be altered. Even

Exhibit 9-1 Mental Status Alterations Caused by Medications

Confusion
anticholinergics
antihistamines
benzodiazepines
cardiac glycosides
cimetidine
muscle relaxants
narcotics
sedative-hypnotics

Depression
indomethacin
muscle relaxants
nonsteroidal antiinflammatory agents
reserpine
sedative-hypnotics

Flashbacks
chlorpromazine

Hallucinations
anticholinergics
muscle relaxants

medications that have been administered successfully to a patient for years can suddenly cause adverse reactions that affect mental status. Drugs should be among the first area of suspect whenever altered mental status occurs. When multiple drugs capable of producing ill effects to mental status are administered concurrently, the physician may need to discontinue all medications and then gradually reintroduce them singularly to determine which of the drugs is responsible for the adverse reaction.

The relationship of the nursing home environment to the patient's mental health also must be assessed. Do behavioral problems stem from patients learning that disruptions elicit more prompt staff reaction than turning on call lights? Are shadows cast by lighting responsible for patients' claims that they see someone hiding in the corner? Is hostility caused by the unfortunate reality of having to live with people different from oneself, or withdrawal associated with the lack of interests to stimulate the patient? Do patients begin to see themselves as feeble and inadequate because that is how staff treat them? The misperceptions and altered behaviors may result from human and structural aspects of the institution rather than psychiatric disorders. Careful evaluation of the physical environment and staff interactions can aid in identifying facility-induced problems.

SPECIAL CARE UNITS

A growing trend is the development of special care units for the mentally impaired. These units may include patients with a wide range of psychiatric problems (e.g., anxiety, depression, dementia), or more commonly, those with Alzheimer's disease and other dementias. There are several advantages to these units.

- Environmental modifications can be made to reduce safety risks and improve function, such as alarming all exits, covering all electrical outlets, color coding rooms, removing nonessential furnishings.
- Selected staff can receive preparation in psychiatric nursing skills and ongoing support.
- Limited mental health resources, such as psychiatrists and psychiatric nurse specialists, can be used more effectively.
- Therapeutic activities can be planned and a milieu created specific to the capacities and limitations of the mentally impaired population.
- Disruptions to cognitively unimpaired patients can be minimized.

Care should be taken in selecting staff to work on special care units. The first requisite is an interest in working with mentally impaired persons; staff who are frightened by mental illness or intolerant of problem behaviors are not ideal candidates to work on a psychiatrically focused unit. Staff need maturity and patience to deal with the repetition and routine associated with the care of cognitively impaired persons. Selected staff should receive education to familiarize them with mental illness and treatment approaches, as well as have role models available on the unit to demonstrate therapeutic techniques. (This can be achieved through consultative services of a geropsychiatric nurse specialist.) Regular group meetings to discuss care problems and ventilate feelings are also useful.

Consistency is important in the care of the mentally impaired. Meals, treatments, activities, and other routine functions should occur at the same time daily. Staff assignments to a specific caseload should be made for a minimum of several weeks to reduce patients' need to adjust to new persons. Furnishings, personal care items, clothing, and other items should be placed in the same locations after use.

SELECTED CARE PROBLEMS

Dementia

The most commonly encountered mental illness in nursing home settings is dementia. Dementias alter cognitive function without affecting the level of consciousness, which is one important differentiation from delirium (acute confusional states). There are a wide variety of causes of dementia, including the following.

- *Alzheimer's disease.* Currently, most dementias are attributed to Alzheimer's disease. With this disease there is a progressive loss of cognitive abilities, dulling of emotions, personality changes, aphasia, apraxia, and, in the later stages, physical deterioration. Because this diagnosis can be confirmed only at the time of autopsy, Alzheimer's disease is usually the label given to a dementia for which other causes cannot be found. A comprehensive evaluation to rule out other potential causes of dementia, however, must be done before this diagnosis is made. Typically the brain pathology includes cerebral atrophy, neurofibrillary tangles, senile plaques, and restricted cerebral blood flow in the temperoparieto-occipital regions.
- *Multi-infarct dementia.* In this form of dementia cerebral lesions cause ischemia of brain tissue.
- *Wernicke-Korsakoff syndrome.* This degenerative brain condition results from alcohol-induced encephalopathy.

- *Creutzfeldt-Jacob disease.* This rapidly progressing dementia is associated with a "slow" virus. It is believed transmission is possible through cerebrospinal fluid and body tissue; thus special handling of cerebrospinal fluid, blood specimens, and tissue is recommended.
- *Sjögren's syndrome.* This autoimmune disease attacks blood vessels and glands, producing severe dryness. Recently, it has been noted that the vasculitis caused by Sjögren's syndrome affects various body organs and can result in dementia in some persons (Edmunds, 1987).
- *Pick's disease.* The senile plaques and neurofibrillary tangles that occur with Pick's disease are similar to those associated with Alzheimer's disease, but with the former cerebral atrophy is confined to the frontotemporal regions of the cerebral cortex. Another characteristic of the disease is the presence of a swollen, degenerative neuron called the "Pick's cell" in the atrophied areas of the brain.
- *Other causes.* Drug toxicity, Parkinson's disease, trauma, and nutritional deficiencies are among the other factors that can destroy cognitive function.

Symptoms of a dementia appear subtly and gradually. At first, affected persons experience memory problems that they and others may attribute to other causes, such as growing older or preoccupation. Abstract thinking is reduced, and demands for conceptual problem solving produce frustration. Changes in affect occur, demonstrated by overreactions, mood swings, anxiety, and depression. (Depression in the early stage of dementia may be associated with the person's recognizing some of the cognitive changes being experienced.) Attention span is reduced, and the ability to focus on complicated tasks lessens. Poor judgment and impaired decision making become apparent. As the disease progresses the person's social world shrinks, and he or she becomes increasingly self-centered. Family members and friends may not be recognized (amnesia), and there may be paranoia. Aimless wandering occurs. Communication is difficult as words cannot be remembered or understood (aphasia); confabulation may be present. Learned motor movements such as walking are impaired (apraxia). There may be catastrophic reactions whereby overwhelming or overstimulating situations cause the person to become agitated and anxious. In the later stages the person is unable to feed, bathe, or perform other activities of daily living independently.

It is often in the later stage of the disease, when the combination of having to cope with the effects of the cognitive dysfunction and provide all physical care needs impacts fully, that family caregivers exhaust their physical, emotional, and financial resources and seek institutional placement for the affected person. Understandably, families may not be at their best at this time. They are drained from sleepless nights of having to monitor wandering and from tiring days of feeding, toileting, and bathing the impaired person. They may be hurt about accusations the ill person makes or angry outbursts directed toward them. Their social world may become nonexistent as friends become uneasy about being near the demented person and the demands of care giving interfere with social activities and friendships. They may be devastated to see a stranger now in the shell of the spouse, parent, or sibling they once knew. Although family members may realize that they are unable to meet the care-giving demands of their loved one, that does not relieve the guilt, frustration, depression, and anger they feel as they seek nursing home care.

Staff often are the recipients of family members' displaced feelings and must be prepared for this consequence. Support, patience, honest explanations, and the including of family members in activities and care-giving tasks can be constructive approaches. It can be beneficial for family members to be encouraged to attend support groups—the nursing home may consider having support groups offered at the facility. Staff must realize that dementias profoundly affect the entire family unit; thus the care of the family must be considered.

Nursing Considerations

Goal: Patient will be free from injury and secondary complications.
Actions:

- Monitor intake and output.
- Check on patient's status hourly.
- Inspect patient's body daily.
- Provide designated, supervised area for wandering.
- Secure and/or alarm doorways and stairways to prevent patient from leaving unit.
- Cap electrical outlets.
- Remove substances from patient's room that should not be ingested (e.g., shampoo, body lotion, treatment solution).

Goal: Patient will perform activities of daily living as independently as possible.
Actions:

- Adhere to a routine schedule for activities.
- Break tasks into single steps.
- Provide periodic reminders and guidance to complete activities.
- Provide finger foods and other easy-to-eat food items.
- Select clothing for patient to wear.
- Reward patient's successes, correct mistakes.

Goal: Patient will live in an environment that minimizes
     misperceptions.
Actions:

- Assure lighting is adequate and does not cast shadows.
- Eliminate or conservatively use intercoms and paging systems in patient's living area.
- Remove confusing stimuli (e.g., mirrors).
- Approach patient from front, identify self.

Delirium

Deliriums, or acute confusional states, are similar to dementias in that cognitive function is altered, but they differ from dementias in that the onset is rapid, level of consciousness is altered, and correction of the condition is possible. Causes of delirium include fever, dehydration, hypoxia, drug toxicity, hypothermia, trauma, and other factors that can disrupt homeostasis.

Patients will demonstrate confusion, agitation, and irritability. They may be restless and unable to sleep. Nightmares, hallucinations (visual or auditory), illusions, and delusions may be present. An increase in pulse rate and blood pressure may be noted. Level of consciousness can range the continuum of hyperactivity to stupor.

Delirium warrants a prompt, comprehensive physical examination to identify the underlying cause. Treatment of the cause usually restores normal cognitive function in a relatively short time.

Nursing Considerations

Goal: Patient will have cause of delirium identified and treated.
Actions:

- Obtain vital signs; assess physical status for changes, abnormalities.
- Request medical evaluation promptly.

Goal: Patient will be protected from injury and secondary
     complications.
Actions:

- Supervise patient closely, check status frequently.
- Keep hazardous items away from patient.

- Monitor intake and output.
- Inspect patient's body daily.
- Ensure patient obtains sufficient rest and sleep.

Goal: Patient will not be overstimulated.
Actions:

- Provide quiet, stable environment.
- Use soft, nonglare lighting.
- Maintain room environment at approximately 75° F.
- Control noise, traffic flow.

Depression

According to estimations, at least half of all nursing home residents have some degree of depression. Patients may have experienced depression throughout their lives or developed it as a new problem in old age as a reaction to illness or other situations they face.

There are a variety of causes for depression. The multiple losses faced by aging persons may lead to feelings of worthlessness and low self-esteem and cause persons to see few satisfactions in their lives. Physical health problems weaken coping capacity and threaten normalcy and independence. Medications, especially antihypertensives and central nervous system depressants, may lower mood. In some persons, reduced levels of norepinephrine or serotonin (or their metabolites) contribute to depression (catecholamine theory).

The low mood—helplessness and hopelessness—associated with depression is usually easy to detect. Depressed patients lack interest in activities. They may express feelings of worthlessness through comments such as, "I don't deserve such a nice family" or "I'm no good; why does God let me live." Physical disturbances may be noted, including slow psychomotor activity, fatigue, anorexia, weight loss, constipation, and insomnia or excess sleeping. The inattention to grooming, slow motions, and secondary effects of insufficient rest and nutrition can cause depressed persons to give the impression that they have a dementia (and consequently, be treated as such by others, further compounding the depression).

Psychiatric evaluation is important to determine both cause of the depression and appropriate treatment. Staff should be prepared for the reality that quick resolution of depression does not occur with most patients. Weeks of antidepressant therapy may be necessary before results are noted; months of adjunct therapy may be necessary to achieve improvement. Staff must exercise patience and support the patient through this process.

Nursing Considerations

> *Goal:* Patient will obtain psychiatric evaluation and plan of care to improve depression.
> *Actions:*

- Refer patient for psychiatric evaluation; even if depression has been a chronic problem, a fresh evaluation may yield new insights.
- Aid in identifying factors contributing to depression.
- Conduct a team conference to discuss the psychiatrist's evaluation and recommendations.
- Follow prescribed treatment (e.g., antidepressant medications, grief counseling, reminiscence therapy, group therapy).

> *Goal:* Patient will have opportunities to improve self-esteem.
> *Actions:*

- Consult with activities therapist, social workers, and other team members to identify daily activities in which the patient can engage that will provide successes and feelings of accomplishment (e.g., making craft items to decorate the facility, doing volunteer work to help others).
- Recognize patient's successes, accomplishments (e.g., efforts to groom self, attendance at activities).

> *Goal:* Patient will be free from injury and secondary complications related to depression.
> *Actions:*

- Monitor nutritional status, elimination, cleanliness, sleep pattern.
- Observe for indications of self-destructive behaviors, suicidal tendencies (e.g., storing medications or matches, refusing to eat, self-inflicted injuries).

REFERENCES

Burnside, I. 1988. *Nursing and the aged. A self-care approach,* 921–22. New York: McGraw-Hill Book Co.

Edmunds, L. 1987. Sjögren's syndrome. *Johns Hopkins Magazine.* April:53–59.

BIBLIOGRAPHY

Brannan, P. 1988. Using nursing skills instead of restraints. *Geriatr Nurs* 9:114–15.

Gaffney, J. 1986. Toward a less restrictive environment. *Geriatr Nurs* 7:94–96.

Glynn, N.J. 1986. The therapy of music. *J Gerontol Nurs* 12:6–10.

Gomez, G.E., and E.A. Gomez. 1987. Delirium. *Geriatr Nurs* 8:330–32.

Hall, G., M.V. Kirschling, and S. Todd. 1986. Sheltered freedom: An Alzheimer's unit in an ICF. *Geriatr Nurs* 7:132–37.

Lipkin, L.V., and K.J. Faude. 1987. Dementia—Educating the caregiver. *J Gerontol Nurs* 13:23–27.

Ronsman, K. 1987. Therapy for depression. *J Gerontol Nurs* 13:18–25.

Ronsman, K.M. 1988. Pseudodementia. *Geriatr Nurs* 9:50–52.

Struble, L.M., and L. Sivertsen. 1987. Agitation behaviors in confused elderly patients. *J Gerontol Nurs* 13:40–44.

Whall, A.L. 1988. Therapeutic use of self. *J Gerontol Nurs* 14:38–39, 46–47.

Chapter 10

Death

Care of dying persons is an extremely important aspect of nursing home nursing. The skill and sensitivity of nurses in this process can place meaning, comfort, and dignity into this significant life event. The last memories families have of their loved ones can be influenced by nursing's efforts, as can the resolution of feelings that staff and patients have for the deceased. Competency in dealing with death and dying is crucial to effective nursing home nursing.

EXPLORING ATTITUDES TOWARD DEATH

One of the first aspects of caring for dying persons is to explore personal attitudes toward death. Is death viewed as an awaited friend at the end of a long life or as a villain that disrupts the foundations on which we have built our lives? Is death considered a natural part of life or an event to be fought and postponed at all costs? Do we value a death with dignity over a sustained life void of meaning? Personal experiences with death, spiritual beliefs, values, and feelings toward one's own mortality influence the manner in which nurses will deal with death.

It is important that nurses become aware of their attitudes toward death. Nurses can be assisted by discussing their experience and feelings about death with clergy, thanatologists, hospice specialists, and other professionals who are skilled in the area of death and dying. Reading literature pertaining to hospice care, thanatology, and ethics also can assist in clarifying attitudes.

Nurses may need to assist other staff in the nursing home with their feelings about dying patients. Other caregivers possess attitudes that will influence their involvement with dying patients. Perhaps they are frightened to work with dying persons because of their inexperience with death, or view patients' deaths as a sign

133

that their care-giving efforts have been ineffective. The care of dying patients may conflict with staff members' own beliefs and cause ethical dilemmas for them.

The reality of death in the nursing home setting should be addressed during employees' orientation. Open discussions that provide an opportunity for feelings to surface should be facilitated. In-service education reviewing the physical, emotional, spiritual, and legal aspects of caring for dying patients and their families can be provided. The problems and feelings pertaining to individual dying patients can be constructively approached in care planning conferences. Because housekeepers, dietary aids, transporters, and other staff build relationships with patients and are impacted by patients' deaths, death education and counseling should be open to all employees of the facility.

PSYCHOLOGICAL SUPPORT OF DYING PATIENTS

In the process of coming to terms with impending death patients experience a wide range of emotions. Kubler-Ross (1969) aptly described these emotions that persons experience on learning that they have a terminal illness through her identification of the stages of dying.

- *Denial and isolation*. Patients may express disbelief about their terminal state or shop for health care providers that will offer a different diagnosis. This stage offers an opportunity for persons to absorb the reality they must face and strengthen their emotional reserves.
- *Anger*. The realization that their lives are limited can cause patients to experience profound anger, often displaced to other persons and situations.
- *Bargaining*. Dying persons may want to negotiate for an extended life. Most of the time bargains are private and may be made through prayer.
- *Depression*. A profound sadness can be experienced as the impending loss of life and its implications are fully realized.
- *Acceptance*. A certain peace may be reached when persons come to terms with their death.

Although described as stages, these feelings are not necessarily experienced in a specific sequence or progression; instead, they are better considered as different hats that dying patients can wear depending on their emotional states. Patients will experience feelings according to their own timetable. Listening and nonverbal support (sitting quietly with the patient, holding the patient's hand) will be most beneficial to patients as they experience these feelings.

Life review or reminiscence aids dying patients in confronting death by placing significance on the lives they have lived. Although the severity of illness and disability may cause them to feel their current lives have little meaning, patients can reflect on past accomplishments and satisfactions to recognize the positive facets of their existence. Nurses can guide reminiscence activities by reviewing the patient's contributions to the lives of children and grandchildren, work accomplishments, community activities, and the past hurdles that have been overcome (e.g., immigration, wars, Great Depression). Family members can be asked to share photographs, records, scrapbooks, and other memorabilia that can assist patients in reflecting on the past. Life review can give dying patients comfort in recognizing that their time on earth had meaning and made a difference.

The anxiety associated with dying can be compounded for patients by concerns about their loss of control. Patients may question if their pain will be managed, their families comforted, and their bodies treated with dignity. The manner in which other dying patients have been treated and the quality of care provided in general influence impressions dying patients will hold about their own care. For example, have patients died in isolation or with caregivers by their sides? Do staff have conversations with each other during care, ignoring the dying person's presence, or do they continue to touch and talk to the patient, even if he or she is nonresponsive? Are deceased patients' memories eliminated when their bodies leave the facility or are they sensitively remembered by staff and patients? The general care of all terminally ill patients will offer clues to individual patients as to how their dying process will be managed and can contribute to or alleviate anxiety.

With all the losses experienced by dying persons control becomes an important issue. Unless they are unable, or it contradicts good health practices, patients should be given the opportunity to choose their sleep schedules, diet, activity patterns, and other issues pertaining to their daily lives. Even seemingly minor choices, such as which nightgown to wear or what time they would like their baths, should be afforded to patients.

PHYSICAL CARE

Pain control is an important aspect of caring for dying patients. In addition to the psychologic distress associated with pain, physical problems can result if patients are reluctant or unable to move, eat, sleep, or excrete adequately because of discomfort. Rather than alleviating pain after it occurs, the focus of pain control should be on *pain prevention*. Regular administration of analgesics can maintain a blood level that will aid in pain control. Habituation or addiction to analgesics should not be a concern that causes drugs to be withheld. Pain may increase or decrease as the patient approaches death; thus regular assessment of the level of pain and effectiveness of the analgesic is essential.

In the final stage of a terminal illness circulation is reduced and a fluid deficit occurs, observed through decreased intake and output. Dehydration actually can alleviate some discomfort as a decrease in fluids leads to a reduction in vomiting, secretions, voiding, and edema. The higher concentration of electrolytes that accompanies dehydration can have an anesthetic effect on the central nervous system and lessen the discomfort perceived by the patient. However, in addition to alleviating some of the uncomfortable symptoms of their illnesses, patients may develop new problems as dehydration leads to drier oral mucosa, weakness, neuromuscular irritability, confusion, and increased susceptibility to infection and skin breakdown.

Every effort must be made to keep the patient comfortable and free from secondary complications from dehydration, however, and careful thought must be given to correcting dehydration in the dying patient with the use of intravenous fluids. The clinical and ethical implications must be explored by the health care team and family. The decision to initiate intravenous therapy must be weighed against the possibility of extending discomfort for the patient. Ideally the patient will have expressed his or her preferences regarding life-sustaining measures before the terminal stage of an illness is reached.

Good basic nursing care becomes crucial for the dying patient, including the following interventions.

- Keeping skin clean and dry
- Providing good oral hygiene (avoid lemon and glycerin swabs as they dry the mouth)
- Offering small amounts of fluid or ice chips to moisten the mouth
- Changing position often
- Protecting bony prominences
- Massaging and touching
- Keeping the patient warm

SPIRITUAL CARE

Many patients, even those who may not have shown an interest in religious activities in the past, may find comfort through spiritual support during their final days. Last rites may be desired by persons who are Catholic, Episcopalian, Greek Orthodox, or Buddhist. The presence of a reader may be important to Christian Scientists. Communion and confession may be requested. It is important for nurses to explore with patients and their families unique religious preferences and practices. If a patient is of a religious belief with which staff are unfamiliar, it is useful to consult with the facility's clergy representative or call the local church, synagogue, or temple that represents that religion. Nurses may want to ensure that all caregivers understand and respect the patient's religious practices. For instance, a Jewish patient may be distressed rather than comforted if a well-intentioned nursing assistant offers Christian prayers and describes the comfort waiting for the patient in heaven.

CARE OF SURVIVORS

Death ends the ordeal for the terminally ill person but it may launch a new maze of feelings for loved ones of the deceased. It may be painful to realize that the person will no longer be present to fill the roles others have learned to expect. Holidays and special events will not be the same. Sadness and guilt may be felt as survivors reflect on how different things could have been or what they could have done to alter the course. Emotional baggage may be carried for the unexpressed feelings, unresolved conflicts, and other unfinished business between the deceased and survivors. Anxiety and fear may surface as the survivors realize how the loss will alter their lives. These feelings can exist in family members, friends, other patients, and anyone else who had a meaningful relationship with the deceased.

Survivors need to be encouraged to express their grief and to be supported as they do so. The nurse may need to sit in private with family members, allowing them to reflect on the deceased person's life and cry. Active listening, touch, and other nonverbal support can be significant for the nurse to offer. Rather than avoiding feelings or encouraging survivors to "cheer up," the nurse should acknowledge that although the intensity of the grief will lessen in time, it is normal to hurt over the loss of a loved one.

There should be a mechanism for tracking and following up on survivors to assess how they are managing their grief. Often, the full impact of the death is not felt until weeks after it occurs. During the first several weeks there are funeral arrangements and decisions to make, and, most frequently, many friends and relatives are in touch. However, as the weeks progress and other people return to their lives, survivors are left to face the harsh reality that their loved one is permanently gone. This can be the time that profound grief develops and ill consequences can be in store for the survivors. A telephone call or visit with the survivors 4 to 6 weeks after the death can be strategic in assessing the need for interventions for survivors. If the nursing staff is unable to make this follow-up contact, a referral to the clergy or social worker may be of value; a volunteer who is experienced in grief counseling also could be utilized. Nurses can make survivors aware of widowhood groups, grief counseling, and other sources of support that may be available locally.

Patients within the facility are also survivors of the deceased. Often, patients have shared close relationships within the institutional setting and become like "family" to each other. They are affected by their peers' deaths and need assistance in managing their grief. Memorial services and other activities that recognize the deceased are valuable in enabling patients an opportunity to express their feelings. Grief counseling may be necessary. By no means should the topic of a patient's death be avoided in the cause of "protecting" patients; death is a natural life event within the community of the nursing home.

Staff are survivors too. Staff develop close relationships with patients and share patients' joys and sorrows. Caring for and talking with Mrs. Jones in room 200 become routine and expected parts of one's day; not surprisingly, there is a void when Mrs. Jones is no longer there. Sensitive staff who sincerely are interested in patients will grieve a patient's death. Nurses may need to arrange staff conferences where feelings can surface about deceased patients, as well as refer staff to counselors, clergy, and other resources who can guide and support them in their grief. It can be important to both staff and families of the deceased for staff to be given time off from work to attend their patients' funerals. Staff must be helped to understand that being affected by a patient's death is not a sign of weakness, but rather a reflection of sensitivity and caring—important assets for a nursing home employee.

REFERENCE

Kubler-Ross, E. 1969. *On death and dying.* New York: Macmillan.

BIBLIOGRAPHY

Carolan, M. 1987. Hospice care: Nursing the terminally ill. *AAOHN J* 35:168–71.

Kerschner, P. 1985. *Taking charge of the end of your life.* Washington, D.C.: Commission on Legal Problems of the Elderly and the Older Women's League.

Lund, D.A. 1984. Can pets help the bereaved? *J Gerontol Nurs* 10:8–12.

Richter, J.M. 1987. Support: A resource during crisis of mate loss. *J Gerontol Nurs* 13:18–22.

Rose, A. 1987. Care of the elderly dying patient. *Geriatr Nurs Home Care* 7:18–19.

Part III

Managerial Aspects

Chapter 11

Managing Staff

Nurse Jennings begins the shift by listening to report, reviewing the patient caseloads for which she is responsible, and thinking through what needs have to be met during the next 8 hours. She notes the staff who are on duty and assigns them responsibilities on the basis of their competencies. On reviewing new orders she identifies the need for medications and supplies and calls in requests to the appropriate departments. Throughout the shift she checks on the care staff are delivering, in turn correcting deviations from acceptable practice and ensuring appropriate services are being rendered. At the completion of the shift Nurse Jennings evaluates the care that was delivered and prepares a status report for the next shift.

The activities performed by Nurse Jennings reflect the basic functions of many nursing home nurses. In fact, these activities are so common as to be automatic to most nurses. Although seemingly minor, these activities reflect managerial functions that are based on complex processes. Consider that Nurse Jennings's activities required that she

- Have knowledge of the usual operations of the nursing home unit and the facility's policies and procedures
- Be familiar with the competencies and work style of each of the unit's employees
- Know the human and material requirements for patient care activities
- Match resource needs to available resources
- Be able to communicate effectively intradepartmentally and interdepartmentally

- Handle unplanned events and solve problems
- Use observational and interview skills to evaluate the care being delivered
- Coach, guide, and educate staff in proper techniques
- Monitor unit activities
- Develop outcome criteria and determine if they have been met at the completion of the shift

The planning, organizing, leading, and controlling activities described above fall within the realm of management functions. There are various levels of management in which nurses may function (Exhibit 11-1). Although the clinical problem-solving skills possessed by nurses assist them in their managerial responsibilities, additional skills are required for nurses to be successful managers.

MANAGEMENT THEORY

Before the twentieth century little consideration was given to how workers were managed. Workers were viewed as machines that completed tasks. A major transformation in this thinking came about when Frederick W. Taylor (1947) published *The Principles of Scientific Management* and identified how effective management of workers could enhance performance. Taylor introduced concepts well familiar to managers of today, such as standardizing job procedures, matching employees to specific jobs, setting clear goals, and offering incentives to motivate employees to higher levels of performance. His basic premise was that to perform optimally, workers needed structures and prodding. Attempts to incorporate the scientific principles of management into industry, however basic at the time, resulted in improvements in many settings and led the way for further exploration into management theory.

Exhibit 11-1 Levels of Management

Executive:	Broad responsibilities for the organization; relates to all departments and to persons outside the organization (e.g., facility administrator).
Middle Management:	Responsibilities within one department; implements plans, relates to other departments (e.g., shift supervisor, assistant director of nursing).
Supervisory:	Narrow scope of responsibility; oversees one specific unit (e.g., charge nurse, unit nurse coordinator).

Another major insight into management arose from the "Hawthorne studies" (Mayo, 1945). The Hawthorne branch of the Western Electric Company initiated research to determine if different levels of lighting had an effect on productivity. To the researchers' surprise, workers' productivity rose when illumination was increased *and* decreased; even more surprising, the control group who experienced no change in illumination also demonstrated increased productivity during the study. Similar studies using other variables were repeated in other settings, and, again, regardless of the intervention, productivity increased during the studies. The conclusion reached was that productivity rose because of the attention being paid to the workers—a phenomenon now known as the "Hawthorne effect." Results of these studies showed that social variables, such as supervisory style and relationships among employees, influenced productivity. From this the human relations element became part of management theory.

In the 1960s a professor at Massachusetts Institute of Technology, Douglas McGregor (1960), reflected on the two major schools of thought on management—the scientific approach and the human relations approach—and labeled the assumptions of each under *theory X* and *theory Y* management styles (Table 11-1). It was believed that the theory Y manager created a favorable work environment that enhanced performance.

Recently, the impressive performance of Japanese industries has stimulated curiosity as to the management style in those organizations. The Japanese style of management, described as *theory Z* by William Ouchi (1981), a professor at the University of California at Los Angeles, takes McGregor's theory Y to new levels. Theory Z management advocates

- Trust between management and employees
- Holistic concern for employees
- Lifetime employment within the same organization
- Slow evaluation and promotion
- Collective values, decision making, and responsibility

Table 11-1 McGregor's Theory X and Theory Y Assumptions

Theory X	Theory Y
People dislike work, avoid it if possible.	People find work as natural as play or rest.
People have little ambition and avoid responsibility.	People are self-directed and seek responsibility.
People are concerned for themselves.	People want to help the organization meet its goals.
People must be threatened to work.	People will perform at work if their efforts are recognized, challenges are afforded.

It is believed that these factors foster the climate for positive group dynamics that in turn promote maximum performance by employees. Although some of the more successful American corporations (e.g., Procter & Gamble, International Business Machines, Eastman Kodak) have management styles consistent with theory Z, this management style has not been widely tested in the United States. Thus its general applicability in the American culture is still questionable.

MANAGERS' ROLES

There are a variety of roles that managers may assume on the basis of their positions and responsibilities. Some of the classic roles are the following (Mintzberg, 1973).

Figurehead: represents the unit or facility to other employees, the public, patients.
Leader: outlines responsibilities and gets others in motion to meet them.
Liaison: networks with others within and external to the organization to get work done.
Monitor: keeps abreast of the quality and quantity of work.
Disseminator: communicates information.
Spokesperson: represents position of unit or organization.
Entrepreneur: improves function of unit or organization.
Disturbance handler: aids in settling disputes and overcoming obstacles to performance.
Resource allocator: decides how time, manpower, and supplies are to be used.
Negotiator: bargains, makes agreements.

Nurse managers may find that some of these roles are filled more often than others; some may never be assumed.

Each role managers assume carries certain responsibilities. Managers are held accountable for their own actions, as well as for those of their subordinates. They must communicate effectively to superiors, subordinates, and peers, as well as to other departments, patients, family members, and the public. They must be cognizant that their actions represent not only themselves but also the facility. They are responsible for planning, organizing, monitoring, and evaluating the work to which they are assigned.

Certain rights accompany managers' position and responsibilities, such as authority for those aspects required to complete their tasks and support for those actions. For instance, nurse managers should have the authority to reject a staff member who is judged to be incompetent for the job or to order the supplies necessary to complete an assignment. Support can be in various forms such as the provision of the necessary resources to get the job done and administrative trust and backing. Nurse managers should determine the rights and responsibilities associated with their managerial roles to ensure there is a healthy balance of both.

LEADERSHIP

Leadership, the ability to influence others to meet goals, is one of the most important components of management. Nurse managers must exercise leadership over their work group or team to achieve patient care goals. However, as can be observed in most work settings, there are different leadership styles that may be displayed.

- *Autocratic, authoritarian.* An autocratic/authoritarian leader makes decisions and orders staff to do tasks, with little or no input from staff. Subordinates are controlled through the leader's exercise of rewards and punishments.
- *Laissez faire.* At the opposite pole from the autocratic leader, the laissez-faire leader gives maximum authority to subordinates to make their own decisions and exercises little or no control.
- *Democratic, participative, consultative.* In between the extremes of excessive and no control over subordinates, democratic/participative/consultative leaders obtain staff input and allow subordinates to make decisions within defined parameters, but ultimately hold responsibility.
- *Inconsistent.* Perhaps the most difficult style of leadership to work with is one that is unpredictable. The inconsistent leader may vary style from day to day. In one situation the leader may encourage staff to make decisions independently and in another similar situation instead chastise staff for not getting direction.

The leadership styles can be viewed on a continuum: on one end the focus is to get the job done and at the other extreme the concern is for sensitivity to subordinates' feelings, views, and problems. These extremes of leadership styles have been identified as "task-centered" and "people-centered" behaviors (Hampton, 1986). To exemplify how each extreme would address a similar situation consider the following.

Staff arrive on duty and learn that one of their favorite patients has died unexpectedly during the previous shift. The patient had resided in the facility for many years and developed close relationships with many of the staff. Her death to many staff was like losing a special family member.

The supervisor who is task-centered may approach this situation by distributing assignments and informing staff, "This is something you have to get used to in a nursing home. Now let's go ahead and get to work . . . we have a lot to do today." The supervisor expects staff to put their feelings aside and complete their assignments satisfactorily.

The people-centered supervisor recognizes how touched the staff are by the death of the patient and decides to hold a staff meeting to allow staff an opportunity to express their feelings. Assignments are delayed until the meeting can be conducted, and throughout the shift the supervisor demands only that essential tasks be completed, allowing employees extra time to exchange emotional support.

Both extremes carry their share of risks: task-centered leaders may cause their subordinates to lack group cohesiveness and have low morale; people-centered leaders may have highly satisfied subordinates, but there is no guarantee that they will get the job done. Ideally, managers will reach a balance between the two extremes and be sensitive to the social and emotional factors that influence subordinates' performance, while assuring that the work gets done. For example:

A nursing assistant reports on duty and immediately begins expressing her concern over having lost her children's babysitter. She continues this conversation throughout report and as the shift progresses is observed talking to other staff in the hallway about her child care problem.

As a manager, allowing the nursing assistant to use work time to discuss her child care problems may be showing her empathy, but it will not aid in getting the work done. Telling her she must "put her personal problems aside and get to work" may result in one unhappy employee who gets the job done, but with a questionable degree of quality. Perhaps a balanced solution would be to ask the nursing assistant to go ahead with her assignment and at break time the two of you will spend some time calling local day care centers and social service agencies to explore resources to aid her.

Various situations may call for different styles of leadership. For instance, when chairing a recruitment committee, comprised of peers who are highly motivated, to develop a plan to attract nurses to the facility, a leader can allow a more democratic, participative, permissive style to be exercised. On the other hand, an emergency situation or other activity that requires firm structure or direction may benefit from an authoritarian leadership style. The group being managed also influences leadership style: a group of 18-year-old nursing assistants who lack work experience may require clear directives of specific responsibilities as they learn acceptable job behaviors, whereas a group of nursing assistants with several decades of experience may be afforded more flexibility in how they complete their tasks.

POWER

By virtue of the fact that they carry the responsibilities or title of "manager," nurses are viewed as leaders in the nursing home setting. However, it can be observed throughout the work environment that many persons without a formal leadership title can influence others. For instance:

- The physician has no authority over nursing documentation, but when he requests that a different form be used for documentation of his patients' vital signs the nursing staff comply.
- The secretary to the administrator is an unpleasant person, but department heads seem to go out of their way to do nice things for her.
- The supply clerk always has ample disposable gloves to fill the orders of nurses he likes, but cannot seem to locate any for the head nurse who has a running battle with him.
- Although she is no more competent or experienced than other staff, Ms. Jones is outgoing and attractive and is frequently selected to represent the facility at community events.
- Nursing Assistant Clark informs Head Nurse James which patients she will accept for her assignment, and the head nurse assigns accordingly.

As described in the examples above, some persons are granted and exercise power without having legitimate leadership roles. This develops because power is derived from a variety of means, such as:

- *Role*. The position or title one holds can carry certain traditional power (e.g., director of nursing, charge nurse, physician, union delegate).
- *Expertise*. Special knowledge and skill can be powerful (e.g., that of the administrative clerk who is familiar with all personnel policies, the gero-psychiatric nurse specialist, or the nurse who is able to cannulate a vein successfully for intravenous therapy).
- *Information*. The ability to obtain and communicate information can command power (e.g., the facility's housekeeper who carries gossip from one unit to another, the administrator's secretary who knows the position her boss takes on an issue, the supervisor who receives schedules before they are posted).

- *Association.* Who one knows or affiliates with can be a source of power (e.g., being related to the administrator, belonging to the same softball team as the director of nursing, sitting at the same lunch table with department heads).
- *Control of rewards and punishment.* There is power in the ability to decide how resources are allocated and to influence outcomes (e.g., the boss whose evaluation determines the amount of one's merit raise, the supply clerk who can delay deliveries if he does not like the nurse who ordered them, the payroll clerk who decides if paychecks will be distributed before or after the bank closes).
- *Personal attributes.* Personality and appearance can create a power image (e.g., the assertive nursing assistant, the nursing administrator who dresses in suits, the "life-of-the-party" employee, the handsome orderly).

Multiple sources of power are at play in every work setting. To be effective, nurse managers must learn to work constructively with other power sources. This begins by identifying the power possessed by significant others. Nurse managers may find it helpful to make a list of all employees in the work setting and then analyze the type of power they possess. (See Exhibit 11-2.) Often, conflict exists because nurse managers are not aware of other power sources or that they threaten the power held by other persons. When possible, respect other power sources. As examples:

- A nursing assistant who has information about the internal operations of the facility because of his years of employment can be an asset to the new nurse manager. In return for his expertise, the nursing assistant's power can be acknowledged by asking him for input on policy and procedure revisions.

Exhibit 11-2 Power Analysis

	Employees												
Power Possessed													
Role													
Expertise													
Information													
Association													
Control of rewards and punishment													
Personal attributes													

- Harmonious relationships between the nursing and housekeeping departments are beneficial. The housekeeping director can be shown the value of her department is realized by asking her for input on a new program being planned by the nursing department.
- When the supply clerk makes an error in filling a unit's order, rather than criticizing the clerk it may be more effective to store that as an IOU to be used against the next mistake the unit makes in ordering supplies.

Nurse managers can find ways to enhance their own power. Examples include

- Developing expertise in a specific area
- Keeping informed of health care issues
- Establishing lines of communication with significant people in the organization
- Joining organizations and networking with power sources
- Assisting others in meeting their goals and maintaining their power
- Being assertive
- Creating a power image (good posture, eye contact, professional dress habits)

MOTIVATION

Motivation is the drive possessed by persons. All employees are motivated: some are motivated to commit 150% to a job and do the best they can, whereas others are motivated to do as little as possible. The challenge to the nurse manager is to motivate employees to optimal performance.

One of the early theories offered to explain employee motivation was based on Maslow's (1971) hierarchy of needs. Various levels of needs were identified.

- Physiologic: food, water, air, rest
- Safety: protection from threats and dangers
- Love: belonging, caring, and being cared about
- Esteem: recognition by others
- Self-actualization: realizing one's full potential

As they apply to the work setting these needs can be interpreted as

- *Physiologic:* clean air to breathe; break times to meet nutritional and elimination needs; adequate earnings to afford food, clothing, shelter
- *Safety:* job security, fair labor practices, protection from exposure to communicable disease and crime

- *Love:* interacting and being accepted by the work group
- *Esteem:* having efforts recognized, feeling pride and accomplishments in work
- *Self-actualization:* opportunity for autonomy, creativity, and challenge in one's job

Maslow claimed that lower level needs must be met before higher level ones can be realized. For example, an employee may not take advantage of an opportunity to attend an extramural class and expand her knowledge of geriatrics if she is preoccupied with meeting her living expenses week to week. Further, Maslow suggested that to motivate employees they must be afforded opportunities to fulfill unmet needs. For instance, an employee who is earning a competitive salary and is treated fairly may invest special effort to improve her unit's quality assurance audits because it is important to the team to do so.

Herzberg (1976) further developed motivational theory with his discussion of the motivation-hygiene theory. Herzberg identified ''hygiene'' factors in the work place, such as:

- Job security
- Fair personnel policies and supervision
- Safe working conditions
- Ample salary
- Satisfying relationships with peers and supervisors
- Status

These factors need to be present for employees to be satisfied; however, their presence does not *cause* employees to be motivated or satisfied. Factors that will influence better performance are those that afford employees opportunities for

- Recognition
- Achievement
- Responsibility
- Challenge

The validity of Herzberg's theory can be observed in the nursing home setting. Traditionally, the hygiene factors in the nursing home have not been competitive with those in the hospital sector. In long-term care facilities salaries are lower, opportunities for advancement are limited, and staff are still plagued by the stigma associated with employment in this setting. As a consequence, recruitment and retention of staff remain difficult processes. Nurses must advocate for working conditions, salary, and benefits for nursing home staff that are competitive with those offered to staff in other sectors to ensure hygiene needs are met and dissatisfaction minimized. (In addition to advocating this position to the facility's administration, nurses also need to advocate through community, professional, and political groups.) Having good hygiene factors, however, is only part of the picture. To promote higher levels of staff performance nurse managers must assist in providing motivators. Examples of motivators include

- Praising good performance
- Teaching and allowing staff to use new skills
- Providing opportunities for staff to use their creativity in solving problems
- Varying assignments
- Identifying staff's accomplishments

CONCLUSION

The work force of today is highly diverse. In a single work unit one can find staff with varying educational levels (from a high school equivalency to graduate degrees), employment histories (from those who have never held a job before to those with decades of experience), and work attitudes (from persons for whom nursing is just a job to those who believe caring for the sick is a special calling). Staff may come from various socioeconomic backgrounds and have different work ethics. Because of this diversity no one approach to managing staff will be adequate. Nurse managers must know their individual employees and have an understanding of their experiences, attitudes, and needs. Once the unique profile of each employee is understood, approaches appropriate to the individual can be planned. For instance, some employees may respond to having their efforts recognized and praised, whereas others may only perform if regularly monitored and coaxed. The effective nurse manager uses a variety of techniques to encourage good performance.

REFERENCES

Hampton, D.R. 1986. *Management*, 455. 3d ed. New York: McGraw-Hill Book Co.

Herzberg, F. 1976. *The managerial choice: To be efficient and to be human*. Homewood, Ill.: Dow-Jones-Irwin.

Maslow, A.H. 1971. *The farther reaches of human nature*. New York: Viking Press.

Mayo, E. 1945. *The social problems of an industrialized civilization*. Cambridge, Mass.: Division of Research, Graduate School of Business Administration, Harvard University Press.

McGregor, D. 1960. *The human side of enterprise.* New York: McGraw-Hill Book Co.

Mintzberg, H. 1973. *The nature of managerial work,* 59. New York: Harper & Row.

Ouchi, W. 1981. Theory Z. Reading, Mass.: Addison-Wesley Publishing Co.

Taylor, F.W. 1947. *Scientific management: The principles of scientific management.* New York: Harper & Bros.

BIBLIOGRAPHY

Blancett, S.S. 1988. *Classics for JONA: Readings in nursing administration.* Philadelphia: J.B. Lippincott Co.

Douglas, L.M. 1988. *The effective nurse leader manager.* 3d ed. St. Louis: C.V. Mosby Co.

Hingley, P., and C.L. Cooper. 1986. *Stress and the nurse manager.* New York: John Wiley & Sons.

Marquis, B.L., and C.J. Huston. 1987. *Management decision making for nurses: 101 case studies.* Philadelphia: J.B. Lippincott Co.

Marriner-Tomey, A. 1988. *Guide to nursing management.* 3d ed. St. Louis: C.V. Mosby Co.

Rowan, R. 1986. *The intuitive manager.* Boston: Little, Brown & Co.

Scalzi, C.C. 1988. Role stress and coping strategies of nurse executives. *J Nurs Adm* 18:34–38.

Sullivan, E.J., and J. Decker. 1988. *Effective management in nursing.* 2d ed. Menlo Park, Calif.: Addison-Wesley Publishing Co.

Vestal, K.W. 1987. *Management concepts for the new nurse.* Philadelphia: J.B. Lippincott Co.

Yager, D. 1988. Long term facilities feel the nursing shortage, too. *Am J Nurs* 88:450.

Chapter 12

Legal Aspects

Situation: A patient complains of fatigue and heaviness on his chest, and you assess that he has a low-grade fever, increased pulse rate, and nonproductive cough. The physician cannot be reached by telephone, and during the next 4 hours you leave several messages with the physician's answering service. Finally, the physician returns the calls, states he will examine the patient in the morning, and, in the interim, orders an antibiotic and acetaminophen. You are uncomfortable that the patient's condition worsens as the shift progresses and again call the physician, who responds angrily, "I told you I'll see the patient in the morning." You carefully document all communication with the physician. Near the end of the shift the patient is found dead. Autopsy results reveal the cause of death as myocardial infarction.

Outcome: You are sued for negligence in not recognizing the severity of the patient's condition and intervening on the patient's behalf by transferring him to a hospital for medical evaluation.

Situation: You are the evening supervisor for the entire facility on a severely short-staffed evening. Multiple crises on one unit prevent you from making rounds to all other units. On one of the other units, a temporary personnel agency nurse does not realize that one of the patients with Alzheimer's disease is missing from the unit. The patient is later discovered in neighboring woods, suffering from hypothermia because of exposure to the cold.

Outcome: You are sued for not providing adequate supervision to ensure staff were correctly fulfilling their responsibilities.

Situation: A patient repeatedly complains about the use of bedrails at night and demands to have them left down. Although the patient has

153

periodic bouts of confusion, she has not been judged incompetent. The facility agrees to comply with the patient's wish and has her sign a release from responsibility, stating the facility will not be held responsible for any injury related to the bedrails being down. The patient falls out of bed several times but continues to demand the rails be left down. The staff feel they are protected from liability because the patient signed the release. After several more falls the patient has a fall that results in a fracture.

Outcome: The nursing staff are sued for failing to protect the patient from injury; the release the patient signed proves to be invalid.

Situation: A patient with dementia has been becoming increasingly agitated and begun having violent outbursts. Although the patient has become more problematic, the staff feel sorry for him because he has no family and the only alternative is placement in a state mental hospital. Thus they try to manage him the best they can. The patient attacks another patient and seriously injures that patient.

Outcome: The facility is sued by the injured patient because it kept a patient in the facility whose care was at a level inappropriate for a nursing home and failed to ensure the safety and well-being of the injured patient.

Situation: You are a charge nurse on a unit and discover that one of your nursing assistants has reported on duty in what seems to be an intoxicated state. You confront him and he denies having ingested alcohol; he then proceeds to become loud and verbally abusive. You feel he is a threat to patients and other employees and request that he leave. The employee refuses to leave and begins to stagger away. You grab him by the arm, pull him to the lobby, and place him in a taxicab with instructions to go home.

Outcome: You are sued by the employee for defamation of character, assault, and battery.

Situations like those described above can easily occur in a nursing home and result in liability for nurses and their employers. Most nurses would not intentionally take risks that jeopardize the facility and themselves, but sometimes short staffing, difficult judgment calls, and choices between two less than ideal options create legal problems. The nursing home is increasingly becoming a high-risk site for litigation. Among the factors responsible for this trend are the following.

- *Patient population.* Most nursing home residents have multiple health problems that increase their frailty and susceptibility to complications. Often, altered mental status prohibits patients from expressing needs; thus early detection of problems is more difficult.

- *Family reactions*. The guilt, anger, and frustration that families feel concerning the realities of having to institutionalize a loved one and watching that person regress may be displaced to staff. Sometimes families have expectations that are impossible to meet or do not accept that complications may be a result of illness and not caused by staff. The misconception held by people about "the horrible conditions in nursing homes" also leads to families believing that problems with their loved ones are a result of negligence or abuse.
- *Staffing*. Most direct nursing care is provided by nursing assistants who have minimal preparation, and the caseloads of those caregivers are heavy. Licensed nurses are stretched to their limits with multiple clinical and managerial responsibilities.
- *Changing care demands*. The care of nursing home patients is becoming increasingly more complex, and staff are expected to provide competent care for persons with a wide range of needs. On a single unit staff may be faced with patients whose care requires monitoring of a ventilator, observation of the effects of psychotropic medications, recognition of altered cardiac status, behavioral modification, and education in the use of assistive devices.
- *Litigious society*. Ours is a society that sues for any minor wrongdoing (or perceived wrongdoing), so it should not come as a surprise that patients and families who have reason to suspect the nursing home has been negligent in its responsibilities and caused them unnecessary harm believe the nursing home should be held accountable.

Complaints about the facility made in the presence of patients and visitors (e.g., "They never give us enough staff," "I hear that physician doesn't know what he is doing"), errors in charting, failure to communicate problems, and not following the facility's policies and procedures are among the factors that can cause legal problems, for the nursing assistant through the director of nursing. Even if the outcome proves staff and the facility to be innocent of the charge, the time, energy, and money invested in a lawsuit can be significant. All levels of staff must realize the legal risks they face and learn how to minimize those risks.

LEGAL PROBLEMS

Malpractice

Nurses are prepared to competently perform nursing functions for patients based on accepted standards of practice. It is expected that when nurses assume responsibility for patients' care they will act in accordance with accepted standards. A deviation of those accepted standards that results in harm to the patient makes a nurse liable for negligence or malpractice. Examples of malpractice include

- Administering a medication to the wrong patient
- Administering an incorrect dose of a medication
- Failing to administer a medication
- Failing to take precautions or follow a special procedure related to medication administration
- Failing to follow a physician's orders
- Following a physician's orders incorrectly
- Omitting treatment
- Failing to recognize and report a change in the patient's status
- Failing to follow established procedure or policy
- Failing to recognize and report safety hazards
- Performing functions outside the scope of nursing practice

To prove liability four basic elements must exist (Feutz, 1989).

1. *Duty:* a relationship between the nurse and patient for the nurse to provide service to the patient following acceptable standards of care
2. *Negligence:* conduct or care fails to meet acceptable standards of practice
3. *Damage:* physical, emotional, or financial injuries
4. *Proximate cause:* damage to the patient resulting from negligence of the nurse

Competency

The high prevalence of mentally impaired patients in the nursing home raises some important issues concerning competency. Unless persons have been judged incompetent by a court of law they have the right to make their own decisions about their care. Thus obtaining permission for a procedure from a confused patient's spouse rather than directly from the patient is not legally appropriate. The physician's or interdisciplinary team's judgment that the patient is incompetent is not legally binding.

Nurses play an important role in competency issues. Documented nursing observations of indications of the patient's incompetency are beneficial. Rather than broad statements such as "patient has questionable judgment" or "patient behaving inappropriately," notations should be as specific as possible: "patient observed giving money to strangers, stating he was paying them for fixing his car"; "patient unable to remember that he had children"; "patient fully dressed at 3:00 A.M. stating he had to go to work." Notations such as these help the court understand the actual mental function of the patient.

Once significant data have been collected justifying the concern for the patient's competency, nurses can refer the matter to the facility's administration and legal counsel. The facility may suggest to family members that they assume responsibility for obtaining guardianship, or it may ask the state agency on aging or other resources to intervene. It is an important advocacy function of the nurse to ensure that patients who are incompetent to make decisions for themselves have legal guardians appointed to assume a decision-making role.

The specific procedure for declaring an individual incompetent varies in each state, but the basic issues that will be of concern are the patient's ability to make decisions and understand the implications of those decisions. Notations from the patient's medical record may be reviewed in making the determination, as may direct testimony from staff. If the court decides that the patient is incompetent, it will appoint a legal guardian. The guardian is not necessarily next of kin, and restrictions to guardianship may apply. Thus it is beneficial for information about the name and responsibilities of the legal guardian to be clearly evident in the patient's record.

Consent

At the time patients are admitted to the nursing home, they usually sign forms that authorize the facility to perform routine and emergency care activities, such as examinations, medication administration, and baths. Consent forms do not grant permission for any or all care activities, however. Any procedure beyond routine care activities requires specific informed consent.

Informed consent is just that: consent based on information. For consent to be truly informed patients need full explanations of the procedures or treatments, including

- Description of what will happen
- Anticipated outcome
- Potential risks and complications
- Alternatives

Information presented to the patient should be documented and often is included in the consent form that the patient signs.

The patient's signing of the consent form is witnessed, and nurses may be called on to act as witnesses. Although there is no legal problem with nurses serving as witnesses to patients' signing of consent forms, facilities may have policies prohibiting such actions. Thus it is essential to review the facility's specific policy. In witnessing the signature nurses are ensuring that the person whose signature appears on the form was the same person who signed the form and that he or she signed the form voluntarily. Witnessing the signature does not mean that the witness participated in the process of giving information to the patient about the procedure or treatment. If there is any indication that the patient has been coerced into signing the consent or lacks an understanding of the procedure or treatment, the nurse should discuss the matter with the physician or nursing supervisor next in the line of command. Failure to obtain informed consent can result in liability for malpractice, assault, and battery.

Patients also have a right to refuse consent or renege consent for a procedure or treatment to which consent has been granted.

Responsibility for Subordinates

Under the doctrine of *respondeat superior* an employer is held liable for the wrongful acts of employees. The facility's liability for its employees exists for wrongful acts committed within the scope of job responsibilities. This doctrine does not relieve employees from responsibility for their wrongful acts: injured parties can still sue the responsible employee, and the employer can sue the employee to recover the losses the facility sustained.

Nursing home nurses commonly must supervise and delegate functions to other nursing staff. Unlike the employer, the nurse manager is not liable under respondeat superior for the negligent actions of subordinates. However, if an employee's wrongful act results from failure of the nurse to carry out appropriate supervisory duties, then the nurse could be held liable. Examples of situations that could result in supervisory liability include assigning a nursing assistant a caseload that requires licensed nursing care, allowing an employee to perform tasks outside his or her job description, incorrectly instructing an employee on the performance of an activity, and not intervening or correcting a known hazardous situation.

References

There has been so much paranoia associated with sharing former employees' job histories on references that many references given provide no meaningful information on which to base an employment decision. Unfortunately, this can result in problem employees repeating their experiences in other settings and jeopardizing the well-being of additional patients and employees. A balance must be achieved between communicating sufficient information on a reference to provide an accurate profile of the employee and avoiding comments that could risk litigation for defamation of character or invasion of privacy.

The first step in ensuring a legally sound reference is to verify that the requesting agency has secured the employee's written consent for obtaining the reference. It is risky to take a person's word over the telephone that the employee granted permission for the reference, even if the caller is known. Instead of giving a full critique of the employee it may be best to acknowledge that the person was employed at the facility and that more information will be provided on receipt of the reference request that bears the applicant's signature.

Once the written request is received a complete profile of the employee's work record can be provided. The *ABCs* to remember in writing a reference are to be

- *Accurate*. Deal only with facts. Hearsay, unsubstantiated allegations, or subjective feelings do not belong in a reference. Negative information can be shared, but it must be valid and supportable (e.g., "received three disciplinary actions during last year of work for forgetting to chart medications," "called in sick on all weekends scheduled to work during May through September," "terminated for striking another employee on the facility's premises").
- *Brief*. Give only the data requested and do it concisely. There is no need to give a chronicle of the employee's employment.
- *Consistent with facility policy*. If the facility has a policy that all references must be communicated through the personnel office or that shared information is limited to certain items, follow the policy.

References can result in a defamation charge if false comments are made that injure the character of the employee or interfere with his or her ability to be employed. Slander is the oral form of defamation, libel the written form. Comments volunteered outside the scope of references also apply, such as stating to a colleague, "I hear Mary Jones is working for you now. I'd watch her. We could never catch her, but it seemed a lot of patients lost their valuables whenever she was on duty."

Protecting against Litigation

Every employee has a responsibility for ensuring that unsound, unethical, and illegal actions do not occur in the work place. Deviations from acceptable standards can jeopardize patients' lives, threaten licenses of the facility and its staff, and be costly to the facility in terms of money, time, and public confidence. In light of the increasingly complex world of the nursing home, nurses must be sensitive to legal risks and actively minimize those risks.

Being informed on the laws, regulations, and standards governing nursing home practice is the first step in avoiding legal problems. Nurses should be familiar with

- Federal, state, and local regulations governing their specific type of facility
- Nurse practice acts for their state
- Scope and limitations of other licensed and certified staff
- Basic civil and labor laws
- Residents' Bill of Rights (see Exhibit 13-2 in Chapter 13)
- American Nurses' Association Standards of Gerontological Nursing Practice (see Exhibit 14-1 in Chapter 14)
- American Nurses' Association Code for Nurses (see Exhibit 13-1 in Chapter 13)
- Standards for nursing homes developed by the American Health Care Facilities Association and other professional organizations

Nurses should ensure they and their facilities are complying with standards and take actions to improve compliance when necessary.

The facility's policies and procedures should be known and followed. A review of policy and procedure manuals during orientation can help staff learn acceptable practices for the facility. Nurses need to ensure that other staff are complying with policies and procedures and take corrective actions when deviations are discovered. Manuals should be readily accessible to all staff and reviewed annually for continued accuracy and relevance.

Nurses need to recognize their limitations and not place themselves in uncomfortable or risky situations. When faced with having to do a procedure for the first time, nurses should ask for assistance and guidance and not attempt to complete tasks for which they lack competence. Responsibilities that are beyond the scope of nursing practice should be refused, and assignments that are unrealistic protested. If a nurse feels there is insufficient staff to adequately meet patients' needs, he or she should notify the supervisor immediately. If the supervisor is unable or unwilling to correct the situation, rather than abandoning the assignment the nurse should (1) document the nature of the concern (including staffing pattern, number and acuity of patients) and that he or she is working with these conditions under protest and (2) present the written complaint to the supervisor (keeping a personal copy). Some state nursing associations suggest that a copy of the memorandum documenting the nurse is working under protest be filed with them; some even have forms nurses can use for this purpose.

Problems identified should be reported and acted on. For example, employees violating acceptable practices, patients who have uncontrollable behavior, and equipment that is malfunctioning require prompt action. Nurses also should feel a responsibility to seek resolution of problems involving other departments. Rather than an ''It's not my job'' attitude, an ''It's everybody's job'' attitude will foster a safe environment.

Documentation plays a crucial role in legal protection of the facility and its staff. In Exhibit 12-1 some of the important points to remember regarding documentation in the nursing home are highlighted. Documentation can

- Determine whether the facility can justify to regulatory bodies and third party payers the services delivered to patients
- Influence the fairness of employees' evaluations
- Provide crucial evidence in a court of law

Exhibit 12-1 Documentation Guidelines

Be objective. Opinions, suppositions, and feelings do not belong in patient charts, employees' evaluations, and other official forms of documentation. For example, notations indicating the frequency of telephone calls to the physician and responses are more appropriate than documenting ''physician reluctant to examine patient.''

State signs and symptoms but do not make the medical diagnosis. It is not within the scope of nursing to conclude the patient has pneumonia. Instead, record vital signs, lung sounds, and other findings.

Avoid drawing conclusions from events. It is more appropriate to record ''employee reported to nurse that she 'slipped on floor and back is now sore''' rather than ''employee injured back from fall on floor.'' Unless you actually saw the fall you have no way of knowing it occurred or if it was the cause of the back injury.

State the date and specific time of the notation; write legibly; and sign.

Use only accepted abbreviations.

Do not obliterate the original entry when correcting errors. Draw a single line through the error and date, time, and initial the error. Make a notation in the record to explain.

Do not alter documents at a later time.

Remember, documentation does not relieve the responsibility for action. Notations in an employee's personnel file regarding poor performance should be accompanied by counseling of the employee; recording of the fact that a physician was notified of a patient's changing condition does not excuse the nurse from taking action if the patient's condition declines before the physician's visit.

Not only patients' records but also correspondence, employees' disciplinary actions and evaluations, and other forms of documentation should be written for the thought that they may be scrutinized later by other parties. Arbitrators, jurors, and others will have no way of knowing that the evaluation of the employee was based on hearsay, or that notations regarding the physician's unwillingness to address a problem were the result of other stresses that day, or that a full patient assessment was done but time did not allow for the assessment tool to be completed. That which is in writing will count! Care needs to be taken to ensure documentation is accurate and legally sound.

It is important for nurses to maintain their competency through continuing education. In addition to the in-service education offered by the facility, nurses bear a responsibility for attending extramural seminars, participating in professional organizations, and reading literature to keep abreast of current knowledge and skills. Membership in the American Nurses' Association and National Association for Licensed Practical Nurses, for registered nurses and licensed practical nurses/licensed vocational nurses respectively, not only shows commitment to staying current but also demonstrates commitment to the profession.

A last, although important, consideration in the efforts to avoid litigation is public relations. No amount of good will and positive attitudes will prevent litigation for gross malpractice or misconduct. However, people who are treated sensitively, courteously, and fairly may be less likely to let small problems grow out of proportion. People who believe they can be heard and achieve results from within the facility may be willing to solve problems there and not resort to litigation.

REFERENCE

Feutz, S. 1989. Legal aspects of gerontological nursing. In *Nursing the elderly: Dynamic roles in diverse care settings*, edited by C. Eliopoulos. Philadelphia: J.B. Lippincott Co.

BIBLIOGRAPHY

Costa, L. 1988a. Computerized records raise questions about patients' right to privacy. *Contemp Longterm Care's D.O.N.* 11:15–16.

Costa, L. 1988b. Monitoring patient care: A standard of nursing practice. *Contemp Longterm Care's D.O.N.* 11:11, 47.

Fiesta, J. 1988. *The law and liability: A guide for nurses.* 2d ed. New York: John Wiley & Sons.

Floyd, J. 1988. Research and informed consent: The dilemma of the cognitively impaired client. *J Psychosoc Nurs Ment Health Serv* 26:13–14, 17, 21.

Fox, T.C., ed. 1986. *Long term care and the law.* Owings Mills, Md.: Rynd Communications.

Henry, K.H. 1987. *Nursing administration and law manual.* Rockville, Md.: Aspen Publishers.

Kapp, M.B., and A. Bigot. 1985. *Geriatrics and the law.* New York: Springer Publishing Co.

Chapter 13

Ethics

To many persons, ethical dilemmas seem confined to the high-technology, acute care arena.

- Should a teen-ager be allowed to have an abortion without parental consent?
- Should efforts be made to save the life of a highly deformed, brain-damaged infant?
- Should persons be able to sell their organs or their unborn child?

These are the highly charged areas that make the headlines and stimulate public debate. Often these issues seem remote to nursing home nurses, causing them to sigh in relief that they need not be involved with major ethical dilemmas in their daily practice.

In reality, nursing home nurses face many ethical dilemmas in their daily practice—dilemmas that may be chronic, subtle, and even unrecognized. These dilemmas can be at the root of conflict, burnout, inappropriate care, and other activities that have negative effects for both patients and nurses. With the many real ethical dilemmas in the nursing home setting, as well as the likelihood that they will continue to grow, nurses should gain a better understanding of this complex area.

WHAT ARE ETHICS?

Basically, ethics are those beliefs held about what constitutes good and bad. For example, people in our society generally believe stealing, lying, cheating, and killing are bad, whereas being helpful, honest, charitable, and fair are good;

discrimination is bad, equal opportunity is good. The framework of society is based on those assumptions. Cultural and religious groups have ethics that further influence persons' beliefs about good and bad. Also, families instill certain beliefs in their members that define right and wrong, good and bad. Even work settings have their "shoulds" and "should nots." All of these systems lead persons to develop the unique set of ethics that guides their lives. Understandably, personal ethics are complex and may vary from person to person.

The nursing profession has ethics guiding its practice based on the principles of

- Beneficence (preventing harm and doing good)
- Autonomy (allowing persons the right to make their own decisions concerning their life)
- Fidelity (being true to one's word, faithful to one's commitments)
- Justice (treating all persons equally)

These principles are integral to the ethical standards for nurses, described in the American Nurses' Association Code for Nurses (Exhibit 13-1).

ETHICAL DILEMMAS

Guidelines for what is right and wrong seem relatively straightforward until attempts are made to apply them to daily life. It is then that the complexities emerge. Some persons' beliefs or understandings of what is right and wrong may be different from others'. These variances are witnessed every day in society, for example when advocates for and against abortion both feel their ethic is the right one. Gray areas emerge that cannot fit neatly into clear categories of right and wrong. For instance, killing is considered wrong, but in situations of war, self-defense, or suffering it may be considered acceptable. Knowing exactly what is right and wrong in all circumstances can indeed be problematic.

Even the seemingly straightforward principles guiding nursing give rise to ethical dilemmas. For example:

- *Beneficence:* Nurses certainly would not cause patients to suffer, but what if suffering is necessary to achieve other goals or to sustain life? If a patient prefers to be left in bed because moving the joints causes him discomfort, does the nurse respect his desire or urge him to move and experience pain for the sake of maintaining joint mobility? At what point does the terminally ill patient's physical and psychologic agony not justify the extended life achieved through intravenous feedings or ventilator support?
- *Autonomy:* Independence for patients is promoted, but what if the patient's desires conflict with what is good practice or what is believed to be in the best

Exhibit 13-1 American Nurses' Association Code for Nurses

1. The nurse provides services with respect for human dignity and the uniqueness of the client, unrestricted by considerations of social or economic status, personal attributes, or the nature of health problems.
2. The nurse safeguards the client's right to privacy by judiciously protecting information of a confidential nature.
3. The nurse acts to safeguard the client and the public when health care and safety are affected by the incompetent, unethical, or illegal practice of any person.
4. The nurse assumes responsibility and accountability for individual nursing judgments and actions.
5. The nurse maintains competence in nursing.
6. The nurse exercises informed judgment and uses individual competence and qualifications as criteria in seeking consultation, accepting responsibilities, and delegating nursing activities to others.
7. The nurse participates in activities that contribute to the ongoing development of the profession's body of knowledge.
8. The nurse participates in the profession's efforts to implement and improve standards of nursing.
9. The nurse participates in the profession's efforts to establish and maintain conditions of employment conducive to high quality nursing care.
10. The nurse participates in the profession's effort to protect the public from misinformation and misrepresentation and to maintain the integrity of nursing.
11. The nurse collaborates with members of the health professions and other citizens in promoting community and national efforts to meet the health needs of the public.

Source: Reprinted with permission from p. 1 of *Code for Nurses with Interpretive Statements*, published in 1985 by the American Nurses' Association, 2420 Pershing Road, Kansas City, Missouri 64108.

interest of the patient? Does the nurse have a right to intervene if a patient decides he would rather shorten his life by living his remaining time uninhibited by the demands of therapeutic measures? Should an institutional committal be aggressively pursued for a person who chooses to live on the streets?

• *Fidelity:* Can nurses always be true to their words to patients? If the patient asks the nurse to be honest and inform him of his diagnosis, does he or she tell the patient he has terminal cancer, despite family protests or the nurse's assessment that he may not be able to cope with the reality?

• *Justice:* With limited resources can all persons be treated equally? Should a 30-year-old person and a 70-year-old person have equal access to an artificial organ or scarce medication? Is it fair that for one couple, who sacrificed and saved throughout life, the husband now has to exhaust all assets to pay for his wife's nursing home care, but for another couple, who lived luxuriously and spent all their income when young, the wife receives Medicaid subsidy?

The answers to these questions may be unclear and could vary depending on the circumstance.

Nurses have to be concerned with ethical dilemmas that arise both in clinical practice and in their managerial roles. As examples:

> The administrator of the facility instructs you to chart that patients received more care than was actually delivered to increase reimbursement for the facility. You know this is improper, but your boss orders you to do so. No one will know what you did. Do you follow proper protocol, even if your job may be in jeopardy for doing so—particularly if you need this job?

> You witness an employee taking a box of disposable diapers from the facility's storeroom to her car. You know that theft is a cause for immediate termination from the facility, but you also know that this employee is the sole breadwinner for her family and has three children and an ill mother for whom she is responsible. Do you follow policy and terminate the employee?

> Staff are complaining that their caseloads are getting heavier and they need higher staffing levels. You recognize their complaints are valid but have been instructed by administration that the facility is trying to save some money by not increasing staff and that staff are to be convinced that their staffing is adequate. Do you support management and comply with administration's demands or fight for more staff, even if it means your job?

> There is suspicion that a patient's narcotic analgesic is being stolen. Facts must be collected to identify who the guilty employee is. The patient has the right to be informed of this potential problem in his care, but to inform him may ruin the investigation. Do you tell the patient, or withhold this information from him to ensure an airtight case against the thief?

> You and the director of nursing have worked together for 12 years and are social friends. The new administrator confides in you that he wants ''fresh blood'' in the nursing department and plans to terminate the nursing director as soon as the candidate for the position is able to begin work. He asks you not to share this with the nursing director. Because of loyalty do you inform your friend she will soon be losing her job or do you respect the confidence of the administrator?

Often it is easy to theorize what is right and wrong, but when faced with the situation personally, decisions become more difficult. Should rules be bent if no one will be hurt? Should a person feel more loyal to the employer than a co-worker friend? Are there situations when it is right to withhold information or mislead subordinates or patients to achieve a noble goal? Would a person risk a desperately needed job for the sake of doing the right thing?

OUTCOMES OF DILEMMAS

Nursing staff face many dilemmas in the work place; some are obvious and others are subtle and may be unrecognized. Whether or not they are aware of these dilemmas, staff are affected by situations that place their value systems in conflict.

One of the ways staff respond to ethical dilemmas is through expression of disagreement and criticism. For instance, a nursing assistant who believes that old people should be allowed to die a natural death may respond to an aggressive treatment approach to the patient with the charge that "the doctors don't know what they're doing" or "they're torturing the patient." Staff who believe devotion to one's parents to be a highly regarded principle may feel impatient and critical of a patient's daughter who has no interest in visiting her mother. A day shift nurse who values patients' independence may argue against the evening shift nurse's practice of restraining wandering patients. An analysis of the issues behind staff bickering, gossip, and criticism often can disclose differences in values at the core.

Sometimes disagreements and criticisms are not verbalized but, instead, are displayed in other ways. A nurse who feels that every attempt should be made to sustain life may ignore the DNR (do not resuscitate) order and institute cardiopulmonary resuscitation on a patient who has ceased breathing. A memorandum directing staff to reduce the theft problem by reporting co-workers seen stealing may be removed from the bulletin board. An overtly racist patient may have her call light answered slowly and her requests "forgotten" by staff members of the race she dislikes. A nurse manager may respect the administration's desire to withhold information from staff about the record profits the facility has made but "accidentally" leave a copy of the annual report in the employees' lounge. Sabotage and game playing may be associated with the inability to solve ethical dilemmas openly.

Burnout is yet another manifestation of ethical dilemmas. Being torn between two conflicting sets of values can take its toll on a person's physical and emotional well-being. Headaches, backaches, fatigue, gastrointestinal upset, overeating, anorexia, insomnia, or excess sleep are among the physical manifestations of the stress associated with ethical dilemmas. There may be high sick time utilization. Irritability, depression, and other emotional reactions may be noted. Some staff may limit their emotional investment in their jobs, perhaps believing that if they are less involved they are less likely to be caught in the middle of uncomfortable ethical conflicts. Some persons may change jobs or specialties as a means to escape ethical dilemmas; unfortunately, some may go as far as leaving the nursing profession. Such outcomes are destructive for patient care, the facility, and the individual employees.

MANAGING ETHICAL DILEMMAS

Ethical dilemmas are ever present in the health care system and, if anything, will grow rather than subside as new technology, scarce resources, and other issues create new issues for health care workers to face. It is unrealistic for staff to think that they can shield themselves from ethical dilemmas. A more constructive approach is to learn effective ways of managing ethical dilemmas.

One of the first measures to deal with ethical dilemmas is for staff to come into touch with their personal ethics. Staff need to reflect on family, religious, cultural, and educational influences on the values they hold and be helped to understand the diversity of values at play in the work place. Through guided learning experiences and discussions of issues and cases, staff can learn their individual positions on what is right and wrong.

Ethical issues in the work place can be identified and discussed, such as the use of life-sustaining measures, unequal access to health care, insufficient reimbursement to meet known care needs, the balance between the patient's right to choose and caregivers' obligation to protect the patient from potentially hazardous choices. An ethics committee can be a useful forum for these discussions. Committee membership could include attorneys, clergy, ethicists, consumers, and other persons who can present added facets to the discussion. Staff at all levels should be encouraged to refer ethical dilemmas to the ethics committee for guidance.

Staff need to become acquainted with the ethics guiding patient care. Direction can be gleaned from the American Nurses' Association Code for Nurses (Exhibit 13-1, *supra*) and the Residents' Bill of Rights (Exhibit 13-2). The principles included in such documents can be actively applied by relating them to issues witnessed in care-giving activities.

The position of the facility on ethical issues must be clarified to minimize confusion and misunderstanding. Is it believed that the facility has an obligation to care for patients who no longer are able to pay for service or that it has no responsibility to those persons? Is it the facility's position to share profits with the staff or to improve the financial return to investors? Will a patient's desire to avoid life-sustaining measures be honored or will that be in conflict with the facility's religious or cultural framework? Are all patients afforded equal care or will private pay patients reside on one unit, with higher staffing levels and a more attractive

Exhibit 13-2 Department of Health, Education and Welfare Residents' Bill of Rights*

These patients' rights policies and procedures ensure that, at least, each patient admitted to the facility:

1. is fully informed, as evidenced by the patient's written acknowledgement, prior to or at the time of admission and during stay, of these rights and of all rules and regulations governing patient conduct and responsibilities;

2. is fully informed, prior to or at the time of admission and during stay, of services available in the facility, and of related charges including any charges for services not covered under titles XVIII or XIX of the Social Security Act, or not covered by the facility's basic per diem rate;

3. is fully informed, by a physician, of his medical condition unless medically contraindicated (as documented, by a physician, in his medical record), and is afforded the opportunity to participate in the planning of his medical treatment and to refuse to participate in experimental research;

4. is transferred or discharged only for medical reasons, or for his welfare or that of other patients, or for non-payment for his stay (except as prohibited by titles XVIII or XIX of the Social Security Act), and is given reasonable advance notice to ensure orderly transfer or discharge, and such actions are documented in his medical record;

5. is encouraged and assisted, throughout his period of stay, to exercise his rights as a patient and as a citizen, and to this end may voice grievances and recommend changes in policies and services to facility staff and/or to outside representatives of his choice, free from restraint, interference, coercion, discrimination, or reprisal;

6. may manage his personal financial affairs or is given at least a quarterly accounting of financial transactions made on his behalf should the facility accept his written delegation of this responsibility to the facility for any period of time in conformance with State law;

7. is free from mental and physical abuse, and free from chemical and (except in emergencies) physical restraints except as authorized in writing by a physician for a specified and limited period of time, or when necessary to protect the patient from injury to himself or to others;

8. is assured confidential treatment of his personal and medical records, and may approve or refuse their release to any individual outside the facility, except in case of his transfer to another health care institution or as required by law or third-party payment contract;

9. is treated with consideration, respect, and full recognition of his dignity and individuality, including privacy in treatment and in care for his personal needs;

10. is not required to perform services for the facility that are not included for therapeutic purposes in his plan of care;

11. may associate and communicate privately with persons of his choice, and send and receive his personal mail unopened unless medically contraindicated (as documented by his physician in his medical record);

12. may meet with and participate in activities of social, religious, and community groups at his discretion, unless medically contraindicated (as documented by his physician in his medical record);

13. may retain and use his personal clothing and possessions as space permits, unless to do so would infringe upon rights of other patients, and unless medically contraindicated (as documented by his physician in his medical record); and

14. if married, is assured privacy for visits by his/her spouse; if both are inpatients in the facility, they are permitted to share a room, unless medically contraindicated (as documented by the attending physician in the medical record).

*DHHS (formerly the Department of Health, Education and Welfare) requires the posting of these rights in a prominent position in all participating facilities.

environment, and Medicaid patients be housed on another unit, with lesser staff and amenities? Articulating the answers to such questions may not be comfortable for facility leadership, but it can save later conflict by clarifying expectations and practices to staff. Policies and procedures should be consistent with the ethical beliefs held by the facility's ownership and/or administration.

As new populations of disabled persons age, life-sustaining technology expands, and resources shrink nursing homes will face an increasing number and complexity of ethical dilemmas. It will be essential for nursing homes to identify these dilemmas and develop constructive means to manage them.

BIBLIOGRAPHY

Callahan, D. 1987. *Setting limits. Medical goals in an aging society*. New York: Simon & Schuster.

Edwards, B.J. 1988. Establishing a nursing bioethics committee. *J Nurs Adm* 18:30–33.

Flech, L.M. 1987. Decisions of justice and health care. *J Gerontol Nurs* 13:40–46.

Last, J.M. 1987. The ethics of paternalism in public health. *Can J Public Health* 78:3–5.

Meier, R.H. 1988. Recent developments in rehabilitation giving rise to important new (and old) ethical issues and concerns. *Am J Phys Med Rehabil* 67:7–11.

Muyskens, J.L. 1987. Acting alone. *Am J Nurs* 87:1141–42, 1146.

Phillips, L.R. 1987. Respect basic human rights. *J Gerontol Nurs* 13:36–39.

Urden, L.D. 1986. Building a case for decision making. *J Nurs Adm* 16:6.

Veatch, R.M., and S.T. Fry. 1987. *Case studies in nursing ethics*. Philadelphia: J.B. Lippincott Co.

Chapter 14

Regulation and Quality Assurance

When nursing homes emerged there was little known about the conditions that ensured good quality in this setting. Vast diversity existed among nursing homes in mission, leadership, resources, and physical plant. As growing numbers of persons began to utilize nursing homes and increasing amounts of government funds were being spent on care for the elderly, concern for the quality of nursing homes heightened, leading to the beginning of licensing of these institutions in the 1950s. Government funding for nursing home construction through the Hill-Burton grants was accompanied by standards for physical design, safety, and basic staffing. With no model to use as a guide, federal standards for nursing homes mimicked those of hospitals in many ways—in fact, facilities constructed during the 1950s followed the traditional hospital layout.

The most profound regulation emerged in the mid-sixties with the passage of Medicare and Medicaid (Table 14-1). Regulatory standards continued to increase thereafter. During the Carter Administration the nursing home industry began to voice considerable concern over the cost of meeting escalating amounts of regulations, and the federal government began studying the problem. With the Reagan Administration came an interest in relaxing regulations; however, public outcry as to the fear of seeing the quality of nursing home care slide caused that administration to refrain from weakening or reducing standards.

Facilities that accept Medicare and Medicaid reimbursement must meet the standards of those programs, which address the following issues.*

- *Abuse.* The facility must have policies and procedures regarding physical and mental abuse and ensure that they are being followed.

---

*Reprinted from *Nursing Administration of Long-Term Care* by C. Eliopoulos, pp. 212–219, Aspen Publishers, Inc., © 1983.

Table 14-1 Differences between Medicare and Medicaid Coverage Pertaining to Nursing Home Care

Medicare	Medicaid
Health insurance financed by the federal government for persons age 65 years and older or for persons who have received Social Security disability benefits for at least 2 years.	Health insurance financed by federal and state governments for persons of any age whose income falls below a designated level (as determined by state).
Covers skilled nursing care that requires daily skilled or rehabilitative services performed by a licensed professional.	Covers intermediate care that is above level of room and board but not of the intensity of skilled care.
Coverage is limited; only 100 days are reimbursed (only a portion of those are covered in full).	No limitation to coverage period.

Chemical and physical restraints used as punishment or for the convenience of staff are considered examples of patient abuse.

- *Administration of medications.* The facility must have written policies and procedures (approved by the pharmaceutical services committee) related to drug administration, stop orders, verbal orders, and other practices that ensure drug safety. Medications must be administered only by physicians, licensed nurses, or other personnel who have completed a state-approved training program in medication administration. Drugs must be administered and monitored on an individual basis, with supporting documentation. The charge nurse should ensure comformance to established practice by supervising personnel who administer medications. Except for single-unit dose administration systems, drugs should be poured and recorded for one medication pass at a time and administered as soon as possible after pouring. Subsequent doses should not be poured until the current ones are administered and recorded. Self-administration of drugs is permitted only upon written order of the attending physician. Verbal orders can be accepted only by a licensed nurse and must be countersigned or confirmed in writing by the attending physician within 48 hours. Drugs and biologicals must be stored in the containers in which they are received; any transfer between containers must be performed by the pharmacist. No discontinued, outdated or deteriorated drugs are to be kept in the facility. Poisons and drugs for external use are to be kept separate from other medications. Controlled drugs must be stored in separate compartments that are locked and permanently affixed.

An emergency medication kit, approved by the pharmaceutical services committee, should be readily available.

- *Administrator.* The governing body must appoint a qualified administrator who is responsible for the management of the facility. Proof of the administrator's current licensure or registration must be available. In the absence of the administrator, an employee who is authorized in writing to act in the administrator's behalf must be appointed. If the director of nursing substitutes for the administrator, a qualified nurse must be available to fulfill the nursing director's usual functions.
- *Changes in patient status.* Written policies and procedures must stipulate notification of a patient's attending physician and family or responsible party about significant changes in the patient's physical, mental, or emotional status or in the facility's billing or administrative practices and about any accidents involving the patient.
- *Complaints and grievances.* The facility must have a written procedure for registering and resolving complaints and grievances and for dealing with recommendations by patients and their representatives. The procedures must also deal with employees' responsibilities for handling complaints, grievances, and recommendations and for implementing investigation processes, resolution processes, and methods of documenting. Records must be maintained of complaints and grievances and of any actions taken. Patients are to be encouraged and assisted to exercise their rights to voice complaints and grievances and to make recommendations to the facility or outside agencies without restraint, interference, coercion, discrimination, or reprisal.
- *Confidentiality of records.* The facility must have procedures to limit access to patients' medical and personal records to those personnel who are involved with the patients' care and services. Patients have the right to request that their records be accessible and that information be released to anyone they desire.
- *Consultants.* When a consultant is used to perform a service in the place of a facility employee, a written agreement to that effect must include descriptions of services to be provided, specific responsibilities and limitations, method of reimbursement, duration of the agreement, staff development responsibilities, and the qualifications and health status of the consultant. A signed, dated agreement between the administrator and consultant, or authorized representative, must be completed.

- *Director of nursing.* The skilled nursing facility must have a qualified registered nurse employed full-time (40 hours a week) in the position of director of nursing. If this individual has other institutional responsibilities, a qualified registered nurse must serve as assistant. The nursing director is responsible for developing and maintaining nursing service objectives, standards of nursing practice, nursing policies and procedure manuals, written job descriptions for each level of nursing personnel, daily rounds to see all patients, and recommendations for the number and level of nursing staff to be employed. The nursing director participates in planning and budgeting for nursing services and ensures that all nursing policies and procedures are being implemented appropriately.

- *Incompetent patients.* There should be documented evidence of patients' incompetence. Incompetent patients are not denied the rights of other patients and should be advised of their rights to the extent to which they may understand them. Patients classified as incompetent should have documented evidence in their records that the patient's guardian has been advised of the patient's rights and is acting on behalf of the patient.

- *Licensed nurses.* The skilled nursing facility must provide 24-hour coverage by licensed nurses. A registered nurse must be present at least during the day shift, seven days a week, unless the facility is waivered for this requirement. A sufficient number of staff must be available to meet the patients' total nursing needs.

- *Medical condition.* Patients must be fully informed of their medical condition by a physician. If the physician decides that informing patients of their condition is medically contraindicated, this decision and its justification must be documented in the patient's record.

- *Medical director.* The facility must have a written agreement with a physician who serves as the medical director. The medical director coordinates medical care, maintains liaison with attending physicians, participates in the development of policies and procedures, serves on committees, ensures that adequate medical services are delivered to each patient, reviews incident and accident reports, and monitors the health of the facility's employees. Each patient must be under the supervision of a physician, who must examine the patient within 48 hours of admission (unless such examination has been performed within the previous five work days) and visit the patient at recommended intervals.

- *Medical emergency.* Written procedures must be available at every nurses' station to describe the procedure to follow in the event of a medical emergency. The names and telephone numbers of physicians to be called in a medical emergency should be posted at each nurses' station, accompanied by procedures to follow if the physician does not respond.

- *Nursing services.* The facility must provide 24-hour nursing service with the number and type of personnel to meet the total needs of the patients. Nursing services must be sufficient to maintain patients' physiological functions, assist patients to learn to live with their condition, increase patients' ability to care for themselves, assist patients in maintaining optimal physical and psychological functioning, encourage out-of-bed activities, protect patients from accident and injury, promptly respond to patient calls, and ensure that routine, special, and emergency needs of all patients are met at all times. Nursing staff should be assigned duties consistent with their education and experience. Weekly time schedules must be maintained, indicating the number and classification of nursing personnel who work on each unit on each tour of duty.

- *Nursing supervision.* The director of nursing must designate a registered nurse or licensed practical (vocational) nurse to be in charge of each tour of duty. This charge nurse evaluates patients' physical and emotional status daily, checks medication orders and charts, reviews patient care plans, delegates responsibilities, supervises and evaluates nursing personnel, communicates with the nursing director on patient and personnel matters, and provides direct patient care when needed.

- *Patient care plan.* A written care plan must be developed and maintained for each patient. The nursing services component of the care plan is based on the documented nursing assessment of the nursing needs of the patient. Patient care conferences or other means of reviewing the care plan should be utilized to keep the plan current. All personnel caring for the patient should have access to the care plan. The facility should have written policies and procedures regarding the development, frequency, and method of review of the patient care plan.

- *Patient care policies.* Written patient care policies must exist in the areas of admission, transfer, and discharge; categories of patients accepted and not accepted; care of patients in emergencies; patient activities; medical records; transfer agreements, utilization review;

personal and property rights; and physician, nursing, dietetic, rehabilitative, pharmaceutical, diagnostic, dental, and social services. These policies are developed by the medical director or organized medical staff with the advice of at least one physician, a registered nurse, and other professional personnel. The medical director or registered nurse (who has a physician advisor for medical guidance) must be designated in writing as having responsibility for implementing the patient care policies. The administrator is responsible for ensuring that the policies are established.

- *Patients' clothing and possessions.* The facility must have policies that permit patients to keep reasonable amounts of clothing and possessions for personal use unless medically contraindicated and documented to that effect. The items are to be recorded on admission, and a receipt is to be given to the patient for all possessions retained by the facility during the patient's stay. Stored items are to be promptly returned to the patient upon request or upon discharge.

- *Spouses.* The facility should have a policy that permits married patients to share a room unless medically contraindicated and documented to that effect. The facility should have provisions to afford privacy in visits by spouses.

- *Patient funds.* Patients may manage their personal financial affairs or be given, at least quarterly, an accounting of financial transactions made on their behalf. A copy of the facility's financial statement to the patient should be maintained in the patient's record.

- *Patient labor.* Patients are not to perform services or be used as a source of labor against their will or against physicians' orders. If patients perform services for therapeutic reasons, there must be written evidence of a physician-approved therapeutic plan and its goals, or of the fact that the patients are acting voluntarily.

- *Patient respect and dignity.* Patients are entitled to respect, individuality, privacy, choice, and involvement in their care activities.

- *Patients' rights and responsibilities.* Written policies must indicate how patients are to be treated by the facility, its personnel, volunteers, and others involved in providing care. Written policies must also describe the responsibilities of patients in their dealings with the facility, staff, and other patients. These rights and responsibilities are formally reviewed in the on-going staff development program. Written copies of the rights and responsibilities should be prominently posted in locations available to all patients. Statements signed by the patients within five working days after their admission, indicating their understanding of these rights and responsibilities, must be maintained on the patients' records. Patients of course maintain their right as citizens when admitted to the facility.

- *Personnel policies.* Written personnel policies, procedures, organizational charts, and job descriptions must be available and discussed with each employee. A complete personnel record must be maintained for each employee. This record is confidential and should include the dated application for employment, verification of references, summary of training and experience, current health status report (including at least annual verification that the employee is free from communicable diseases), and evaluations of work performance.

- *Rehabilitative nursing care.* The facility must have an active program of rehabilitative nursing care as an integral part of its nursing service, and staff must be trained in the skills of rehabilitative nursing. Routine rehabilitative nursing measures in daily care should include maintaining good body alignment and positioning, encouraging and assisting bed patients to turn at least every 2 hours (day and night), keeping patients active and out of bed, assisting patients to adjust to their disabilities, aiding patients to perform prescribed therapy exercises between the therapist's visits, helping patients with their routine range-of-motion exercises, and instituting bowel and bladder retraining programs. Planned rehabilitative nursing measures should be written in the patient care plan.

- *Research.* A patient considered for participation in experimental research must be fully informed of the nature, risks, and possible consequences of participating and not participating. The patient's written consent must be obtained prior to participation in such research.

- *Restraints.* Chemical and physical restraints are not to be used to limit patient mobility for the convenience of staff. Restraints should be used for patient behavior that may result in injury to the patient or to others, but only after other treatment plans have proved unsuccessful. The use of restraints must be authorized in writing by a physician, stipulating the type of restraint, the specific reasons for its use, and any time limitations. Unless the patient's condition warrants, restraints should not be used for longer than 12 hours. The restrained patient must be checked at least every 30 minutes and exercised at least 10 minutes during each 2-hour period during the daytime.

- *Staff development.* Each facility must have an on-going staff development program. Each employee must receive orientation to the facility and its policies and to the specific responsibilities of the employee's job. Annual in-service training for each employee must include, but not be limited to, the topics of prevention and control of infection, fire and safety, accident prevention, confidentiality of patient information, and preservation of patient dignity. Continuing education should be provided to address the specific needs and interests of staff. Policies should address staff's attendance at educational programs outside the facility. Records must be maintained to indicate the content of and attendance at educational programs.

- *Staffing pattern.* The facility must be able to furnish a staffing report to the state. This report must include the patient census and a list of each shift's personnel by name, title, and total hours worked. Administrative personnel who contribute directly or indirectly to patient care must be included; administrative personnel who perform managerial and financial functions can be excluded. In a multistory building, the staffing pattern for each floor must be included. The state survey agency will review at least one week's staffing pattern during each quarter.

- *Supervision of patient nutrition.* Nursing personnel must be aware of patients' nutritional needs and ensure that prescribed diets are served. Prompt assistance must be available for patients who cannot eat independently, and the need for assistance is to be noted in the patient care plan. Adaptive self-help devices should be provided to increase patients' independence in eating. Deviations from normal patterns of food and fluid intake should be documented in the patient's record. A written procedure must describe the method used for the transmission of diet orders and patient requests to the dietetic service.

- *Transfer and discharge.* Patient transfer and discharge within units of the facility or to an outside facility may occur for medical, social, emotional, or financial reasons. Policies and procedures must stipulate the process for transfer and discharge, including mechanisms for providing the patients with reasonable advance notice. (In medical emergencies, patients may be transferred or discharged without advance notice.) Verification procedures must be instituted to ensure that the policies and procedures are utilized.

- *Visitation and communication.* Policies and procedures must ensure that patients have access to and can communicate with the community. A visitor may not be restricted unless the patient refuses to see the visitor, the physician contraindicates the visit (giving specific rationale), or the visitor's behavior is disruptive to the facility. Comfortable, private space should be available for visitation. Telephones must be available and accessible for patients to make and receive calls in privacy. Mail is to be received and sent unopened, unless medically contraindicated. Assistance should be provided to patients who cannot read or send mail independently. Patients have the right to participate or refuse to participate in social, religious, or other activities in or outside of the facility.

There are additional standards that outline the conditions other departments must meet, including administration, dietary services, rehabilitative services, pharmaceutical services, laboratory and radiologic services, dental services, social services, patient activities, and medical records. Still other standards address specific issues, such as transfer agreements, the physical environment, facilities for the handicapped, unit features, infection control, disaster preparedness, utilization review, the budget, disclosure of ownership of the facility, and sanitation.

These are minimum standards required by the federal government for facilities that accept Medicare and Medicaid reimbursement. State regulatory agencies can add to the federal standards, making them more stringent, but cannot weaken them. (Nurses can obtain a copy of their state's regulations through the state's licensing and certification division). Of course, individual facilities also can choose to upgrade quality by striving to meet standards that surpass those mandated by government agencies.

THE SURVEY PROCESS

The announcement "the health department surveyors are here" can cause panic in some nursing homes. However, an understanding of the survey process can not only reduce anxieties but also assist in improving compliance with regulations. There is nothing devious or mysterious about the surveyors' actions; they are merely determining how well the facility is meeting standards.

The survey begins with an entrance conference in which surveyors meet with key administrative personnel. During this time the surveyors will introduce themselves and request necessary paper work, such as records of fire drills, inservice education programs, and staffing patterns. Any change in administrative policies, procedures, and personnel will be reviewed.

The surveyors will ask nursing service for the numbers of patients in each of the following categories.

- Completely bedfast
- Chairbound
- Ambulatory
- Restrained
- Confused or disoriented
- Possess decubiti
- Receive special skin care
- On bowel and bladder training programs
- Receive intravenous therapy or blood transfusions
- Require no assistance with activities of daily living
- Self-administer medications
- Require tube feedings
- Incontinent
- Use indwelling or external catheters

In addition, the number of patients requiring assistance in each of the activities of daily living—bathing, dressing, toileting, transferring, feeding—will be requested.

A resident sample is then selected and reviewed to determine if appropriate care is being provided. For the selected patients the surveyors will observe care activities, review the medical record, and interview those patients. Attention will be directed to

- Provision of treatments, medications, and diet as prescribed
- Cleanliness, grooming, oral hygiene
- Prevention of skin breakdown and promotion of healing of decubiti
- Proper application and release of restraints
- Infection control techniques
- Rehabilitative nursing care to promote maximum function and prevent complications

The observation of drug administration also is an important component of the survey. (See Chapter 7 for a discussion of this process.)

The facility's attention to patients' nutritional needs is determined through observation of mealtime activities. Not only the appropriateness of food and fluid intake but also the assistance and supervision provided to patients in eating and drinking are noted. The surveyors may review records of patients' weights and evaluate if nutritional intake is adequate to maintain a minimum average weight for individual patients. The dining area will be observed for adequacy, comfort, and cleanliness.

At the conclusion of the review the surveyors will prepare a deficiency statement and reveal their findings in an exit conference. It is beneficial for unit level staff to attend the exit conference to learn about deficits in meeting standards and suggestions for improvement. Administrative nursing personnel should make notes of the surveyors' findings so that they can communicate survey findings to staff and begin corrective actions as necessary. Nurses should feel comfortable asking the surveyors for clarification or questioning findings that seem incorrect. Rather than assuming a defensive posture, the facility should be open to surveyors' constructive criticisms and attempt to use the survey process as a stimulus to correct problems and improve quality.

Nurses have a responsibility for meeting regulations and ensuring that good standards of practice are in place. Active attention should be paid to preventing deficiencies, rather than waiting for surveyors to detect them on inspection.

REGULATIONS AND QUALITY ASSURANCE

Complying with regulations is an important component of the nursing home's quality assurance program; however, it is just one piece of the total program. Regulations define the minimum standards that a facility must meet. The nursing profession demands that nurses strive beyond minimum standards to reach the highest possible level of care attainable in the nursing home setting. To accomplish this, nurses must

- Be familiar with the American Nurses' Association Standards, Joint Commission on Accreditation of Healthcare Organizations Standards for Long Term Care Facilities, and the standards of other agencies involved in long-term care.
- Define the standards desirable in the specific nursing home through policies, procedures, and protocols. (See Exhibit 14-1 for suggested standards set by the American Nurses' Association.)
- Facilitate staff competency in fulfilling standards through sound hiring practices, ongoing in-service education, close supervision, and regular performance appraisal.
- Evaluate the quality of services rendered through rounds, observation, audits, and various feedback mechanisms (e.g., staff meetings, resident counsels, informal conversations with visitors).

Exhibit 14-1 Standards of Gerontological Nursing Practice

Standard I. Organization of Gerontological Nursing Services
All gerontological nursing services are planned, organized, and directed by a nurse executive. The nurse executive has baccalaureate or master's preparation and has experience in gerontological nursing and administration of long-term care services or acute care services for older clients.

Standard II. Theory
The nurse participates in the generation and testing of theory as a basis for clinical decisions. The nurse uses theoretical concepts to guide the effective practice of gerontological nursing.

Standard III. Data Collection
The health status of the older person is regularly assessed in a comprehensive, accurate, and systematic manner. The information obtained during the health assessment is accessible to and shared with appropriate members of the interdisciplinary health care team, including the older person and the family.

Standard IV. Nursing Diagnosis
The nurse uses health assessment data to determine nursing diagnoses.

Standard V. Planning and Continuity of Care
The nurse develops the plan of care in conjunction with the older person and appropriate others. Mutual goals, priorities, nursing approaches, and measures in the care plan address the therapeutic, preventive, restorative, and rehabilitative needs of the older person. The care plan helps the older person attain and maintain the highest level of health, well-being, and quality of life achievable, as well as a peaceful death. The plan of care facilitates continuity of care over time as the client moves to various care settings, and is revised as necessary.

Standard VI. Intervention
The nurse, guided by the plan of care, intervenes to provide care to restore the older person's functional capabilities and to prevent complications and excess disability. Nursing interventions are derived from nursing diagnoses and are based on gerontological nursing theory.

Standard VII. Evaluation
The nurse continually evaluates the client's and family's responses to interventions in order to determine progress toward goal attainment and to revise the data base, nursing diagnoses, and plan of care.

Standard VIII. Interdisciplinary Collaboration
The nurse collaborates with other members of the health care team in the various settings in which care is given to the older person. The team meets regularly to evaluate the effectiveness of the care plan for the client and family and to adjust the plan of care to accommodate changing needs.

Standard IX. Research
The nurse participates in research designed to generate an organized body of gerontological nursing knowledge, disseminates research findings, and uses them in practice.

Exhibit 14-1 continued

Standard X. Ethics
  The nurse uses the code for nurses established by the American Nurses' Association as a guide for ethical decision making in practice.

Standard XI. Professional Development
  The nurse assumes responsibility for professional development and contributes to the professional growth of interdisciplinary team members. The nurse participates in peer review and other means of evaluation to assure the quality of nursing practice.

Source: Reprinted with permission from *Standards and Scope of Gerontological Nursing Practice*, published in 1988 by the American Nurses' Association, 2420 Pershing Road, Kansas City, Missouri 64108.

In Figure 14-1 the cyclic nature of the quality assurance program is exemplified. The quality assurance program begins with a clear definition of standards. Standards are expressed in a manner specific to the individual nursing home through policies, procedures, and job descriptions. For example, one regulatory standard requires that a care plan exist for every patient. A nursing home may apply that standard in its setting through a policy that states a registered nurse should complete an initial care plan for newly admitted patients within 48 hours of admission and develop a comprehensive care plan within 7 days. A related procedure could outline the specific form that should be used, components of the plan, and where the plan is to be placed on completion.

Staff require resources, assistance, and support to enable them to meet standards; this is another component of the quality assurance program. For example, to fulfill the standard of completing a patient care plan staff must be skilled in assessment and care plan development, have access to the form on which the plan is written, and possess sufficient time to invest in this activity.

MECHANISMS TO ASSURE AND EVALUATE QUALITY*

Audits

Audits are an important means of determining if actual practice matches the expectations defined through standards. Three types of audits can be performed.

1. *Structure audit.* This type of audit answers the question, "Were the correct elements present for care?" It includes a review of procedures, protocols, standards, and the number and level of staff.

---

*Adapted from *Nursing Administration of Long-Term Care* by C. Eliopoulos, pp. 178–194, Aspen Publishers, Inc., © 1983.

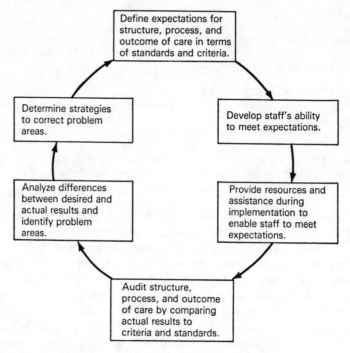

Figure 14-1 The Quality Assurance Program. *Source:* Reprinted from *Nursing Administration of Long-Term Care* by C. Eliopoulos, p. 178, Aspen Publishers, Inc., © 1983.

2. *Process audit.* This is an examination of what occurred during care. It explores how, when, where, and by whom care was given.
3. *Outcome audit.* Whereas the above two types of audit evaluate the care-giver's actions, this type investigates the patient to determine if the desired results for the patient were achieved through the care given.

Audits can be conducted by the nursing department, or they can be a multi-disciplinary effort. Some facilities have an audit committee that conducts regular audits throughout the facility; others have staff from one unit audit another unit. Each facility must determine the approach that best suits its needs. A combination of retrospective review (evaluating past efforts, for example, by reviewing the charts of all diabetics residing in the facility over the past year) and concurrent review (evaluating care as it is being delivered, for example, by examining the care currently being received by all hypertensive patients) is useful.

The most significant phase of the quality assurance program comes next—analysis of the audit results and determination of methods to improve deficits. Finding that 50% of all patients with grade I decubitus ulcers are not turned hourly and thus develop more severe decubiti are meaningless unless that information is used to change care activities and to improve patient outcomes. Specific recommendations for change should be developed from the audit. These could include a variety of measures, such as use of different equipment, more staff supervision, special training, or modifications in the procedures. The recommendations are then implemented, with subsequent audits determining their appropriateness. Thus, the cycle continues.

From the input of the quality assurance committee, nursing administrators should develop general standards for all patient care. An example of a general audit form is presented in Exhibit 14-2. Facilities may find it useful to develop similar audit forms tailored to their expectations for care. In addition to the general audit, facilities may want to develop audits for specific categories of patient care or nursing diagnoses, for example, the diabetic patient or the patient with altered thought processes.

Nurses may find it beneficial to establish with each audit measurable goals for improvement. For example, if an outcome audit in January determined that 50% of all charts were complete, goals can be established to raise the amount of complete charts to 80% in February and 100% in March. It is advisable to strive for 100% attainment of standards; but, in reality, perfection will not be consistently found in all aspects. Thus, realistic, acceptable standards must be developed; for example, at least 90% of all treatments must be correctly documented. Comparing audit results among units can aid in identifying specific problem areas that may need special intervention. Also, by posting all units' audit results, healthy competition can be fostered and efforts toward improvements can be reinforced (see Figure 14-2).

Utilization Review

In an effort to ensure that patients' care is necessary and appropriate, the federal government has mandated utilization review programs for nursing homes. A committee—usually composed of the medical director, at least one other physician or nurse practitioner, the nursing director, social worker, administrator, medical records coordinator, and other representatives—performs the utilization review function (physicians may not review their own cases). Some facilities contract with external groups, such as private firms or local hospitals, to conduct utilization reviews. Professional Standards Review Organizations (PSROs) may also be delegated responsibility for utilization review.

The utilization review committee inspects the documented care of patients at designated intervals to determine if

- A physician has certified need for admission based on real medical/nursing problems.

Exhibit 14-2 General Nursing Audit Form

	Yes	No	Comments
Admission note:			
1. Date and hour of admission			
2. Age or date of birth			
3. Sex			
4. Nationality			
5. Religion			
6. Mode of arrival			
7. Place from which admitted			
8. Admitting physician			
9. Statement of general physical status			
10. Statement of general mental status			
11. Family contact			
12. Current drug regimen			
13. Current treatment regimen			
14. Vital signs			
15. Patients' Rights and Responsibilities form completed and signed by patient and admitting nurse			
16. Personal property form completed and signed by patient and admitting nurse			
17. Consent to treatment form reviewed and signed by patient			
Initial nursing assessment:			
18. Height			
19. Weight			
20. Skin condition			
21. Hair condition			
22. Allergies			
23. Known diseases			
24. T.P.R.			
25. Sputum sample obtained			
26. BP (sitting, standing, lying)			
27. General mobility			
28. Range of joint motion			
29. Condition of oral cavity			
30. Presence of teeth or dentures			
31. Eating habits			
32. Diet			
33. Appetite			
34. Voiding pattern			
35. Urine sample obtained			
36. Bowel elimination pattern			
37. Stool sample obtained			
38. Hearing			
39. Vision			

Patient name: _____   Unit: _____

Exhibit 14-2 continued

	Yes	No	Comments
40. Presence of eyeglasses			
41. Speech pattern			
42. Olfaction			
43. Condition of genitalia			
44. Sexual history			
45. Level of consciousness			
46. Affect			
47. Memory			
48. Personality			
49. Emotional status			
50. Sleep pattern			
51. Goals			
52. Significant problems			
53. Completed and signed within one week of admission			
Care plan:			
54. Lists patient problems			
55. Reflects priority of problems			
56. Contains nursing approaches to problems			
57. States long-term goals			
58. States short-term goals			
59. Evaluates patient's response to care			
60. Completed and reviewed within designated time frame			
61. Dated and signed			
Documentation:			
62. Daily note during first seven days after admission			
63. Weekly note during weeks 2–4 after admission			
64. Monthly summary by each shift after first month of admission			
65. Shift documentation for significant change in status or special problem			
66. Vital signs every two weeks			
67. Weight every month			
68. Daily elimination			
69. Daily nutrition			
70. All treatments signed			
71. All medications signed			
72. Other ordered care documented			
Nursing care:			
73. Patient observed to be clean, well groomed, free of odors			
74. Food intake adequate			
75. Intake and output balances			
76. Measures for physical activity employed			
77. Measures for mental stimulation employed			
78. Attention to prevention of complications			
79. Family kept abreast of care plan and progress			

Exhibit 14-2 continued

	Yes	No	Comments
80. Rehabilitative measures employed			
81. Emotional support given			
82. Diversion provided			
83. Attention to increasing or maintaining self-care capacity			
84. Health teaching provided			
85. Specimens obtained as ordered			
86. Evidence that nonprofessional staff supervised in care activities			
87. Patient environment clean and safe			
88. Observed procedures performed according to standards			
Total			

Note: Each item on the audit can be given a separate weight according to its significance.

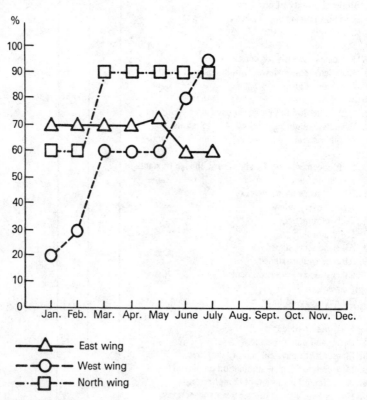

Figure 14-2 Audit Results

- Continued stay in the facility is based on real need and accompanied by recertification of need by the physician.
- The services that are provided are justified by patient need.
- Care is being provided in the most cost-effective manner at the appropriate level of care.

The coordinator or chairperson of the utilization review committee must ensure that the appropriate forms are completed for each patient and the committee minutes are recorded and maintained. Findings during the utilization review process may prove beneficial to nursing administrators, for example, by showing that documentation did not support the ordered care, or that 60% of all patients are more dependent and require a higher level of nursing care 2 months after their admission. Such findings may necessitate further investigation, perhaps through a nursing audit. A utilization review, in addition to facilitating reimbursement for services, can aid in ensuring that patients receive an appropriate level of care that neither ignores their needs nor fosters dependency.

Employee Health

Ensuring that all caregivers are in good physical and mental health is an important means of protecting patients and the facility. Ongoing efforts must be made to monitor employees' health. All new employees should have preemployment physical examinations to ensure that they do not have infections, diseases, or disabilities that will interfere with their safe performance in the facility. It is advisable not to allow employees even to attend orientation classes until they have been cleared for employment.

Once employed, personnel require periodic checks on their health. Each facility should develop their own employee health standards, which may include such practices as annual screening for tuberculosis and evaluation by the medical director after an extended illness or hospitalization. Policies should be established relating to employee health, for example, regarding care of injuries, emergency treatment, clearance for return to work after hospitalization or extended illness, and management of alcoholic employees. Special education programs on the health of employees can be presented. Some facilities may wish to offer periodic screening programs for employees; such programs not only aid in detecting illnesses that can impact employee performance but also demonstrate to employees that the facility is concerned about them as people.

Work in a nursing home is not easy. The physical and emotional wear and tear experienced by staff can be significant and may take its toll. Nurses should keep abreast of signs of stress among employees and intervene when necessary. It is useful to have a person designated as a resource with whom staff can discuss problems and from whom they can seek help. Frequently, the personnel director or social workers are effective in this role because they possess special counseling skills and are not in a superior-subordinate relationship with the employee. Counseling and referral to the appropriate agencies when necessary can benefit employees in solving their problems and aid the facility in maintaining effective, healthy employees.

Fire and Safety

The nature of the patient population in nursing homes necessitates that staff be particularly skilled in the prevention and management of fire and safety hazards. Fire and safety education is an essential component of all employees' orientation and needs continued emphasis in regular in-service education.

Fires can be a devastating experience in nursing homes. Sensory deficits, common among older persons, may prevent patients from smelling smoke and hearing alarms. Slower mobility and confused states can delay their safe evacuation from the fire area. A large number of patients may be wheelchair-bound or bed-bound and be totally dependent on staff to remove them from dangerous areas. These factors compound the usual hazards associated with fires and place a tremendous responsibility on staff to prevent and manage fires efficiently and effectively.

Each facility should develop a procedure for fire emergencies that is appropriate for it and should ensure that staff are skilled in following the procedure (see Exhibit 14-3). Fire drills should be conducted regularly for all shifts, with an evaluation by a designated person to detect weak areas in the staff's performance (see Exhibit 14-4). Follow-up training can emphasize detected areas for improvement. Special training for patients and visitors can be extremely beneficial in facilitating understanding of the procedure for fire emergencies.

Fire and safety prevention teams, consisting of representatives from all levels of all departments, can assist in identifying and correcting risks. These teams can survey the facility with a critical eye to discover actual or potential hazards in the environment or mode of practice; for example, housekeepers leaving their buckets and mops in the hall when they take breaks, unapproved appliances used in patient rooms, and confused patients sneaking cigarette smokes in the linen closet. Team members can be trained to serve as fire and safety resource persons in their departments. Such teams extend nurses' ability to monitor the facility and to develop a core of resources to serve as effective role models for their peers.

Infection Control

The fact that elderly nursing home residents are highly susceptible to infections requires that the facility have a strong infection control program. In fact, this is of

Exhibit 14-3 Fire Procedure

- Remember the basic ABCs when a fire is detected:
  A ssure patient safety.
  B eckon for help.
  C ontrol the fire.
- The individual discovering the fire should:
  1. Remove patients from the site of the fire.
  2. Pull the nearest fire alarm.
  3. Page the fire code: "Dr. Red for _____ unit."
  4. Use the proper extinguisher to begin fighting the fire.
- Nursing and nonnursing staff on the unit where the fire is located should:
  1. Check all rooms and areas to locate patients and ensure their safety.
  2. Close all windows and doors, marking rooms containing patients.
  3. Turn off all oxygen and electrical equipment.
  4. Clear hallways, elevators, and exits.
  5. Instruct visitors to leave the building through designated stairway exits.
  6. Assist in extinguishing the fire.
  7. Keep patients calm.
- Nursing staff on other units should:
  1. Remain on their units and listen for a potential page for a request for help at fire area.
  2. Instruct visitors to leave the building.
  3. Continue normal activities.
- If a request for assistance to the fire area is paged, all nursing assistants (except those performing a patient care activity) should report to the area. No less than two staff members should remain on the unit.
- Nonnursing staff throughout the facility should:
  1. Report to area of fire immediately.
  2. Assist in extinguishing fires.
  3. Obtain additional extinguishers from other areas if necessary.
  4. Follow instructions of the unit nursing staff.
- If instructed by the facility administrators or nursing administrators, all staff should be prepared to begin evacuation efforts.

such importance that the federal government requires infection control programs in long-term care facilities as a condition of participation in the Medicare and Medicaid programs.

There are three basic elements of an infection control program.

1. *Infection control committee*. Because infection control is a multidisciplinary responsibility, this committee should have representatives from nursing, medicine, administration, dietary, housekeeping, maintenance, and any other department that might assist in infection prevention and control. There must be a physician advisor to the committee. The function of this group is to establish policies and procedures for investigating, controlling, and preventing infections and to monitor the facility to ensure the policies and pro-

Exhibit 14-4 Form for Evaluating Fire Drill

	Yes	No	Comments/ Corrective Plan
Unit:_____ Date:_____ Time:_____ Staff participating:_____			
1. Patient(s) removed from immediate danger			
2. Fire alarm pulled			
3. Fire code paged correctly			
4. Staff mobilized to area			
5. Doors to patient rooms and other areas closed			
6. Rooms containing patients marked			
7. Oxygen turned off			
8. Electrical equipment turned off			
9. Hallways cleared of equipment			
10. Elevators and exits cleared			
11. Correct number of fire extinguishers present			
12. Assistance provided to patients and visitors			
13. All-clear code paged			
14. Personnel able to verbalize evacuation measures			

cedures are adhered to. Quarterly meetings must be held, with additional special meetings if necessary, and minutes must be kept.

2. *Regular surveillance*. The chairperson of the infection control committee or a designated infection control coordinator should monitor the routine activities of the institution. The monitoring should include making rounds; routine microbiological sampling of equipment, environment, and personnel; reviewing patients' microbiological laboratory results; and investigating suspected or actual infections. Because urinary tract, wound, and respiratory infections are the most common in the nursing home, mechanisms should be developed to detect these problems readily. Daily reports from each patient unit, like that presented in Exhibit 14-5, can help the coordinator keep abreast of potential and known infections. It is also useful to maintain individual infection reports (see Exhibit 14-6). Nosocomial infections (those developed within the facility) must be analyzed in an attempt to reveal possible causative factors that can be corrected. Daily attention to infection control is as necessary as the daily review of staffing.

Exhibit 14-5 Infection Control Report Form

	Total Cases	New Cases	Comments
Unit: _____ Census: _____ Date: _____			
Diarrhea			
Vomiting			
Temperature $\geq 100°$ F			
Decubiti			
Urinary tract infection			
Respiratory tract infection			
Productive cough			
Draining lesion			
Discolored urine			
Foul-smelling urine			
Foul-smelling vaginal discharge			
Purulent eye drainage			
Purulent ear drainage			
Furuncle			
Jaundice			
Indwelling catheter			
Intravenous therapy			
Inhalation therapy			
Sterile dressings			
Antibiotic therapy			

3. *Control measures.* Controlling the spread of infection is a full-time job that involves every person in the facility. Measures for controlling infections include preemployment screening of personnel for infections, regular monitoring of employee health, in-service education, preadmission screening of patients for infections, patient education, visitor control, good housekeeping, pest control, safe handling of food, proper disposal of waste, use of clean or sterile (as appropriate) supplies of materials, practice of good care techniques, and reinforcement of infection control principles.

Supply Usage

One of the often-overlooked ways to monitor a facility is to analyze its use of supplies. This is useful not only for cost control, but also for detecting possible problems. For example, if East Unit, with twice the number of incontinent patients

Exhibit 14-6 Individual Infection Report Form

Patient's name:
Unit:
Physician:

Infection:
Date of onset:
Signs displayed:
Possible causative factors:
Nosocomial:

Treatment:

Laboratory Findings

Date					
Test					
Results					

Outcome:
Recommendations for prevention:

as West Unit, has used half the number of underpads as West Unit, it could indicate one of several things to the nursing administrator: (1) East Unit may be utilizing an effective toileting program, (2) West Unit may be using underpads unnecessarily, (3) East Unit may not be changing patients frequently enough, or (4) West Unit may have a theft problem. Keeping supply usage records, preferably by unit, can aid in identifying a variety of such causative factors.

Feedback of information on supply usage and cost to the staff can be effective in influencing change. If reminded that the spill they clean with an underpad costs $0.15 more than the spill they mop, that the special treatment tray they mistakenly open costs $12 to prepare, and that the stethoscope they carelessly misplace costs $25 to replace, the staff may become more aware of the fiscal impact of their actions.

Staff suggestions for supply control should be elicited and recorded. Some facilities have saved significant amounts of money from employee suggestions. All employees must understand that cost containment is a significant responsibility to their patients, employer, and fellow taxpayers. If less of the limited health care dollar is wasted, more can be made available for direct service benefit.

Complaints

An unpleasant aspect of nursing is receiving patient and family complaints. As though hearing criticism of the department is not bad enough, the critical remarks may be presented in a less than tactful manner by very irate persons. It is not uncommon for the nurse to become defensive toward the complaining party, angry toward staff, frustrated with the total situation, or exhibit a combination of all these reactions. Complaints are never easy to hear, but they are an anticipated reality in a setting such as a nursing home. In fact, they should be neither avoided nor discouraged. Complaints can provide significant insights into problems that may otherwise be missed through the usual monitoring measures.

Nurses should receive complaints openly and objectively, without reacting to the anger or accusations of the complaining party. It may be unnerving to have a family member march into the office, point a finger, and shout, "What kind of nursing director are you to have staff who steal old people's belongings?" but if, in fact, there is a theft problem among staff members, the nursing director would want to learn of it, regardless of the manner in which it was presented. If possible, the complaint should be referred to the unit nurse manager for resolution, with the option of returning it to the nursing director if no satisfactory solution is reached. Notes should be kept on each complaint, indicating the unit and staff involved, the nature of the complaint, the action taken, and the resolution. When specific staff members are accused of wrongdoings, it may be useful to send a note to the staff outlining the complaint and requesting their response. This serves the purposes of presenting the complaint directly to the staff, offering members an opportunity to react, and having a written record of the charge and explanation to file in the employee's record. Staff should understand that the nursing administrator will investigate each complaint fairly and not immediately judge them to be guilty of the offense. On the other hand, staff must understand that they will be held accountable for their improper actions.

Periodically, the nursing administrator may review all complaints received and attempt to categorize them by type of complaint and unit. This can reveal specific problem areas for which intervention is required.

Incident and Accident Reports

Incident and accident reports are also an important source of data and are discussed fully in Chapter 15.

CONCLUSION

Nurses are involved in a wide range of complex clinical and managerial activities in the nursing home setting. Tasks often must be delegated to persons with limited education and experience, increasing the risks associated in caring for the highly vulnerable nursing home population. The nature of nursing home practice demands that nurses develop meaningful and realistic standards, assist staff in achieving desired standards, monitor and evaluate nursing practice, and continuously advocate for improved levels of nursing service.

BIBLIOGRAPHY

Brower, H.H. 1988. Determinants of quality nursing care. *J Gerontol Nurs* 14:7, 41.

Dailey-Murray, M. 1988. *The new long term care survey process: A facility guide*. Owings Mills, Md.: National Health Publishers.

Herbelin, K. 1988. Components of a quality assessment and assurance program. *Contemp Longterm Care* 11:70–72.

National Health Publishing Editorial Staff. 1980. *Director of nursing manual. Federal regulations and guidelines* (annual updates). Owings Mills, Md.: National Health Publishing.

Patterson, C.H., D. Kranz, and B. Brandt. 1986. *A guide to JCAH nursing service standards*. Chicago: Joint Commission on Accreditation of Hospitals.

Chapter 15

Incidents and Accidents

Incidents and accidents are more than inconveniences that create additional paper work. They are serious situations for patients, nurses, and the facility. Incidents and accidents can result in injury that can cost patients their function, comfort, and lives; nurses their licenses; and facilities millions of dollars. It is particularly important for nursing home nurses to understand the causes and impact of incidents and accidents and learn ways to prevent them from occurring.

INCIDENT OR ACCIDENT?

Nurses are responsible for preventing, identifying, managing, and reporting incidents and accidents; thus it is basic that the difference between these two events be understood. Incident and accident should not be used interchangeably. An *incident* is something that happens that is not ordinary or usual, such as a patient falling from bed, a nurse sticking a finger with a needle, a medication being administered incorrectly, an employee slipping on the floor, or a patient wandering off the premises. An event does not have to result in an injury or residual problem to be an incident; documenting the incident only implies that something unusual occurred.

An *accident* is an unintentional injury. The ecchymosis resulting from a fall, the break in the skin from a needle stick, the hypoglycemic reaction caused from an incorrect insulin injection, the back pain and stiffness resulting from a slip on the floor, and the jewelry stolen from the patient when she wandered off the premises are examples of the accidents caused by incidents.

Incidents and accidents can be experienced by patients, staff, and visitors to the facility. All unusual events and unintentional injuries occurring in the facility, or to patients while in or away from the facility, should be documented.

197

DOCUMENTING INCIDENTS AND ACCIDENTS

Facilities usually have their own accepted forms for recording incidents and accidents. Although the forms seem relatively simple, carelessness and poor judgment by nurses in completing the incident and accident forms can have serious implications.

Incident and accident forms should be completed immediately after the event. Waiting until later to record the event can cause details to be forgotten and witnesses or evidence to be unavailable. Also there is the risk that the nurse may need to leave the facility before the documentation is completed.

Legibility of the form is important, as is attention to detail—such as the patient's full name, whether the event took place at 2:15 A.M. or P.M., and associated factors (e.g., urine on floor, bedrails up, call light at bedside, Nursing Assistants Jones and Green assisting with lift). It is important to remember that years after the event took place incident and accident forms can be used to prove details related to an injury.

Only observed facts should be recorded without drawing conclusions. If a patient is found on the floor next to his bed in the middle of the night, there is a good possibility that he fell from bed; but, unless the fall is witnessed, the only accurate statement that the nurse can make is:

"At 3:15 A.M., while making rounds, I found the patient sitting on the floor next to the bed. Patient stated that he tried to crawl over bedrails alone."

Similarly, if the patient walks to the nursing station and reports she just fell from bed, the nurse should record:

"At 1:00 A.M. patient walked to nursing station and reported she fell from bed approximately 30 minutes ago."

rather than:

"Patient fell out of bed at 12:30 A.M."

The documentation also should reflect who observed and reported the incident. If it was the nursing assistant who found the patient on the floor, the report should reflect that fact.

Likewise, diagnoses should not be concluded from injuries. For instance, when documenting a back injury that an employee claimed to experience while lifting a patient, the nurse should not make statements such as "employee strained back while lifting," or "employee appears to have ruptured her disk again." Instead, state only what is known or reported:

"Employee states that while lifting patient she felt a sharp pain in right side of the lower part of back. Employee is walking bent to right side and complaining of back pain."

The immediate actions taken and related times should be documented carefully to avoid any question at a later date. For example:

"Patient immobilized immediately and sent to emergency department for x-ray films at 2:20 P.M."
"Employee placed in wheelchair and wheeled to employee health clinic for examination."

Refused care should be indicated in the documentation:

"Employee did not want to use wheelchair or to be examined by facility's physician. Instead, she walked from unit alone at 1:45 P.M., stating she was going directly to personal physician."

Statements on the form regarding corrective actions to prevent the incident from recurring should be realistic and achievable. To write as a corrective action for falls for a patient with Alzheimer's disease "Reinforce to patient the importance of ringing call light for help with toileting" ignores the actual cognitive limitations of the patient. Also, to recommend that "patient's status be checked every 15 minutes during the night shift" may be unrealistic within the staffing constraints of most facilities.

Incident and accident forms provide information about quality of care and the facility's operations that assist the facility in its risk management efforts. In essence, they are tools to assist with internal investigations of facility problems, and, for this reason, only a limited audience within the facility should have access to completed forms. The forms should not be kept in the patient's record. The only documentation of the incident or accident in the patient's record should be facts pertaining to what the patient experienced, patient status, and related care.

Most facilities require that copies of incident and accident forms be forwarded to the administrator (or designated risk manager or quality assurance manager), director of nursing, and the facility's malpractice insurance carrier or legal counsel (or both). In some facilities the medical director and quality assurance/risk management committee also receive copies. Nurses should check their individual facility's policy related to completion, distribution, access, and use of incident and accident reports.

IDENTIFYING PROBLEMS AND TRENDS

It is easy for multiple incidents and accidents to occur involving one specific person or factor. For instance, in a given month 12 of 15 patient falls could have occurred from a wheelchair, 10 of 11 employee injuries may have been pulled back muscles related to lifting, and 13 of 20 medication errors may have been caused by one nurse. Unless all incident and accident data are analyzed and organized, specific problem areas may go undetected. Increases in the number of specific incidents and accidents also give clues to problems. For example, perhaps the number of incidents related to patients striking employees has increased steadily, possibly reflecting a change in the patient population or ineffective behavioral management techniques by staff.

Identifying trends and specific problem areas can be a relatively simple process. The first step is to develop a tool that will enable data to be centralized, such as that shown in Exhibit 15-1. On a monthly basis, the number of incidents and accidents for each category can be transferred to the form from individual incident and accident records. This tool can be used to compile incident and accident data for the

Exhibit 15-1 Incident/Accident Record

Event:	Jan.	Feb.	Mar.	Apr.	May	June	July	Aug.	Sept.	Oct.	Nov.	Dec.
Fall on misplaced object												
Fall on stairway												
Fall on wet floor												
Fall outdoors												
Struck by patient												
Struck by equipment												
Medication: Omitted												
Wrong dose												
Wrong drug												
Wrong patient												
Burn												
Cut												
Needle stick												
Back injury												
Other (state)												

entire facility or for individual nursing units. Incident and accident data presented to this format can enable the facility to detect trends; further evaluation of specific problem areas can then be planned.

As one example, the facility may experience a steady increase in the number of wheelchair-related falls. Additional information is necessary to determine if this is related to

- An increase in the number of wheelchair users (The actual number of injuries per wheelchair user could actually be lower, although the total number of incidents is higher if more patients are using wheelchairs.)
- Improper sizing or use of wheelchairs
- Poor staff supervision of wheelchair-bound patients
- Other factors

Interventions addressing the specific problem can then be arranged, such as physical therapy assessment before wheelchair use, in-service education, staff counseling, or improved wheelchair maintenance. Problem-specific interventions have a good likelihood of correcting the underlying cause and preventing future incidents and accidents. Audits and other forms of follow up at a later date can determine if corrective actions were successful in bringing about a reduction in incidents and accidents.

FALLS

Among the most frequently experienced incidents and accidents in the nursing home are falls. There are many factors that cause falls to be a risk (Exhibit 15-2).

Exhibit 15-2 Factors Contributing to Falls

Decreased vision
Impaired mobility
Dizziness
Orthostatic hypotension
Insomnia
Incontinence
Altered mental status
Depression
Medications (e.g., psychotropics, sedatives, antihypertensives, analgesics, antidepressants, diuretics)
Environmental hazards
History of previous falls

Falls are serious to the elderly because of the higher risk of disability and death from this injury in advanced age. Studies have shown that

- An estimated 30% of the elderly experience a fall each year, with the highest rate among the ill elderly (Myers et al. 1987).
- One in five fatal falls occurs in the nursing home setting (Baker, Karpf, and O'Neill 1984).
- Most falls occur near the patient's bed or while the patient is traveling to the bathroom; one in five falls involves a wheelchair—pulling wheelchair over on oneself, getting out of restraints, missing seat (Myers et al. 1987).
- Falls play a major role in hip fractures being the most frequently occurring serious injury of the elderly and the most common cause of surgery in the population over age 75 years. In one study of nursing homes, results showed 30% of the patients who experienced a hip fracture died within 5 months (Baker and Harvey 1985).

Falls can cause both physical injuries and psychologic trauma, which can influence patients' functional abilities. Patients who escape injury from a fall often fear falling again and may be reluctant to ambulate. Unnecessary immobility, dependency, and wheelchair use may result.

Nurses can aid in decreasing the risk of falls in nursing homes (Exhibit 15-3). Management of risks associated with falls can enable patients to achieve maximum independent function safely.

Exhibit 15-3 Hints to Reduce Risk of Falls

Ensure handrails and grab bars are present in hallways, stairways, and bathrooms; encourage patients' use of these safety aids.

Use night lights.

Have stairways lighted at all times.

Use caution signs and contrasting colors to warn of changes in levels, stairs.

Do not leave clutter on floor.

Remove carts and equipment from patients' rooms and walking areas when not in use.

Use nonskid strips or surface finishes in tub and shower areas.

Clean spills promptly; place "caution floor wet" sign over wet area.

Avoid having floors mopped and waxed during times of peak activity.

Filter sunlight and use nonglare lighting.

Ensure environmental problems are reported and corrected promptly.

Have alarms or bells installed on exit doors and stairways of units on which confused patients are housed.

Identify high risk patients for falls (see Exhibit 15-2, *supra*); include goals and actions to prevent falls in care plans.

Exhibit 15-4 Principles of Good Body Mechanics

Push or pull instead of lifting (whenever possible).
Keep the body in proper alignment; avoid twisting body during lifting, pulling, pushing.
When lifting:
- Use as many muscles as possible, particularly arm and leg muscles to avoid back strain.
- Bend knees and keep back straight.
- Use both hands.
- Hold load as close to body as possible.
- Lift by pushing up and straightening legs.

EMPLOYEE BACK INJURIES

The care of nursing home patients often is physically demanding of staff. Because of the frail, dependent status of many patients caregivers do considerable pulling, turning, and lifting. Not surprisingly, the physical challenges of care giving can tax staff's muscles and bones, particularly those of the back, resulting in back injuries being common incidents and accidents of employees.

The high incident of back injuries supports the need for staff education for good body mechanics. The principles of good body mechanics should be taught and reinforced (Exhibit 15-4). Further, individual employees who experience repeated back injuries should be counseled and educated when observed to use poor body mechanics. Disciplinary actions may be considered for employees who fail to demonstrate good body mechanics as they are jeopardizing the safety of themselves and patients.

REFERENCES

Baker, S.P., and A.H. Harvey. 1985. Fall injuries in the elderly. *Clin Geriatr Med* 1:501–8.

Baker, S.P., R.S. Karpf, and B. O'Neill. 1984. *The injury fact book*. Lexington, Mass.: Lexington Books.

Myers, A.H., S.P. Baker, E.G. Robinson, H. Abbey, E. Timms, and S. Levenson. 1987. Injurious falls among institutionalized elderly. Findings of the Johns Hopkins Falls Study, Baltimore, Md.

BIBLIOGRAPHY

Baker, S.P., and A.H. Harvey. 1985. Fall injuries in the elderly. *Clin Geriatr Med* 1:501–8.

Baker, S.P., R.S. Karpf, and B. O'Neill. 1984. *The injury fact book*. Lexington, Mass.: Lexington Books.

Mossey, J.M. 1985. Social and psychological factors related to falls among the elderly. *Clin Geriatr Med* 1:541–52.

Tideiksaar, R. 1988. Environmental fall prevention in nursing homes. *Contemp Longterm Care's D.O.N.* 11:25–27.

Chapter 16

Time Management

No nurse has to be told that time is a precious and fleeting commodity. Twelve-hour days, perpetual motion, and paper work taken home do not seem to dent the workload. Consider the following situations.

Mr. Simon, the unit clerk, tries to keep pace with orders so that he won't run late; but more often than not, a last minute request from the evening supervisor causes him to leave work a half hour late.

Answering call lights, supervising subordinates, and making rounds with the physicians leaves little time for the charge nurse, Mrs. Clark, to document in patients' records. She has resorted to spending 1 hour after the shift's end to catch up.

The day supervisor, Mrs. Bell, is well liked by personnel in her department because she always pitches in and helps them. But at the end of the day when her subordinates leave, she remains to complete her own tasks.

Everyone admires the group process skills of Mr. Harvey, the gero-psychiatric nurse specialist. As a result he is invited to serve on most committees. He spends so much time and energy in meetings that he has little to invest in monitoring his patients. To his surprise, his caseload had the greatest number of documentation deficiencies during the last audit.

The nursing director, Mrs. Glass, has an open-door policy that staff and residents' families readily use. In fact, staff have learned that it is easier to drop in and get her thoughts than to wait for her to weed through the mounds of paper work on her desk to answer their correspondence.

Most likely, nurses can find at least one of these examples in their long-term care facility; perhaps they are the example. In any event, situations in which nurses lose control of their time are not unusual. Inefficient time utilization can result in serious consequences, including low productivity, health problems, dissatisfaction with work, and poor personal relationships. Because the demands on nurses' time increase continuously and the number of hours in the day are finite, nurses must learn to use effective time management strategies.

IDENTIFYING TIME WASTERS

The first step toward improving time utilization is to assess current time wasters. A checklist of time wasters that can help in self-evaluation is shown in Exhibit 16-1. From this list major problem areas can be identified, such as those discussed in the following pages.

Exhibit 16-1 Checklist of Time Wasters

_____ Not having goals and plans
_____ Not prioritizing activities
_____ Dealing with all issues as they occur
_____ Cluttered desk
_____ Reading/handling same mail several times
_____ Lack of private work area
_____ Reluctance to delegate
_____ Poor delegation techniques
_____ Answering all incoming calls (unscreened)
_____ Open-door policy at all times
_____ Trying to do several tasks simultaneously
_____ Unnecessary meetings
_____ No agenda for meetings
_____ Discussion of nonagenda items during meetings
_____ Gripe sessions
_____ Being unassertive
_____ Personal calls
_____ Discussion of personal problems
_____ Long breaks or lunches
_____ Insufficient experience or skills to do job
_____ Fatigue
_____ Personality conflicts with co-workers
_____ Unnecessary perfectionism
_____ Wanting to be involved in all activities
_____ Equating long hours with high performance

Poor Organization

Long hours and constantly being busy do not necessarily relate to a higher level of performance. Two nurses in the same situation may appear to be equally productive. However, a closer look reveals Nurse A always seems relaxed and leaves work after a normal shift and Nurse B, with the same workload, appears hassled and hurried and puts in 10- to 12-hour days. The difference between these nurses could be in their degree of organization.

Organization begins with planning—a process often shortchanged by nurses who believe they are too busy *doing* to plan what they need to do. Lack of planning activities can have the same result as driving cross-country without a road map: one's destination may eventually be reached but perhaps not along the quickest or best route possible.

Planning begins by looking at the broad picture first. For example, what are the major activities that need to be completed over the next year: update a policy manual? relocate to a new wing of the facility? develop a new service? write performance-based job descriptions? The annual assessment of needs and development of plans gives a sense of direction that can help goals be reached. Nurses should be familiar with the plans for the entire facility to be in a better position to assess the challenges they will face in the coming year. If these plans are not formally shared through management meetings or reports, nurses should ask the administrative staff for their thoughts. Subordinate staff also should be asked about their needs and goals for the next year. With this information goals and plans can be outlined.

The next step is to plot the plans on a calendar (Exhibit 16-2). This can be helpful in judging if the plans can be accomplished realistically and in identifying conflicts between plans and other factors. As an example, the in-service education director may want to start a nursing aide II training program to upgrade entry level staff. She discovers her plans allow her to implement the program from June to September. However, when she looks at the broader calendar she discovers that during those same months annual evaluations are due, a major health department survey is expected, and vacations peak. Thus that would not be the best time to implement the training program.

From the annual calendar, nurses can outline their monthly and weekly goals and plans. Weekly plans can be outlined on an index card or calendar; for example:

Week of October 1

- Review sections B and C of procedure manual.
- Meet with evening shift employees.
- Interview job applicants.
- Review attendance records of day shift staff.

Exhibit 16-2 Plotting Annual Activities

	Jan.	Feb.	Mar.	Apr.	May	June	July	Aug.	Sept.	Oct.	Nov.	Dec.
Inventory equipment												
Review/update policy manual												
Conduct "Fire" in-service												
Conduct "Infection" in-service												
Review attendance files												
Plan vacation schedules												
Develop orientee manual												
Plan budget												
Develop budget												
Present budget to director												
Prepare staff evaluations												
Give staff evaluations												
Write proposal for new project												
Supervise visiting students												
Plan employee recognition month												
Conduct employee recognition events												
Learn use of new computer												
Put files on computer												
Teach staff to use computer												

- Meet with medical director to discuss department's role in new outreach service.
- Begin preliminary planning for next year's budget.

Of course, many unplanned activities will confront nurses, so plans should not absorb all or even most of one's time.

Plans should be prioritized. This can be done by keying each activity (e.g., A, urgent; B, moderately important; C, important, but not urgent). With this exercise, nurses can differentiate among activities and address urgent ones first and those that are important but not necessarily urgent at a later time. Important activities are those with a high value, such as meeting with employees on a regular basis or keeping current on professional journals. Urgent activities are those that must be done soon, such as correcting a malfunctioning fire alarm system or removing an intoxicated employee from the facility. Nurses may run themselves ragged responding to every problem as though it was urgent rather than weighing the need for immediate action. On a daily basis nurses can evaluate the amount of time they spend on low- versus high-priority activities and modify it as necessary.

In addition to scheduling, the organization of material used in daily activities can influence time utilization. Factors such as inaccessible forms, non-alphabetized files, a cluttered desk, or the lack of a desk or "thinking area" can interfere with work flow. An effort should be made to keep the desk top clear. Papers should be filed as soon as possible or quickly disposed of (either through action or in the trash can). A three-tiered tray can be used to store incoming and outgoing mail and active files. A supply of forms and files that are used frequently should be kept in the desk drawer.

Nurses should have a desk or work area to call their own. If permanent space is unavailable, arrangements should be made for a locked file cabinet in an office area that can be used when necessary. A quiet area with desk space is an important tool, especially for the nurse manager.

Inappropriate Delegation

Getting the job done through others is an important management task. Part of what nurse managers are expected to do is to identify tasks that must be completed, assign qualified staff to complete the tasks, and ensure the tasks are completed in a timely, correct manner. But nurses sometimes experience difficulties delegating assignments because of a variety of reasons.

- *Feeling delegation is an imposition.* Some nurses feel guilty giving assignments to staff: "Gee, I hate to make you do this, but we have 10 extra trays to prepare today." "Would you mind very much cleaning wheelchairs today because it is Thursday and we usually clean wheelchairs on Thursdays?'' ''I'm sorry to make you get up again, but East Wing needs this chart delivered.'' No apology is necessary to assign employees reasonable tasks that they are hired to do. This does not imply that nurses should hand out orders in a dictatorial fashion but, rather, that assignments should be delegated courteously and directly: ''There will be five admissions today.'' ''This is bedside table cleaning day.'' ''East Wing needs these supplies delivered.''

- *Fearing poor completion of the job.* There may be concern that an employee will not complete the job correctly or on time. This can be based on a real assessment of staff's deficits or an invalid perception. Staff who lack the competencies to fulfill the responsibilities in their job descriptions should be helped to gain the skill they need (e.g., through in-service training, working with the manager to see how the job is done). Discipline should be considered for unimproved performance, or for poor performance in employees who are competent. ''Dead wood'' on the team creates an added burden for other employees and the manager.

- *Fearing exceptional performance.* At the other extreme, some nurses are afraid that competent employees could ''show them up'' and threaten their positions. This may relate to the nurse's own insecurity. Actually, it is the effective, confident nurse who develops competency in subordinates.

- *Preferring the task to management responsibilities.* Functions that could be delegated to less-qualified staff may instead be performed by nurses because tasks are more familiar or less stressful than management functions. For example, the nursing director may dislike the task of reviewing her department's personnel files or developing the budget for a new program, so she may spend her time intervening with family complaints that the unit nurse manager should handle. The charge nurse may choose to answer all incoming calls himself rather than allow the unit clerk to screen calls. The director of nursing may use the excuse of having to feed a patient to be relieved of a department head meeting.

- *Delegating improperly or over delegating.* Delegation problems can result when functions are not delegated carefully. Tasks may be delegated to staff who lack the knowledge, skills, time, or resources to get the job done. Incorrect or insufficient information may be provided to the employee, or there may be no monitoring of how the employee is progressing with the task.

Because delegation is essential to effective management and nurses remain accountable for delegated functions it is important to minimize the associated risks. This requires careful thought and action. The competencies of staff must be known before tasks are delegated to them. (This reinforces the importance of performance appraisal.) When nurses accept incompetent subordinates that someone else has hired and evaluated they also are accepting responsibility for the consequences of those subordinates. As mentioned, if performance deficiencies exist they should be corrected. The appropriate employee should be matched to the task.

Specific directions should accompany delegation, including the exact task to be completed, expected outcome, and time frame for completion. Nurses should be clear as to how much they wish to be involved in the task; instructions can range from

- here is the problem; come back and discuss your approach with me before taking action, to
- here is the problem; take action and keep me informed of your progress, to
- here is the problem; solve it, and there is no need to get back to me unless you have any difficulty.

The type of task and the specific employee's competencies determine the level of involvement of the manager.

Employees need the resources to complete the task. A charge nurse who is told to teach a class to visiting students needs the time to prepare and conduct the class. A payroll clerk assisting with the implementation of a computerized time clock needs support and training from the computer specialist. A food service supervisor who is asked to place a special holiday treat on the food trays needs extra funds to purchase the treat. The support and availability of the manager also are important resources to employees as they complete delegated tasks. Progress of the delegated task should be followed, and the outcome evaluated. It is beneficial for employees to receive feedback to reinforce positive behaviors and improve negative performance. Correctly delegating tasks can help nurses to use time more effectively and employees to develop new skills.

Interruptions

By keeping a one-day diary of activities (Exhibit 16-3) and analyzing planned versus unplanned activities, nurses may learn surprising facts about the number of interruptions in their average day. Short of absolute isolation, there is little that can be done to eliminate all interruptions. However, interruptions can be reduced by controlling the unnecessary or preventable ones so that only truly urgent and important issues cause interruptions.

Some interruptions can be eliminated by such measures as

- Having calls screened
- Limiting "open door" times

Exhibit 16-3 Activity Log

Time	Activity	Issue	Person(s) Involved	Scheduled?	Priority

- Changing office layout (e.g., not facing door)
- Informing the interrupter, "This is not a good time, and to do justice to the discussion let's schedule a time to meet."
- Scheduling regular meetings with frequent interrupters (e.g., if the purchasing agent calls or drops in several times during the week to discuss purchasing requests establish one regular meeting each week at a mutually convenient time)
- Confronting the interrupter with the problem

Time saved on dealing with (and recovering from) interruptions can be put to more productive use.

Meetings

Meetings are often viewed as major time wasters, and they certainly are if conducted inefficiently or unnecessarily. There are valid reasons to have meetings.

- To share information in a timely, consistent manner
- To obtain immediate feedback
- To complete a task
- To fulfill regulatory requirements

There also are bad reasons to have meetings.

- Tradition (e.g., supervisors have always met on the third Tuesday of the month)
- Unstructured griping
- Need of meeting chairperson to feel important
- Delegation to a group a task that could be completed by one or two people

Effective meetings begin with adequate planning. Composition of the group should be clearly thought through, and only those persons who have a contribution or need to participate should be in attendance. An agenda should be developed and distributed to members before the meeting. During the meeting deviations from the agenda should be controlled. For example, if the topic of the meeting is to review the last quarter's employee incidents and accidents, members should not be allowed to digress into a discussion of the problems with the new time clock. The meeting's chairperson could control this by saying, "It sounds as though that is a problem for several of you. Because it doesn't happen to be on our agenda today, I'll forward it to the Finance Director for followup." Putting times alongside agenda items also will serve to control discussion. If there are insufficient items for an agenda, there is probably little need for the meeting. To meet just because it is the usual day of the month to meet when there is nothing on the agenda can be a costly waste of time.

Sometimes separate meetings of groups can be combined into one major one as a time-saving measure. For instance, rather than meeting individually, the Utilization Review, Procedure, Medical Records, Fire and Safety, Infection Control, and Patient Care committees can be combined under the umbrella of Quality Assurance Committee and be placed on the agenda for one afternoon's meeting. Specific times can be allocated for each of the subcommittees. Because many of the same persons serve on all of these committees time commitments for key staff can be decreased considerably.

Meetings that develop into gripe sessions are not only a poor use of time but also can have many destructive effects. Complaining about an issue without resolution can deepen frustration, anger, and resentment. Complaints that were insignificant can become major crises when the fire is fueled through a gripe session. This is not to imply that problems should not be discussed but, rather, that staff need to be guided through the steps of problem solving. Staff can be assisted in identifying causes of and methods to manage their problems. No purpose is served by dwelling on problems that cannot be solved; time is better spent addressing resolvable issues.

Personal Problems

Individual personality traits and behaviors can be causes of time wasted at work. Some persons need to be needed or want to make themselves indispensable, so they foster staff's dependency on them. The lack of assertiveness prohibits some persons from setting limits and delegating responsibilities. Allowing personal calls or excessive discussion of personal problems during working hours can rob valuable time, as can extending breaks and lunch times. Of course, attempting to fill a job for which one is not qualified can result in tasks taking longer to complete than would be necessary for a more-qualified person. Health problems, insufficient rest, poor nutrition, inadequate activity, anxiety, depression, and drug or alcohol abuse are among the additional factors that can affect productivity. Nurses need to be honest in evaluating personal problems that impact on time utilization and identify specific measures to improve them.

CONCLUSION

The object of all time management efforts is to control time, rather than be controlled by it. Effective time management can positively impact job productivity, satisfaction, and morale. Perhaps more importantly, improving time utilization at work can lead to having more time and energy available for one's personal life.

BIBLIOGRAPHY

Rowan, R. 1986. *The intuitive manager*. Boston: Little, Brown & Co.

Scalzi, C.C. 1988. Role stress and coping strategies of nurse executives. *J Nurs Adm* 18:34–38.

Vestal, K.W. 1987. *Management concepts for the new nurse*. Philadelphia: J.B. Lippincott Co.

Chapter 17

Performance Appraisal

Performance appraisal brings to mind several images, ranging from some complex, sophisticated activity that is irrelevant to daily work to the annual evaluation that is scanned over, filed, and forgotten. In reality, performance appraisal is an ongoing process, affecting the facility's quality of services, legal protection, and reputation. Whether conscious of it or not, nurses will invest considerable time and effort in monitoring, evaluating, and improving employees' performance.

STEPS IN EVALUATING PERFORMANCE

There are many steps in the performance appraisal process (Figure 17-1), and the one that lays the foundation is that of developing good job descriptions. Job descriptions clearly outline the responsibilities and expectations of the employee. Every type of position should have its own job description that states the title of the position, qualifications, general description, and specific responsibilities.

The responsibilities are perhaps the most important component of the job description; they should be:

- *Clear and specific.* Comments such as "will deliver basic patient care" or "perform routine supervisory duties" are so broad as to risk being misinterpreted by staff. Does basic patient care mean baths and toileting or personal care, vital signs, and treatments? Do supervisory functions include making assignments and trouble-shooting or also disciplining, completing evaluations, and attending interdisciplinary team conferences? The expectations of employees in previous jobs in other facilities may differ from what is expected of those employees in your facility. To prevent misunderstanding

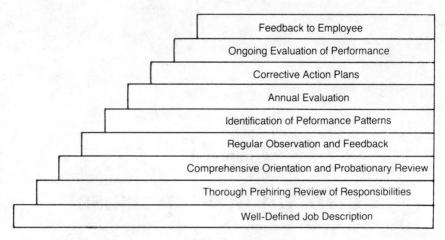

Figure 17-1 Steps in Performance Appraisal Process

and performance problems responsibilities should be described as specifically as possible (e.g., give or assist with bed, tub, and whirlpool baths; feed patients with utensils or syringe; discipline staff as necessary; make staff assignments; refer clinical problems to assistant director of nursing).

- *Realistic.* Stating that the employee will be responsible for ''maximizing staff productivity'' or ''meet all patient and family needs'' is so ambitious and global as to have little meaning. The object is not to have impressive sounding responsibilities but, rather, ones that are attainable.

- *Legally sound.* Responsibilities should be consistent with the legally accepted functions of the employee and the facility. For example, a nursing home is not licensed to serve as a community emergency department, so it is unsound to state in a nurse's job description that the nurse will initiate intravenous solutions and other emergency measures for any person coming to the facility for assistance. Likewise, to authorize a nursing assistant to give medications in an emergency situation is inconsistent with who is allowed legally to administer drugs.

A sample job description is shown in Exhibit 17-1.

Careful prehiring screening is the next step of the performance appraisal. The job description should be reviewed in the prehiring interview with applicants for the position. Again, it is important to reinforce that the responsibilities of employees in similar positions can vary from facility to facility. The only way to ensure the prospective employee understands the expectations in your facility is to review the job description. Applicants can be asked about their experiences and competencies with the various responsibilities listed to evaluate their appropriateness for the job.

The responsibilities on the job description continue to play an important role as employees are oriented to their jobs, the third step of the performance appraisal. This step involves closely observing and evaluating employees' competencies in fulfilling responsibilities. When areas of weakness are detected, plans should be made to assist employees in improving those skills (e.g., referring them to the in-service instructor, pairing them with experienced employees, giving them literature to read). A useful feedback mechanism is to list the responsibilities stated in the job description on an orientation form with evaluation columns (Exhibit 17-2) and then to review the evaluation of each responsibility with the orientee. Having both the manager and the orientee sign the evaluation form acknowledges this review and could aid at a later time if the employee denies being aware of a responsibility or the manager expects competency in an area that was not part of the original job for which the employee was hired.

Perhaps the most extensive step in performance appraisal (the fourth step) is the day-to-day evaluation of employees that enables managers to compile fair, meaningful annual evaluations. Regular, informal evaluation of performance is important to ensure work is being completed in a desirable fashion and to correct problems in an early stage. It is a risk to the facility and an injustice to the employee to allow a problem to persist or not be addressed until the annual evaluation. Sufficient information should be collected to give a comprehensive view of performance. The relationship of external factors on the employee's performance also must be considered. For instance, a nursing assistant may not complete his assignment in a timely fashion because the physical therapist was teaching the patient exercises for 45 minutes. Added demands, low staffing, and insufficient or a low quality of supplies can negatively impact employee performance. In addition to learning about employees' performance, regular observation and evaluation demonstrates management's interest in employees.

Positive and negative feedback of employee performance can be summarized as anecdotal notes (Exhibit 17-3). Notes can be kept on index cards or in a notebook. Recording observations of employees' performance on a regular basis supplies specific examples to support claims made on the annual evaluation and helps managers avoid the trap of basing the evaluation on a major or recent incident, without taking the whole picture into account.

Notes can be reviewed periodically to detect performance patterns (the fifth step in performance appraisal). For example, in a 2-month period an employee may have on five different occasions left a dirty linen hamper unemptied at the end of the shift; in the past month three letters may have been received praising the new charge nurse; and since the unit clerk was hired 3 months ago, 15 visitors may have called or sent comments to the administrator commenting on how easy it has become to communicate with the nursing staff. Of course, managers need not wait until the annual evaluation to react to the positive or negative patterns they detect. Giving positive feedback can reinforce the good behaviors of employees, whereas reviewing poor patterns may help to salvage a potentially good employee.

Exhibit 17-1 Sample Job Description

Head Nurse

Qualifications:

- Registered nurse licensed in this state
- Five years' nursing experience (minimum)
- One year's experience in a nursing home (minimum)
- Managerial experience preferred

Position description:
The head nurse is responsible for the 24-hour operations of the unit, including assignments, staffing, monitoring staff performance, communicating changes in patients' status to physicians, ordering supplies, and ensuring the safety of the environment. All unit nurses, nursing assistants, and ward clerks are responsible to the head nurse; the head nurse is responsible to the associate director of nursing.

Duties:
1. Assesses all new admissions to the unit.
2. Initiates care plans on new admissions.
3. Communicates care plans to:
   - Patients
   - Family members
   - Nursing staff
   - Other disciplines as necessary
4. Monitors care delivered to patients.
5. Identifies and communicates changes in patients' condition to physician.
6. Leads care planning conference.
7. Ensures appropriate documentation on all patients.
8. Conducts staff meetings as required.
9. Meets with families as necessary.
10. Gives patient care when necessary:
    - Bathing
    - Dressing
    - Feeding
    - Lifting, transferring, mobility assistance
    - Toileting
    - Medication administration
    - Treatments
11. Evaluates performance of all nursing employees on unit for all shifts.
12. Orders supplies for unit.
13. Identifies need for and requests maintenance repairs.
14. Communicates with other departments.
15. Audits charts monthly.
16. Spot-checks evening and night operations of unit at least once a month.
17. Attends head nurse meetings.

Figure 17-1 continued

18. Provides unit-level educational programs to staff at least monthly.
19. Arranges for staff to attend facility in-services.
20. Maintains own competency with continued education.
21. Compiles annual evaluation and goals of unit to assist with departmental planning.
22. Discusses budget status monthly with associate director of nursing.
23. Serves on internal and external committees as assigned.
24. Tours outside groups through unit as requested.

Employees can be asked to complete a self-evaluation before their formal performance appraisal. This can aid in determining how realistically employees perceive their strengths and weaknesses. Also, problems and needs of employees that are unknown to the manager can surface.

The annual performance appraisal (the sixth step) judges actual performance observed throughout the year for those responsibilities listed on the job description. Here again, the job description responsibilities can serve as the skeleton for the evaluation tool, with evaluation columns added (Exhibit 17-4). It is acceptable to include a similar section on all employees' evaluation pertaining to basic work habits (e.g., attendance, tardiness, courtesy, adherence to policies). Although responsibilities evaluated will vary based on the specific job, the performance appraisal process should be basically the same for all employees. The employee and manager should sign the evaluation, and, ideally, a copy should be given to the employee. If the employee refuses to sign the evaluation, a witness should be present to observe the evaluation discussion. This should be documented on the evaluation form. (Having a witness prevents that employee from being able to claim that the manager never evaluated the employee or discussed problems with performance.)

The seventh step in performance appraisal is developing a corrective action plan to improve problem areas. The corrective action plan includes the desired goal, specific behaviors/actions to achieve the goal, the time frame in which the problem is to be corrected (stated as part of the goal), and the consequences for not correcting the problem. The employee and manager can develop this plan jointly. For example, the corrective action plan for an employee with a chronic lateness problem could be:

Goal: Employee will reduce lateness to no more than two occurrences during the next 2 months.
Actions:

- Ask to join co-workers' car pool on days car is malfunctioning.
- Set two alarm clocks to ring 5 minutes apart.

Exhibit 17-2 Orientation Evaluation Form

Head Nurse

Responsibilities	States Understanding	Demonstrates Competency	Needs Improvement
1. Assesses all new admissions to the unit.			
2. Initiates care plans on new admissions.			
3. Communicates care plans to:			
• Patients			
• Family members			
• Nursing staff			
• Other disciplines as necessary			
4. Monitors care delivered to patients.			
5. Identifies and communicates changes in patients' condition to physician.			
6. Leads care planning conference.			
7. Ensures appropriate documentation on all patients.			
8. Conducts staff meetings as required.			
9. Meets with families as necessary.			
10. Gives patient care when necessary:			
• Bathing			
• Dressing			
• Feeding			
• Lifting, transferring, mobility assistance			
• Toileting			
• Medication administration			
• Treatments			

11. Evaluates performance of all nursing employees on unit for all shifts.
12. Orders supplies for unit.
13. Identifies need for and requests maintenance repairs.
14. Communicates with other departments.
15. Audits charts monthly.
16. Spot-checks evening and night operations of unit at least once a month.
17. Attends head nurse meetings.
18. Provides unit-level educational programs to staff at least monthly.
19. Arranges for staff to attend facility in-services.
20. Maintains own competency with continued education.
21. Compiles annual evaluation and goals of unit to assist with departmental planning.
22. Discusses budget status monthly with associate director of nursing.
23. Serves on internal and external committees as assigned.
24. Tours outside groups through unit as requested.

Exhibit 17-3 Sample Anecdotal Notes

7/6   Left dirty bucket on unit when going off duty.
7/10   Did not report supply needs to supervisor.
7/11   Returned patient to unit; patient was found wandering in facility parking lot.
7/18   Volunteered to stay after work to clean flooded basement.
7/29   Reported by Head Nurse Jones for smoking in linen closet.
7/30   Observed puffing on cigarette in patient's bathroom at 9:30 A.M.; threw cigarette in
       toilet when approached.

- Lay out next day's clothes before retiring.
- Plan to eat breakfast at home, rather than stopping at the carryout en route to work.

Consequences: Employee will receive written warning if late more than two times within the next 2 months, and 1-day suspension if late additional two times within the 2-month period after that.

For the nurse who has a pattern of forgetting to record medications the corrective action plan could be:

Goal: Employee will have no omissions or erroneous recording on medication records during the next 2 months.

Actions:

- Carry medication record on drug cart and sign off as soon as drug is administered.
- Review medication records during afternoon break.
- Ask charge nurse to audit medication records for 1 week.

Consequences: Employee will receive written warning for next medication recording error within the next 2 months.

The employee and manager should sign the plan, and the employee should be given a copy for reference. The manager should make a notation on his or her calendar of the date on which a corrective action plan is to be evaluated. With many employees to supervise it is easy for the manager to overlook this type of detail and for the employee not to be held accountable for the lack of improvement or not to be rewarded for correction of the problem.

Ongoing evaluation of employee performance is the eighth step in performance appraisal. The manager must assure that the employee is competently meeting expectations outlined in the job description and adhering to desired practice standards. The manager should not assume that an employee is regularly meeting job responsibilities satisfactorily just because he or she was once judged to have satisfactory performance. Personal problems, changes in patient acuity level, poor morale, and many other factors can reduce work quality and quantity. Continued supervision and observation of performance are essential.

Although feedback to the employee is identified as the last step of performance appraisal, communication between the manager and employee permeates every step of the evaluation process. The protection of patients demands immediate correction of care delivery problems rather than waiting for a formal, scheduled evaluation. Likewise, employees should be provided opportunities to improve their skills and increase their competency through constructive criticism and instruction on ways to improve their practice. Managers should be certain to not only provide feedback on poor performance, but also to acknowledge good or improved performance.

DISCIPLINE

At times, lack of improvement or the seriousness of an offense warrants disciplinary action. Although often seen as punitive, discipline can serve as a corrective means to improve behaviors before they become habitual or result in serious problems. Progressive discipline typically follows the stages of

Facilities may vary as to the type of infringement that qualifies for a specific type of warning. For example, in one facility an employee may issue an oral warning for an unexcused absence whereas another facility may give a one day suspension for the same offense. There also can be variation in how many similar types of warnings will be given before discipline progresses to the next step. For instance, in one facility the first infringement may result in an oral warning, the second in a written warning, the third in a suspension; in another facility the practice may be to allow several written warnings before suspending an employee. Managers need to become familiar with the practices within their own facilities to ensure appropriate application.

Exhibit 17-4 Annual Evaluation Form

Head Nurse

Responsibilities	Always	Performs According to Standards		Never
		Most of Time	Seldom	
1. Assesses all new admissions to the unit.				
2. Initiates care plans on new admissions.				
3. Communicates care plans to:				
• Patients				
• Family members				
• Nursing staff				
• Other disciplines as necessary				
4. Monitors care delivered to patients.				
5. Identifies and communicates changes in patients' condition to physician.				
6. Leads care planning conference.				
7. Ensures appropriate documentation on all patients.				
8. Conducts staff meetings as required.				
9. Meets with families as necessary.				
10. Gives patient care when necessary:				
• Bathing				
• Dressing				
• Feeding				
• Lifting, transferring, mobility assistance				
• Toileting				
• Medication administration				
• Treatments				

11. Evaluates performance of all nursing employees on unit for all shifts.
12. Orders supplies for unit.
13. Identifies need for and requests maintenance repairs.
14. Communicates with other departments.
15. Audits charts monthly.
16. Spot-checks evening and night operations of unit at least once a month.
17. Attends head nurse meetings.
18. Provides unit-level educational programs to staff at least monthly.
19. Arranges for staff to attend facility in-services.
20. Maintains own competency with continued education.
21. Compiles annual evaluation and goals of unit to assist with departmental planning.
22. Discusses budget status monthly with associate director of nursing.
23. Serves on internal and external committees as assigned.
24. Tours outside groups through unit as requested.

Before the disciplinary session, managers need to do their homework. Facts should be validated. For example, if the employee is being disciplined for lateness the specific dates he or she was late should be documented on the disciplinary action form; if an employee is being disciplined based on the observations of a co-worker, a signed statement of the incident should be prepared by that co-worker.

To prepare the employee for the disciplinary action arrange a mutually convenient meeting time and explain the purpose of the meeting. This should be done in private, not in front of other employees. If the employee is represented by a union, a union delegate has the right to be present during the disciplinary session.

During the meeting the discipline should be presented assertively and directly: "Ms. Clark, we are here to discuss the eight times you were late for work this month, for which I am giving you an oral warning." There is no need to be defensive or apologetic ("I'm awfully sorry to have to do this to you, but I have to follow the rules"), nor harsh and aggressive ("Just who do you think you are being late so many times?"). State the facts and your expectations. It is important to hear the employee's perspective, but care should be taken not to allow the discussion to stray from the problem being discussed. For example, if the employee responds "You just don't like me . . . I know you're friends with Mary and that is why you never pick on her the way you hassle me . . . I always do my work," there is no need to react to the charges. Instead, return the discussion to the problem at hand: "Ms. Clark, we are discussing your tardiness and the need to correct it." A corrective action plan (as previously discussed) should be developed and given to the employee, and progress should be monitored.

Ideally, the disciplinary session should be a win-win situation for the manager and employee: the manager receives the employee's compliance with expected standards, and the employee is given an opportunity to correct performance (and stay employed) in a manner that preserves his or her self-esteem and dignity.

Employees do have a recourse to discipline through grievances. Each facility may have its own procedure for the grievance process, and this must be well understood by the manager to ensure that employees' rights are protected. Employees have the right to involve outside agencies for some issues, such as discrimination. The personnel department or administration can assist managers in learning more about specific laws pertaining to employee relations.

CONCLUSION

Poor performance in industries can result in a lower quality product or reduced profits. Poor performance in nursing homes can threaten human lives. Whether or not employees have limited direct contact with patients, their actions can affect the health, safety, and well-being of the patient population. The quality of performance also affects employees themselves in terms of its relationship to morale, job satisfaction, and the continued security of their jobs. The manager's responsibility for ensuring and promoting good performance, therefore, is a significant one.

BIBLIOGRAPHY

Eliopoulos, C. 1983. *Nursing administration of long-term care*. Rockville, Md.: Aspen Publishers.

Henry, K.H. 1987. *Nursing administration and law manual*. Rockville, Md.: Aspen Publishers.

Murphy, E.K. 1985. What is the potential liability for negligence in supervision? *AORN J* 41:523–25.

Chapter 18

Public Relations

There are a variety of persons who come in contact with the nursing home, including

- Patients and their families, who look to the facility for the provision of long-term care services
- Nursing employees, physicians, consultants, temporary personnel, and other staff, who provide service and obtain employment
- Trustees, who monitor and guide operations
- Students, who use the resources of the facility as a learning laboratory
- Vendors, who supply goods
- Surveyors, who evaluate the facility's compliance with acceptable standards
- Media representatives, who communicate newsworthy items
- Community residents, who exchange neighborly assistance and concern

The public, who is important to the nursing home and for whom the nursing home is important, is indeed wide and varied.

A nursing home must be concerned with the public. The ability to maintain an adequate census, recruit and retain staff, satisfy consumers, and portray a positive image to the community is determined by the quality of the facility's public relations. In the current competitive health care system survival and success of a facility are strongly influenced by public relations.

Public relations is not a Madison Avenue gimmick, nor is it a business activity restricted to administrative personnel. Instead, public relations is the quality of relationships that the facility has with all significant persons. The actions of every staff member influence the quality of the facility's public relations. One of the important responsibilities of the nurse is to ensure that positive public relations exist.

IMAGE

Although it is often said "you can't judge a book by its cover," the reality is that most people do make qualitative evaluations based on first or single impressions of people and physical plant. Many persons may

- Conclude that a service agency is insensitive if a call was put on hold for 15 minutes
- Determine that a grocery store is unsanitary if one roach was spotted crawling across the floor
- Believe that a whole business is poorly managed if several employees were seen socializing with each other, rather than waiting on customers

Conversely, people may

- Feel that a business really cares about them if a sales representative made special attempts to offer assistance
- Judge that a dental practice offers state-of-the-art dental technology because of the modern offices and waiting area
- Choose to patronize a grocery store where prices are slightly higher but the butcher addresses customers by name and remembers their preferences

Nursing homes are service businesses and are impacted by the same factors that create positive and negative impressions in other service businesses. A nursing home can provide expert care to patients but suffer a poor image because of the impressions the public gains from other aspects of the facility. Picture the impression made on Mrs. B., a first-time visitor to the nursing home, who has come to see her newly admitted sister.

The only area of the facility's parking lot with available spaces is one in which the lighting is not functioning. Somewhat frightened, Mrs. B. parks her car and travels through the dark lot alone. She approaches a door, which is locked, and continues traveling around the building to find a second door, also locked. Finally, she reaches an entrance that has "Lobby" printed on the door and enters.

There is a reception desk but no one is present. After waiting several minutes she begins to walk down the hallway and approaches a nursing station where several staff are engaged in a heated conversation about how "the supervisor expects you to work miracles while being short-staffed" and how the staff "aren't going to break their backs for the little money this place pays."

Because the staff have ignored her presence and continued their discussion, Mrs. B. interrupts and asks where she might find her sister. The staff respond that the patient is not on their unit and return to their conversation. Mrs. B. again interrupts to ask how she can locate her sister; the staff tell her to go to the supervisor's office on the second floor and ask.

A frustrated Mrs. B. walks toward the stairway, noticing a few patients lying uncovered and several calling for assistance. In the stairway, Mrs. B. notes debris on the stairs and several roaches.

On reaching the second floor Mrs. B. sees no staff, so she travels along the hallway looking for the supervisor's office. After walking the entire second floor without seeing any office she decides to ask for help and waits at the nursing station for someone to come. Minutes pass, and while waiting Mrs. B. sees several opened charts on the desk. A nursing assistant finally comes to the desk and directs Mrs. B. to the supervisor's office, which is an unmarked door at the end of the hall.

Mrs. B. knocks at the supervisor's door and is greeted by a woman in a tight, wrinkled uniform who is holding a cigarette in one hand and cup in the other; Mrs. B. learns that this woman is the supervisor. When asked where Mrs. B.'s sister is located the supervisor responds "I think she is the new admission on the garden wing but I'm not sure . . . Is she the red head with Alzheimer's? . . . How about waiting until I finish my break—as crazy as this place is tonight I'm not likely to get another one—and I'll check at the front desk for you . . . I'm only temporary and don't know the patients that well."

By the time Mrs. B. reaches her sister she may have determined that the facility is unsafe and unclean, morale is low, personnel are uncaring and unfamiliar with patients, staffing is low, patients are poorly supervised and unattended to, and patients' privacy is unprotected. Imagine the anxieties Mrs. B. has regarding her sister's care. The expertly written care plan, fine reputation of the medical director, excellent health department survey findings, and good physical care provided will be overshadowed by the general image created during Mrs. B.'s first experience with the facility. Mrs. B. may carry away negative impressions that could cause her to believe her sister has been admitted to a horrible facility, to transfer her sister from the facility, and to discourage others from using the nursing home.

A variety of items contribute to the image presented by the nursing home. Some of these items are listed in a self-assessment format in Exhibit 18-1. Strategies should be developed to improve deficits identified during the assessment. Improvements need not be sophisticated or expensive, but can include practical measures such as

---

Exhibit 18-1 Self-Assessment of Facility Image

Service
Care delivered according to acceptable standards
Patients, families, and significant others participate in assessment, care planning, and evaluation of services
Health department surveys reflect no major or recurring deficiencies
Patient preferences honored in care activities
Food served attractively and at correct temperature
Call lights and requests responded to promptly
Individuality of patients promoted

Staff
Work performed confidently and competently
Appearance neat, clean
Manner courteous, polite
Attitude pleasant, cheerful, and one of helping
Information given to patients and families is factual and clear
Criticism and complaints accepted and managed in a constructive manner
Team effort exhibited
Privacy of patients, visitors, and co-workers respected
Criticisms and complaints not expressed about patients, visitors, co-workers, and facility

Communication
Patients, visitors, and personnel addressed by name
Information shared in timely manner
Eye contact, body language, and voice tone reflect interest in conversation
Complaints accepted, investigated, and resolved
Telephones answered within three rings
Telephone calls returned same day
Printed matter available to describe policies and practices

Physical Environment
Clean atmosphere, free of litter and clutter
Attractive decorations
Safe grounds and building
Controlled noise
Sitting areas, snacks available for visitors
Signs posted to enable areas to be located easily
Convenient parking
Physical plant, equipment in good repair

- Using proper telephone courtesy (Exhibit 18-2)
- Exercising discretion regarding comments made in public (Exhibit 18-3)
- Avoiding discussions pertaining to patients or work problems in public areas
- Wearing clean, well-fitting uniforms
- Greeting visitors courteously and with a smile; offering to assist
- Giving clear directions and explanations
- Using signs to direct visitors and identify areas
- Accepting and resolving complaints
- Maintaining the physical plant; reporting maintenance problems
- Providing sitting areas, snack bars, vending machines
- Having well-lighted parking and walking areas

Exhibit 18-2 Telephone Courtesy

Answer telephone within three rings.
Identify self and location.
Greet the caller, and acknowledge by name.
Wear a smile while speaking.
Avoid using medical jargon or slang terms (e.g., "They're in ITC now"; "Okay, sweetie?").
Speak clearly and courteously.
Do not chew gum or eat while talking.
Ask the caller if it is convenient *before* placing caller on hold, or if the caller prefers to call
  again.
Check on holding calls frequently, and give status report (e.g., "Mrs. B. is still with a patient";
  "Dr. Smith hasn't finished with the other call.").
Offer to take a message.
Inform caller of action before transferring call.
Assist caller who has incorrect number in finding correct number.
Return call when promised.
Say goodbye before hanging up.

Exhibit 18-3 Killer Phrases To Avoid

It's not my job.
What now?
That was the last shift's job.
Yeah?
This place is a zoo.
We're always understaffed around here.
What's wrong with you people?
We cover the doctors' hides all the time.
The lab always messes up.
It's a wonder we don't get sued every day.

MANAGING COMPLAINTS

The nursing home is a fertile environment for complaints to flourish. The "customers" being served are ill, debilitated, and dependent—conditions that can cause them to become extremely impatient with minor inconveniences. Family members may be guilty, anxious, and depressed at the status of their loved ones—conditions that cause them to be extra sensitive to situations that even hint at being adverse for their relatives. Some persons assume that staff need to be scrutinized closely to assure adequate care is given; others are unrealistic about the level of care that can be expected. These and many other factors lead to many unfounded, as well as valid, complaints.

Staff must be prepared to manage complaints. This begins by preventing situations in which complaints can arise. Patient and visitor requests should be addressed promptly; reasonable explanations can be offered to help patients and visitors understand the reasons why their requests are not met in a timely or complete manner. For instance, a visitor who asks if his mother can be returned to bed may understand having to wait 20 minutes if told "I need to finish feeding two patients and will be sure to help your mother next," rather than being told "I'll be right there" and having to wait.

Preparing patients and family members for situations and keeping them abreast of changes or problems can minimize complaints. A patient who is informed that "a plumbing problem will delay baths this morning" is less likely to complain of not being bathed before breakfast; likewise, telephoning a family member before he or she visits and explaining that the patient had a fall that left a bruise can avert complaints that result from relatives being surprised about a situation. Active prevention of complaints can be beneficial for all parties involved.

The manner in which a complaint is managed can make the difference between a problem being diffused early and it becoming a major crisis. Clumsy complaint management can cause a small problem to snowball easily. Consider the following scenario and unfortunate sequence of events.

> One of the patients, Mrs. N., is upset because she cannot find her new sweater. She approaches the nursing assistant in the hall, and the following conversation ensues.
>
> Mrs. N.: "Somebody stole my new sweater."
> Nursing Assistant: "Mrs. N., I'm in the middle of doing something important. Your sweater is probably in the back of your closet."
> Mrs. N.: "It is not! Somebody took it. They're always stealing around here."

Nursing Assistant:	"Who would want to steal your sweater?"
Mrs. N.:	"You all are always taking our things. How can you steal from old people?"
Nursing Assistant:	"My mother didn't raise a thief. Nobody wants your stupid sweater. Quit accusing people and being such a grouch."
Mrs. N.:	"You have no right to talk to me that way. You people have no respect."

Mrs. N. then telephones her daughter and tells her that staff are not only stealing from her but also "yelling and calling me names too."

An irate daughter, in turn, visits the administrator and emphatically states that she will not tolerate her mother having things taken from her and being spoken to disrespectfully, and "If that is the way things are around here, I'll transfer my mother to another facility."

The administrator calls the director of nursing, reminding her that they cannot afford to lose patients, and that she "needs to reprimand staff for their attitude problem." The administrator demands a full investigation today so that he can report back to the patient's daughter. The director of nursing, annoyed at having yet another demand made on her time, confronts the nursing assistant and reviews the problem. The nursing assistant reluctantly apologizes to the patient.

In the situation above, a missing sweater has led to

- A patient feeling she is being treated rudely
- A family member feeling that she is not getting the service she is paying for
- Key administrative staff investing extra time and energy soothing the feelings of a patient and family member
- A nursing assistant feeling that the patient has caused trouble that could threaten the nursing assistant's work record

Of course, other persons may have been drawn into this web by the patient and her daughter expressing their dissatisfaction and by the nursing assistant telling other staff how "administration always sides with patients and families." No one wins in this type of situation. All parties feel they have been unnecessarily imposed on, and residual negative feelings may affect future interactions among these parties.

Consider how Mrs. N.'s situation could have been managed differently.

Mrs. N.:	"Somebody stole my sweater."
Nursing Assistant:	"The sweater may be misplaced . . . sometimes laundry is returned to the wrong person. As soon as I'm finished giving this bath I'll help you find your sweater."
Mrs. N.:	"They're always stealing around here."
Nursing Assistant:	"I'm sure we'll find your sweater. I'll be right with you as soon as I'm finished with Mr. J."

In this scenario the nursing assistant is neither fueling Mrs. N.'s anger about the missing sweater nor reacting to the accusation of theft. Instead, the nursing assistant has focused on the issue of the missing sweater. Mrs. N. may still be annoyed about not having her sweater, but she does not have cause to further her anger. Consequently, staff time and energy are spared from investigations, apologies, and calming unhappy patients and visitors. Some guidelines for complaint management are outlined in Exhibit 18-4.

KEEPING IN TOUCH

In one of the most popular management books of the 1980s, *In Search of Excellence*, Peters and Waterman (1982) identify that a trait of successful businesses is that they keep in touch with their customers. Learning what customers need and want and obtaining feedback about customer satisfaction can aid businesses in providing services that are appropriate, effective, and successful.

Nursing homes need to keep in touch with their customers (patients and families), and there are several mechanisms that can be used to accomplish this.

Exhibit 18-4 Guidelines for Complaint Management

Take the time to hear the complaint.

Listen to the complaint attentively and with interest.

Clarify issues (e.g., "You say that when you asked the nursing assistant to take you to the bathroom she ignored you and left the room?"; "The new robe you gave your mother last week is now missing?").

Do not react to accusations or emotionally charged statements; focus on the issue.

Acknowledge the person's feelings without placing blame (e.g., "I can understand your anger at not receiving help"; "It is distressing your new robe is missing.").

Offer assistance in solving the problem, and inform the person as to what the next step will be (e.g., "I'm going to find out why the nursing assistant did not help you"; "I'm going to go through all the closets and see if the robe is misplaced.").

Elicit help or refer the complaint to a superior if the situation seems to be getting out of control.

Follow up and ensure a satisfactory resolution has been achieved.

Resident and family councils are important means of communication between the facility and its customers. The concerns of patients and families can be channeled through the councils and presented in a structured manner to the facility. This format allows persons who do not feel comfortable expressing negative views to be able to channel their comments through others. In turn, the facility can communicate its own views and problems through the councils.

Special groups can be convened to offer insight into the facility's operations and input into planning. For example, the facility may note that few family members attend activities planned for patients and families. Staff may attribute this poor attendance to lack of interest. By gathering a group of family members together to discuss the reasons for the situation it may be learned that the events are announced on a bulletin board that most families do not read, the events are scheduled for the evening and most persons fear leaving the facility in the dark, or the patients are disinterested in the events and inform their relatives that they do not want to attend. Obviously, more suitable solutions to problems can be planned once the nature of the problem is understood.

Questionnaires and surveys can be used to obtain feedback. They can be broad and cover a variety of areas or focus on one specific topic, such as menu, laundry services, or courtesy of staff. Provisions should be made for questions to be read and explained to patients who may have difficulty understanding the tool independently.

The value of being accessible to patients and visitors cannot be overestimated. Making a point of conducting rounds, greeting visitors, asking patients and visitors how things are, and being visible can demonstrate an openness to communication.

Also important is keeping in touch with staff perceptions, attitudes, and morale as this can yield clues to the quality of public relations. Staff comments, such as "All these patients do is complain" and "These families are always picking on something," may reflect a problem in the quality of services rendered or indicate unrealistic expectations on the part of patients and their families. Staff who have the attitude that patients should be appreciative for any care they receive and not expect anything beyond basics may manage patient and family requests inappropriately. Staff who feel that they are treated impersonally and unfairly may not be predisposed to treat patients and families with sensitivity and warmth. Every employee represents the facility and serves as a good will (or bad will) ambassador.

Everyone wins with positive public relations. The facility can avoid a poor reputation, lost revenue, and potential litigation by having dissatisfaction and problems prevented and corrected early. Staff can share a pleasant relationship with patients and families, rather than a stressful adversarial one. Families can be spared frustration and anger and be made to feel like valuable partners in the care process. Most importantly, the quality of services delivered to patients can be affected positively by good public relations.

REFERENCE

Peters, T.J., and R.H. Waterman. 1982. *In search of excellence*. New York: Warner Books.

BIBLIOGRAPHY

Allaire, B., and R. McNeil. 1982. *Teaching patient relations in hospitals. The hows and whys*. Chicago: American Hospital Publishing Co.

Eisenberg, B., and M. Gardella. 1985. Assessing readiness for guest relations programs. *Hospitals* 4:128–29.

Eliopoulos, C. 1986. Customer relations in the health care setting. *Health Care Superv* 4:19–31.

Chapter 19

Challenges of the Future

Nursing homes are undergoing dramatic changes. No longer residences for those in need of basic personal care and supervision, nursing homes are rapidly becoming complex care centers for patients having a diverse range of physical and mental health problems. Although the percentage of the aged institutionalized at any given time will remain at 5%, the growth in the numbers of elderly persons will result in this 5% representing greater numbers. It is estimated that by the year 2000, the nursing home population will increase 47% (Callahan, 1987). As advances in medical technology allow more persons to survive conditions that may have been fatal in the past, a growing number of persons will age with health problems and benefit in late life from a wide range of life-sustaining measures. Consequently, nursing home patients of tomorrow increasingly will require more complicated and sophisticated care than the institutionalized population of today.

Obviously, the number of personnel employed in nursing homes must increase to meet the future demands of this care setting. The mix of this staff also must change to meet the complex care needs of the nursing home population. In-depth nursing assessments, the formulation of nursing diagnoses, development of appropriate care plans, performance of highly skilled procedures, monitoring of unstable conditions, coordination of multiple services, and evaluation of outcomes will require the most competent professionals that nursing has to offer. The Division of Nursing (1986) of the Department of Health and Human Services projects that by the year 2000 the upper bounds of requirements for nursing home personnel will reach 971,800 for registered nurses, 407,700 for licensed practical nurses, and 530,000 for nursing assistants. Nursing home nurses will need to be highly competent persons, knowledgeable of current practices, who can function independently and, most importantly, demonstrate leadership characteristics.

ACTION VERSUS REACTION

An important trait of nurse leaders in the nursing home setting is a predisposition to action rather than reaction. Nursing's history is heavily laced with reactive behaviors that place nurses in the role of powerless pawns in the health care system. The need for this behavior to change is especially relevant in the nursing home industry, where the care system is being redefined. Whether nursing emerges as a leader or victim when the dust settles will be determined by nurses' ability to use broad vision in defining needs, revolutionary approaches in providing nursing care, and possessed power in negotiating increased control and resources for nursing services.

Action demands that nurses be knowledgeable not only of nursing practice but also of other factors that impact nursing homes, such as legislation, demographics, labor dynamics, and consumer trends. Publications such as the *Wall Street Journal* may be as essential to nurse-leaders' reading as the *American Journal of Nursing*. Likewise, nonnursing educational programs can expose nurses to new ideas that can be applied to nursing and aid nurses in understanding factors that influence their practice. The rapidity of change prohibits nurses from investing scarce time in reinventing the wheel. A great deal can be learned from other disciplines and industries. Borrowing theories and practices and adapting them to nursing can yield innovative approaches.

Rather than wait for directives, nurses should take responsibility for proposing changes and new services. For example, instead of waiting for administration to solve nursing assistant recruitment problems, nurses can recommend strategies to assist with recruitment, such as the development of a child care program on the facility's grounds, provision of certified geriatric aide training programs, and private shuttle bus service for employees with transportation problems. Likewise, nurse leaders must be entrepreneurial in identifying new business ventures for the facility that can generate revenue, in addition to meeting community needs. Nurses should even consider opportunities that they can independently pursue as private business ventures for themselves; owning a health-related business affords nurses the maximum opportunity to impact the quality of services delivered and increase their earnings.

The predisposition for action requires behaviors that break from the traditional nursing mold and thrust nurses into a more assertive position. Nurses need to recognize the power they possess and find ways to broaden their power base. This power can be used to negotiate change and increase nurses' authority over practice. There must be a willingness to take risks. The status quo may be comfortable but will not advance practice. Nurses need to accept criticism, resistance, and failure as they tread on new territories to discover innovative approaches. Established rules must be challenged because yesterday's methods may be irrelevant for tomorrow's nursing home practice.

ECONOMIC INCENTIVES

An enormous challenge to nursing home nurses is to compete with other sectors in the recruitment and retention of staff. The difficult nature of the work and the residual stigma associated with nursing home nursing are real deterrents to practice in this setting; noncompetitive salaries compound the problem. Health care resources are not infinite, the likelihood of obtaining significant increases through third party reimbursers is slim, and the current era of growing restrictions and rationing of health care resources will continue. New financial incentives to make employment in the nursing home more attractive must be sought. Some possible incentives to recruit and retain staff include the following.

- *Child care*. A free or low-cost child care center on the facility's premises could offer a competitive advantage to a nursing home. The fact that the nursing home already operates dietary, housekeeping, and laundry services could make the extension of these services to the child care center economical. The worry of picking up the child late if overtime delayed the parent's departure from work could be eased by knowing that the child was in good hands on the premises. Such a center could be opened to the neighboring community to help with operating expenses.
- *Discounts*. Food cooperatives and other discount programs organized by the facility could save employees considerable money in their personal budgets. Local merchants may be willing to offer discounts for public relations purposes and as an act of good will.
- *Caseload payment*. Traditionally, nursing employees receive a flat wage regardless of the number of patients they serve. Perhaps a program by which employees receive a set wage for a minimum number of patients and an extra amount for each additional patient cared for could enable more work to be completed with fewer staff and offer an incentive for staff to assume more responsibility.
- *Profit sharing*. It should not be surprising that many employees do not view cost cutting and increasing the institution's profits as their priorities, particularly when it is the owners and stockholders who benefit from such measures. Perhaps employees would take greater interest in increasing the facility's earnings if they knew there would be a bonus for them in doing so at the year's end.

MAINTAINING COMPETENCY

To meet current and future practice demands nursing home nurses must make an intentional effort to maintain competency and keep abreast of new information pertaining to their practice. In-service education is an important means to achieve this goal. It is easy for in-service education to be given low priority in the total scope of the nursing home operations. However, this function is crucial to the quality of services provided. Educational needs of staff can be identified by evaluating practice deficiencies; reviewing problems identified through incident and accident, as well as other, reports; and reviewing the literature for new practices and trends. Not to be overlooked is the value of asking staff to identify their educational interests and needs.

Didactic classroom teaching can be unexciting for both instructor and staff. On-the-unit demonstrations, discussions of actual cases, debates, role play, and field trips can afford opportunities for learner participation in the educational experience. Attendance at extramural continuing education programs not only provides a learning experience but also can afford an opportunity for networking and sharing among peers.

Every nurse has an obligation to support in-service education. The attitude of nurses toward education will strongly influence subordinates' commitment to learning. For example, a charge nurse who states that it is a waste of time for staff to attend an in-service class or who does not arrange the schedule to allow staff time to attend an educational program clearly demonstrates that education holds a low priority. The inconvenience of having staff absent from the unit for a temporary period of time can be a small price to pay for increasing their competency.

The in-service education provided by the employer is hardly enough to maintain professional competency. It is important for nurses to read a variety of journals and texts and attend professional meetings and educational programs. This may require personal expenditures to maintain competency; rather than being viewed as an expense, such educational costs should be considered investments in oneself.

ADVOCATING AN ETHICAL PRACTICE

The demographic realities of an aging population have begun to create concern as to how society can meet the health and social needs of the elderly. More directly, the growing concern seems to be how can society *afford* to meet the needs of an ever-increasing old population. With competition for a finite amount of resources, challenges to the services offered to older adults will abound. Difficult questions may be posed, such as

- Should life-sustaining measures be limited to persons under a certain age or who have a reasonable likelihood of good physical and mental function?
- Can society afford to promote a longer life expectancy for all its members?

The possibility that decisions could be made that are contrary to the best interest of the aged is a risk. As advocates for the elderly, nursing home nurses must be alert to policies that may hinder the quality of care afforded to the aged and ensure that the elderly's rights and needs are not compromised. When nurses detect a threat to the well-being of the nursing home population they should mobilize professional and community groups to improve the situation. Nurses are potentially the most powerful and credible group to influence the direction of nursing home care.

REFERENCES

Callahan, D. 1987. *Setting limits. Medical goals in an aging society*. New York: Simon & Schuster.

Division of Nursing, Bureau of Health Professions, Health Resources and Services Administration. 1986. Projected requirements for full time equivalent nursing personnel according to criteria-based model, by field of employment, 1990 and 2000. U.S. Dept. of Health and Human Services.

BIBLIOGRAPHY

Brock, A.M. 1988. The necessity of change. *J Gerontol Nurs* 14:7.

Callahan, D. 1987. *Setting limits. Medical goals in an aging society*. New York: Simon & Schuster.

Carter, M.A. 1988. Professional nursing in the nursing home. *J Prof Nurs* 3:325,376.

Kalisch, P.A., and B.J. Kalisch. 1987. *The changing image of the nurse*. Menlo Park, Calif.: Addison-Wesley Publishing Co.

Lambert, J.G., and T. Davis. 1987. Staffing: The most critical issue. *Contemp Longterm Care's D.O.N.* 10:14.

Peters, T. 1987. *Thriving on chaos. A handbook for management revolution*. New York: Alfred A. Knopf.

Shape, J. 1986. Nurses' attitudes to the care of the elderly. *J Adv Nurs* 1:569–72.

Index

Note: Pages in italics refer to material in illustrations.

About the Author

Charlotte Eliopoulos, R.N.,C., M.P.H., has demonstrated leadership in gerontological nursing as an author, lecturer, and initiator of new roles. At the Johns Hopkins Hospital during the 1970s she developed a gerontological clinical nurse specialist position considered to be the first such position in an acute care setting in the United States. She went on to serve as the first state-level specialist in gerontological nursing for the Maryland Department of Health. Later she became the director of nursing for the Levindale Geriatric Center and Hospital in Baltimore where she demonstrated progressive leadership. Currently, she is a consultant providing clinical and managerial expertise in geriatrics and long-term care services.

Ms. Eliopoulos holds a diploma in nursing from Sinai Hospital in Baltimore, a baccalaureate and master's degree in public health from Johns Hopkins University, and is certified in gerontological nursing by the American Nurses' Association.

Nursing Administration of Long-Term Care, Gerontological Nursing, Health Assessment of the Older Adult, A Guide to the Nursing of the Elderly, and *Gerontological Nursing Review: A Self-Instructional Text* are among the books Ms. Eliopoulos has written. She also has written numerous articles and serves on the editorial boards of *Health Care Supervisor, Contemporary Longterm Care,* and *Senior Care.*